FROM THE CAMPUS

FROM THE CAMPUS

Perspectives on the
School Reform Movement

Edited by

Sol Cohen
&
Lewis C. Solmon

New York
Westport, Connecticut
London

Library of Congress Cataloging-in-Publication Data

From the campus : perspectives on the school reform movement / edited
  by Sol Cohen and Lewis C. Solmon.
       p.   cm.
    Bibliography: p.
    Includes index.
    ISBN 0–275–93263–X (alk. paper)
    1. Public schools—United States.   2. Education—United States—
Aims and objectives.   3. Teaching.   I. Cohen, Sol.   II. Solmon,
Lewis C.
LA217.F748   1989
370′.973—dc20   89–33960

Library of Congress Catalog Card Number: 89–33960
ISBN: 0–275–93263–X

First published in 1989

Praeger Publishers, One Madison Avenue, New York, NY 10010
An imprint of Greenwood Publishing Group, Inc.

Printed in the United States of America

∞

The paper used in this book complies with the
Permanent Paper Standard issued by the National
Information Standards Organization (Z39.48–1984).

10 9 8 7 6 5 4 3 2

Contents

Preface

Lewis C. Solmon

This volume had its beginning in an attempt by one of its editors, Lewis C. Solmon, to put together a collection of essays by the faculty of the Graduate School of Education (GSE) at UCLA on the implications of their research for the classroom practitioner. Subsequently, as a result of conversations involving Professor Sol Cohen, the editors of several publishing houses, officials of UCLA's GSE alumni and support groups, Noelle Tisius (then director of public information at GSE), and myself, for reasons to be explicated in the Introduction, it was decided that a volume on the implications of educational research for the classroom teacher could wait and that we should proceed with a volume that would deal with the present crisis in American education.

I asked Professor Cohen to assume the immediate responsibility for soliciting, accepting, and editing contributions, and to help shape this volume into its current form. His vision of how faculty scholarship relates to the current school reform movement has enabled our colleagues to make a unique contribution to the debate about reform in American education. We owe special thanks to Noelle Tisius and our alumni and support groups for helping us to get the right "perspective" on the current needs of American education and for encouraging us to seize the opportunities it offered.

FROM THE CAMPUS

Introduction: A Role for Faculties of Education

Sol Cohen and Lewis C. Solmon

The current school reform or excellence movement may be dated from the National Commission on Excellence's 1983 publication of *A Nation at Risk*. The decline of high school student test scores in the United States had been a troublesome news item for a number of years by that time. But now middle-class parents were becoming apprehensive about their children's preparedness to compete for admission to the nation's more prestigious colleges and universities; enrollment in private schools was increasing dramatically. In addition, many Americans were alarmed at the perceived decline in the quality of our civic and political life and discourse, and worried that as a nation we were becoming morally adrift. The finger of blame was pointed at the schools.

Moreover, substantial declines in American productivity growth indicators and the simultaneous emergence of Japan as a powerful global competitor in international trade and the world economy caused even greater anxiety about the quality of our elementary and secondary schools. It has been generally acknowledged that education imparts knowledge, skills, and attitudes that enhance productivity in the work force. Although this is true for both developed and underdeveloped nations, the development of human capital in the United States through our public system of schools and universities has been credited, along with our abundant natural resources, with America's preeminence as a global industrial and financial power.[1] Now the National Science Board was publicizing the sad state of precollege mathematics and science education, as illustrated by deteriorating performance of high school students on math and science achievement tests, declining SAT scores, and declining interest in academic (versus general or vocational) high school programs and in careers in math, science, and engineering.[2] Given the increasing reliance of industry on advanced technology, these findings were particularly disturbing.

In sum, the capacity of our public schools to meet the country's educational needs was being questioned on varied grounds and from many quarters. Thus, the appearance of the National Commission on Excellence in Education's 36-page report, *A Nation at Risk: The Imperative for Educational Reform*, with its sensational, even apocalyptic proclamation that a "rising tide of mediocrity" was engulfing the country's educational foundations—and continuing, "If an unfriendly foreign power had attempted to impose on America the mediocre educational performance that exists today, we might well have viewed it as an act of war. . . . We have, in effect, been committing an act of unthinking, unilateral disarmament"—tapped a deep reservoir of discontent with the public schools and quickly became a national best seller.[3]

Although scholars and researchers in the fields of school administration, psychology, sociology, testing and evaluation, curriculum theory, and learning and instruction, among other specialists in schools of education, have built their careers around studying effective schools and methods of improving the educational process, this latest school reform movement was not led by these education specialists. Rather, leadership of the reform movement was assumed by the U.S. Office of Education—first under Terrel H. Bell and then under his successor, William J. Bennett—allied with an impressive array of elected officials, especially state governors and their legislatures, and foundation heads and civic and business leaders outside the education profession in general and schools of education in particular. This latter point is the one we wish to stress here. The involvement of faculties of schools of education—we will call them "educationists" for short—in the school reform movement has so far been negligible.

We would like to venture some reasons why educationists have, with some exceptions, stayed on the sidelines during the current debates over school reform. First, though university-affiliated schools of education presumably have the expertise needed to address the problems of education, the reward structure for faculty is based upon research and scholarly publication. Faculty members at such institutions are reluctant to slow down or postpone their discipline-oriented research and publication agendas in order to focus upon the ramifications and implications of their research for public school policy and practice because they may then suffer delays in promotion or in receiving tenure.

Second, the participation of schools of education and professors of education in the school reform movement seems to be neither valued nor wanted by reformers. We think it fair to state that by and large the current school reform movement views educationists as an obstacle, barrier, or source of resistance to reform. *A Nation at Risk* simply dismissed the professional education community from its purview. Some school reformers use a pre-emptive strike strategy. According to California State School Superintendent Bill Honig, "Many of the reform steps we have taken in California have had their critics in the schools of education, some of whom have been downright personally abrasive in their attacks."[4] Some of the most visible and vocal of the school reformers assume a more explicit adversarial stance toward educationists. Chester Finn, assistant secretary of education, declared: "The [education] profession did not initiate it [the excellence movement], is not leading it, and in many instances is opposing key elements of it.'' Despite ''some recent—and opportunistic—attempts by parts of the profession to climb onto the 'excellence bandwagon,' '' Finn continued, ''we must understand that that very bandwagon is rolling over some of the best-loved (if also most vulnerable) beliefs of the educational profession.''[5] The whole field of educational research has been derided by Finn.[6] Little wonder then, that education faculties would be affronted by the reform movement's implication that they are not or have not been committed to excellence in education, or that their research efforts are trivial or esoteric and have contributed little over the years to the improvement of educational practice—and consequently would want to have nothing to do with the reform movement.

In any event, many educationists think the reform movement's analysis of the causes of the school crisis are simplistic and prone to scapegoating the professional educational community. For example, any explanation for the deterioration of our nation's educational effectiveness must pay attention to the changing demographics of the student body. It is clear that by the end of the century our student population will be preponderantly Black, Asian, and Hispanic, and the proportion of whites attending our public schools will plummet. This trend is magnified if immigration from Central and South America and the Caribbean is taken into account.[7] The educational achievement scores of Blacks and Hispanics at the high school level is substantially inferior to that of whites and Asians, especially whites and Asians from the middle socioeconomic status; the dropout rates for Blacks and Hispanics are substantially higher and their progression rates into college lower. As whites decline from 55 to 36 percent of 18-year-olds, and Blacks and Hispanics increase from 35 to 48 percent, it will be unacceptable that so few Blacks and Hispanics will receive college degrees. As Lewis Solmon stated, ''We must dramatically reduce the loss of talent which results when members of minority groups do not achieve the success in college (or precollege education) that is achieved by whites and Asians.''[8] It is clear, he concludes, that we must be concerned with the quality and effectiveness of precollege education available to Blacks, Hispanics, and new immigrants, a problem exacerbated by the fact that these groups often seek to maintain their cultural and linguistic identity. Yet the school reform movement has been oblivious to the implications and ramifications for public education of these demographic trends.

In addition, the breakdown of the traditional nuclear home and family, and weakening of religious institutions in many communities, have created enormous problems among children and youth that exacerbate all the schools' problems. When the public schools are asked to deal with issues like teenage pregnancy, drug and alcohol abuse, and a general breakdown of home and community bonds, it is quite understandable that schools are unable to devote the same efforts to teaching academic subjects as they have in the past. Yet the out-of-school environment that precipitates such problems is beyond the jurisdiction or the power of intervention of the school itself or of the education profession. Consider the impact of television. By the time American youngsters graduate from high school, it has been estimated that they will have spent an average of 17,000 hours in

front of the TV set, compared with the approximately 14,000 hours they will
have spent in school. Time spent watching television surpasses any other single
activity except sleeping.[9] What are the effects on school achievement of spending
so much time watching television? What can the professional educator do while
lamenting the educational quality of television programming, except to say that
the time could be better spent?

Other changes in our society have impacted the problems of the public schools.
Consider the results of the women's rights movement. In the past several decades
much broader opportunities have opened to women in business, law, medicine,
and the sciences. The salaries in many of these careers are substantially higher
than for public school teachers, so it is no wonder that many of the most highly
qualified women have opted for careers other than teaching.[10] This development
has resulted in decreasing the pool from which many talented prospective teachers
might be drawn while leaving the public school responsible for surrogate functions that inevitably complicate, if not interfere with, the school's more formal
educational responsibilities. It is only natural that educationists resent being
scapegoated for trends like these over which they have no control. Finally, the
friction between the excellence movement and educationists may in the end
reflect the fact that different and competing sets of values and philosophies or
ideologies of education are being contested.

What is at stake in school reform has been succinctly and authoritatively
depicted in an important article describing the marked shift in values guiding
pre–1980 federal educational policy, and federal educational policy since the
election of Ronald Reagan as president. The pre–1980 federal agenda for education emphasized equity, needs and access, social welfare concerns, regulation
and enforcement, and the public common school. The post–1980 federal agenda
in education emphasizes excellence, standards of performance, deregulation,
parental choice, privatization, and institutional competition.[11] If educationists
are suspicious of or opposed to the school reform movement (or vice versa), it
would be understandable, since it is the pre–1980 agenda to which most educationists are still committed. Many educationists fear that the excellence movement stands for an elitist and exclusionary doctrine that would jeopardize the
egalitarian and progressive educational gains since the 1950s.

For all these reasons, if school of education faculty have greeted the school
reform movement with hostility or anxious silence or suspicion, again, it is not
surprising. Educationists may talk to one another about the school reform movement in books and in the professional educational journals, but in the public
debate about school reform, with some notable exceptions, their voices have
been very quiet.[12] This is where this volume hopes to make its contribution. Its
aim is to give educationists in at least one school of education, UCLA's Graduate
School of Education, a chance to join the debate.

The school reform movement has in part been aimed at making the public
more aware of educational issues and at placing the issue of educational excel-

lence high on the national agenda. The reform movement has succeeded in accomplishing this aim. Both candidates for the U.S. presidency in 1988 for a time emphasized the need for educational reform. In any case, thanks to the school reform movement, since 1983 the public's level of concern about the quality of our nation's educational system has been raised. How and in what ways this increased public awareness of education will be converted into school reform is quite another matter. Although the reform movement has enjoyed some successes, the direction educational change will take in the future is problematic and will necessitate a public dialogue about the purposes and means of education. It is a dialogue faculties of education should be eager to join.

The time seemed opportune for the faculty at UCLA's Graduate School of Education to join the debate. Our assumptions are several. Of course we assume that educationists have an obligation to conduct research and advance the frontiers of educational knowledge. Nevertheless, although it is difficult to argue that there will ever be "enough" research on the problems of educational effectiveness, the vast outpouring of educational research threatens to overwhelm or confuse judgment.[13] We therefore assume that it is not more educational research that is needed right now but enlightenment of the public as to what all this research means. Education faculties have a responsibility to help illuminate the vital educational issues of the day that preoccupy us as citizens and parents and school board members as well as practitioners. Faculties of education must reach out to the concerned public that does not read the professional education literature, and do so in a language that the public can understand.

On the other hand, we assume that the school reform movement cannot long continue to dismiss or deprecate educationists or faculties of education. Some prominent activists in the school reform movement have a refined historical sensibility and should recall earlier "excellence" movements, like that of the 1950s, that did not hesitate to attack the "interlocking directorate of professional educationists" while attempting to bypass the educationists yet force change in the public schools. That school reform movement was also marked by fervent enthusiasm, zeal, and optimism. Yet its ultimate impact was patchy and ephemeral.[14] Given the history of post-Sputnik school reform movements, it would seem only prudent for today's school reformers to seek the involvement and cooperation of faculties of education in school reform. More than prudence, however, should dictate a rapprochement between the school reformers and educationists.

The school reform movement has provided the stimulus for many important changes taking place in many state and local public school systems. And now that the 1988 election results are in, it seems that the momentum of and popular support for the school reform movement will be sustained and the pace of reform even accelerated: George Bush has stated that he would like to be known as the "education president"; U.S. Education Secretary Lauro F. Cavazos has called for increased federal aid to education. But how reform intentions will be translated into public school policy and practice in the next few years is still uncertain. For example, it is not clear that the school reform movement has at its disposal very much pedagogical expertise to guide state and local school districts in achieving educational excellence or in spending whatever incremental funds should become available for education.[15] Educational research has made substantial contributions to the instructional process since the 1970s. Yet the school reform movement shows little evidence that it is aware of—let alone that it has utilized—any of this body of research.[16] One thing is certain: if the school reform movement is to achieve its goal of excellence, it will have to enter a new phase in which problems of pedagogy—of how to teach, what to teach, when to teach, and in general how to transform a body of subject matter into a curriculum of instruction suitable for diverse groups of children and adolescents—are moved front and center. And problems of pedagogy are the domain of schools of education and their faculties.[17]

The current situation, it should be made clear, offers opportunities as well as problems and dilemmas for educationists. Even if unwelcome and uninvited by the reform movement, and even if suspicious of or opposed to the reform movement, it is time for schools and faculties of education to become involved in the school reform debates now under way, lest by default they concede the issue of educational "excellence" to the reform movement. Educationists must speak up publicly not only in defense of their values but also in defense of their claim to pedagogical expertise, lest they risk becoming irrelevant in the debates that may help shape American education for the 1990s. If educationists refuse to join the debate or engage in massive resistance to the excellence movement, they run the risk, as Finn warns, of encouraging more radical educational reform proposals, with consequences for the public "common" school, as we have traditionally known it, that are hard to predict.[18]

The primary intended audience for this volume is interested parents, school board members, lay educational policymakers—in short, the public that is concerned about our current educational problems. Of course, we hope to reach the education practitioners, as well as school administrators and teachers in training or in service. One of the problems we faced was finding the proper voice in which to address this audience. The contributions in this volume are presented in a serious and scholarly but accessible style, so far as possible. For many contributors it is a first attempt at reaching out to a general, as opposed to a professional educationist, audience. The essays are authored by nationally and internationally prominent figures in the field of education, representing widely divergent interests, fields of expertise, and experience. They reflect the extraordinary diversity of disciplinary domains and languages characteristic of our highly compartmentalized and specialized education faculty, one that we believe is fairly typical of every major university-affiliated school of education faculty in the country.

Although our authors hold widely differing points of view on the school reform movement, they assume that it has something positive and valuable to offer our schools. This is not to say they do not take a critical stance. But they are not interested in polemics. Some of our authors are concerned with the reformers' omissions or oversights, the unfinished agenda of the school reform movement. Others point to what they perceive as the lack of balance in the school reform agenda. Others are concerned that the school reform agenda is not radical enough. Others fault the reform movement's parochialism or provincialism. Whatever their position, our contributors hope to stretch the boundaries of thought that currently define our educational debates in America; to provide the noneducation specialist, the general public, and educational policymakers—and not excluding teachers in training, school administrators, and educational practitioners in general—with "perspectives" on the central educational issues of the day that have been raised by the school reform movement; and to introduce readers to the concepts, literature, and "languages" in which these issues are addressed and with which anyone wishing to be informed about or to participate in the current educational debates should be familiar. In short, their ultimate aim is the improvement of public discourse about education. The coherence of this collection of essays stems from this and not from any consensus about the school reform movement or the purpose or future course of American public education.

The opening essay, by Sol Cohen, points out that current public school practices are undergirded by a tradition or paradigm of education he calls "therapeutic," a tradition he traces back to the mental hygiene movement of the 1920s and 1930s. As depicted by Cohen, the therapeutic tradition of education is comprised of a mixture of psychiatric and psychoanalytic norms, concepts, and language, and embodies a view of children and youth as highly vulnerable to psychological problems, the family as the seedbed of maladjustment, the school as a kind of clinic or strategic center for applied mental hygiene, the teacher as a therapist, and the overriding concern of the whole educational enterprise as being to promote the student's psychological adjustment or to heal the afflicted. Cohen does not discount the humanitarian impulse behind the mental hygiene movement in education that helps account for the tenacious appeal and widespread acceptance of therapeutic concepts of education. He points out, however, that the notion of the school as clinic is an example of our faith in the omnicompetence of the public school and of our limited vision of possible alternative sites for intervention. Whatever the social problem, pressure is put on the public school to adopt ever-widening surrogate functions and to burden the teacher with new responsibilities, leading to slackness in the school's instructional effectiveness and leaving its aims and purposes confused and unfocused.

Cohen goes on to cite two specific areas of everyday school practice, grading and discipline, where entrenched therapeutic values and concerns pose a challenge to the reform movement. He notes that if the school reform or excellence movement is to make any deep and lasting impact, it will have to contest therapeutic concepts of education and open for public debate the entire question of the school's responsibility for the mental health and psychological adjustment of students, what has merit in the idea and what has not.

In Chapter 2 Carl Weinberg considers the school reform movement's emphasis on excellence a serious and worthy one, but calls attention to the movements' limited understanding of excellence. He is disturbed by the reform movement's emphasis on a narrow, standardized curriculum for all and opposes what Theodore Sizer has called the reform movement's "rhetoric of toughness." Weinberg accuses the school reform movement of insensitivity to the full range of individual potential for excellence. He seeks to remind school reformers of progressive and humanistic or neo-humanistic educational ideals: creativity, self-expression, aesthetic development, and interpersonal competence. Weinberg has a warning for the school reform movement. He is convinced that reformers who wish to return schooling solely to the training of the intellectual faculties "are naive in not recognizing that a large segment of the informed public is sympathetic to having expressive and interpersonal goals for the classroom."

Weinberg observes that the reason our high school students fail to achieve "excellence" and realize their true potential has little to do with course requirements or standards, and everything to do with the way they are miseducated and mistreated in school: "Students are multidimensional, expressive, confluent beings who would love to know and appreciate the world, if only it weren't made so unpleasant for them to do so." Weinberg concludes that the holistic, expressive, and interpersonal goals of humanistic education are not only a good in themselves; if seriously pursued by the public school, they might mitigate not only some of the problems of our "at risk" school population but also some of the problems of our "at risk" nation.

James E. Bruno also has no quarrel with the school reform movement's goal of excellence, but points to its questionable reliance on standardized tests of achievement to measure its progress toward that goal. He distinguishes between summative or "thermometer"-type tests, upon which the reform movement currently relies to drive its reform agenda, and formative or "thermostat"-type tests. Bruno criticizes widely used standardized tests like the SAT because they only provide a gross number or score or grade, and serve simply as placement and selection devices while contributing little or nothing to "formative evaluation," the aim of which is to provide diagnosis and feedback to the student, the teacher, and the instructional process *before* summative evaluation occurs.

Bruno depicts standardized multiple-choice tests as especially unhelpful and even counterproductive for at-risk, low-achieving students—those whom, in the interests of equity, the school reform movement is presumably concerned to help. "The breakdown in the formative evaluation process," he claims, "places low-achieving students at risk since they are promoted through the grades independent of their skill levels in language arts, math, and science." But Bruno's criticisms of the widespread utilization of summative, thermometer-type standardized tests go further. He concludes that they impinge on local control of schools, lead to curricula and instructional procedures that are test-driven, and have resulted in the emergence of standardized testing as a big business and an influential but shadowy player in education. Bruno is especially concerned to call attention to the recent phenomenon of "testwiseness" or "teaching to the test" and its adverse consequences for public education. He calls upon the reform movement to make the development of instrumentation for formative evaluation a top priority.

Harry F. Silberman and John E. Coulson point to an irony of school reform. The school reform movement emphasizes that educational "mediocrity" places the United States at a competitive disadvantage in the world marketplace because the public schools turn out an untrained and uneducated labor force while it is silent about or rejects altogether the subject of vocational training or education for work. Silberman and Coulson fault the school reform movement's limited definition of educational excellence and express reservations about its proclaimed commitment to equity. They do admit that improvements in vocational education are necessary, that they can be made and are being made; and they give credit to the school reform movement for providing the spur for needed improvements. But, they continue, the school reform movement's commitment to the education of the collegebound, and its lack of understanding and sympathy for the educational needs of the non-collegebound, only makes the vocational educator's task that much more difficult while raising questions about the school reform movement's commitment to equity.

Silberman and Coulson conclude that through vocational education or education for work the country's manpower needs can be better met, the ideal of equity served, and the cultural and cognitive aims of education, especially with low-achieving and minority, inner-city youth, advanced. They call for a broadening of the school reform movement's agenda to include not only a sympathetic interest in and support for vocational education but also more attention to parenting and early child care, to community housing patterns, to the status needs of the ordinary wage earner, and to the work place as a site for education, training, and retraining.

Frank M. Hewett and Virginia Wagner are concerned with children and youth whose presence in the public school has so far been ignored or neglected by the school reform movement: the physically, emotionally, or mentally handicapped with their special problems and needs. They discuss recent developments connected with the enforcement of federal school legislation on behalf of the handicapped, specifically PL 94–142, the Education for All Handicapped Children Act, signed into law by President Gerald Ford in 1975, which mandated "mainstreaming" of handicapped students, that is, their placement, so far as possible, in regular, not special, classes.

PL 94–142 flowed directly from the equity concerns of minority groups in this country in the 1960s and early 1970s; the handicapped were entitled to as good an education as everyone else. Hewett and Wagner agree that the goal of educational equity must be served. Then they raise the fundamental issues: Can the excellence movement accommodate this special group of students? What are the problems of integrating large numbers of visually impaired, physically disabled, emotionally disturbed, mildly mentally retarded, or otherwise handicapped students into regular or "mainstream" educational programs with nonhandicapped students? What will be the effect on the handicapped of attending regular classes? What will be the likely outcomes in relation to the goals of the school reform movement in, for example, the areas of academic achievement and class-room discipline? Hewett and Wagner conclude that what happens will depend ultimately on the classroom teacher. They assume "that some sort of teacher heroics will surface and save the day." In fairness to the teacher, however, they urge that school reformers "had better begin assembling the resources, supportive services, and funding necessary to nurture and develop" the extraordinary teacher motivation and effort that will be called for.

Burton R. Clark calls attention to the dysfunctional bureaucratic and organi-zational features of our public comprehensive high schools that, unless remedied, make problematic any fundamental and enduring school reform at the secondary school level. Clark looks at the dysfunctional bureaucratic and standardized features of the American public high school thrice, so to speak: once as seen in the mirror of recent scholarly literature on the American high school, and then as seen through the "mirrors" of Japanese secondary education and American higher education. He includes that current proposals for school reform, such as those contained in the Carnegie Foundation's *A Nation Prepared: Teachers for the 21st Century*, are useful but "likely to be short-lived" unless the high school's governance, organization, and structure are drastically altered.

Can our public secondary schools move beyond bureaucracy to become dis-tinctive, teacher-oriented organizations "that motivate teachers and elicit their commitment"? Are there school structures "that activate students rather than bore them"? Clark suggests that the answer lies in high schools that are inten-tionally specialized rather than the all-embracing, comprehensive public high school. Individual high schools should strive to be distinctive in some component of their educational makeup. Differences among high schools should be grounded not in the accidents of neighborhood location but in special educational interests, approaches, and subjects. Clark's chapter is a powerful argument against the public comprehensive high school of the sort that has rarely been heard in this country. Clark emphasizes, however, that the effort should be "not to abandon the public school." The schools' salvation, he concludes, lies in diversity, specialization, decentralization, autonomy at the level of the individual high school, competition among school districts, and a system of dual or shared governance of the high school between teachers and the formal bureaucratic authority structure.

Richard C. Williams makes two major points: (1) that true educational reform must begin in the primary grades; (2) even if the reform movement turns its attention to the elementary school, as it must eventually, it will not have any fundamental, long-term impact unless it undertakes "second order" (as opposed to "first order") school reforms. By "first order" school reforms Williams means the more or less conventional or traditional school reform demands for more or higher or tougher: more courses, higher standards, tougher discipline. By "sec-ond order" reforms he refers to a different, more radical set of reforms having to do with the working climate and staff relations at the individual elementary school site.

Williams demands that a new, more collegial relationship between teachers and administrators, between public school staff and parents, and between public school and community must be created if school reform is to succeed. He gives the teacher a critical role as change agent. Williams insists, however, that it will not be enough to increase standards of academic preparation of prospective teachers, increase teacher salaries, and certify minimum teacher competence through rigorous testing, as the Carnegie Forum or the Holmes Group calls for, without taking steps to improve teacher morale, including making teachers partners in the management of the individual school. Further, any proposals for teacher empowerment will be ineffective without special training of teachers. It is not enough, Williams concludes, for every teacher to know his or her subject thoroughly. Teacher training will also have to emphasize group dynamics, small-group leadership techniques, and interpersonal relations.

Along parallel lines, Donald A. Erickson emphasizes that "technical" reforms cannot achieve the goals of the school reform movement. He stresses that the heart and soul of a school is its "communal system." Erickson emphasizes the connection between the school as a miniature community and school effectiveness or excellence, illustrating his observations from investigations of private schools, especially Catholic schools. He points out that schools do matter, and that it is the school's communal ethos—which powerfully affects students, teachers, and parents—that matters most. Erickson's chapter is ultimately an argument on behalf of parental choice; choice and a positive communal ethos go hand in hand. Erickson emphasizes that the educational achievement of minority and inner-city students especially is enhanced where there is a positive communal ethos in the school. In fact, Erickson observes, a positive communal ethos can enhance student learning in spite of poor teachers, inadequate curriculum, or a school's lack of material or financial resources.

Erickson raises the troubling questions of whether the public school can produce the kind of favorable communal environment more commonly found in private schools; whether it would require that the compulsory aspects of the public school be fundamentally altered first; or whether it would require that the public school be privatized and parents enabled by allocation of public resources to send their children to schools of their choice, public or private. If the responsibility and the means for educational "choice" are not given or returned to parents, Erickson doubts that the public school system can ever achieve any kind of excellence or retain the support of its essential middle-class constituency.

Concepción M. Valadez respects the school reformers' goal of excellence. In her view the reform movement was launched to improve education for all students, to provide all an equal opportunity to succeed at the highest levels of which they are capable. But if large numbers of children and youth, largely Black and Hispanic, are unprepared to profit from excellence in education, the reform movement becomes a mockery. This is indeed what is happening, she says, where standard academic curricula are prescribed for all high school students while many students enter high school to undertake studies for which they have no preparation and in a language in which they are not proficient. Valadez's point is that higher standards, restructuring the organization of the school, or even empowering teachers is insufficient to attain the goal of excellence and equity if the needs of inner-city, minority, and especially language-minority students are ignored. She is especially troubled that the school reform movement is going forward on a foundation that does not concern itself enough with the special needs of language-minority children and youth. The results are irrefutable: the unacceptably high dropout rate for Black, and especially Latino, high school students.

Valadez stresses that the key ingredient in a successful program for language-minority students, especially Latino students, is bilingual education—instruction primarily in the first or home or native language until English proficiency is secured. In her words, "begin by using the first language, with a shift to instruction totally in English as the students become proficient [in English]." She acknowledges the controversy surrounding bilingual education. Valadez depicts the views of the "English only" movement as defensive and revelatory of a lack of confidence in the assimilative capacity of America. She also notes the irony of reformist calls for multilingualism while rejecting bilingual education. Valadez finally makes the case for bilingual education on the reform movement's own grounds—as the most effective instructional means to help language-minority students achieve educational excellence.

Valadez looks for support for her position in current research on the concept of "common underlying proficiency" (CUP), as opposed to the concept of "separate underlying proficiency" (SUP). That is, if one learns something—a subject or a skill—through one language, it is not stored separately in the brain from what is learned through another language; rather, the mind develops a "common underlying proficiency" that can be accessed through any language the person speaks and understands. Valadez's chapter provides a stark reminder that in many areas of the country the minority and language-minority population of our public school system are growing faster than the Anglo student population. She concludes that the school reform movement must support bilingual education (by whatever name it is called) and must supply the resources so that its goal of excellence can be attained by language-minority students.

Barbara Hecht takes up and broadens the discussion initiated by Valadez. The school reform movement is very articulate and even persuasive about its goals of excellence for all. But, she notes, although its spokespersons are aware that language proficiency is the underpinning of educational excellence and of the entire educational process, the school reform movement is virtually silent about the instructional means for attaining language proficiency. Lacking any concrete suggestions for improving students' language arts acquisition and communication, the reform movement runs the risk of making no progress in its drive for educational excellence for all.

Hecht points out that the problem of language arts acquisition is especially problematic for low-income, inner-city minority and other at-risk student populations. The question Hecht poses is "How do we help such students to achieve excellence?" While the excellence movement focuses largely on the high school and secondary education, Hecht identifies the major problems as being in the home, the community, the kindergarten, and the elementary school. One problem is that the language or dialect learned at home and in the community differs from the language of the public school. The task of the public school, Hecht stresses, is to respect the linguistic heritage of minority students while helping them to attain proficiency in Standard English. If, on the one hand, the home language poses a problem, on the other hand and more positively, Hecht identifies the home as our "most effective language school" because it provides opportunities for sustained oral or verbal communication that are essential for language development, opportunities that are absent in most classrooms. One implication Hecht draws for school reform is that teachers must be persuaded to abandon their passive, recitation methods of teaching, ubiquitous even in elementary school, and give children more opportunities to talk and communicate, especially in the context of small-group peer interaction.

On the teaching of literacy, by which she means reading and writing, Hecht points out that many children enter elementary school prepared for literacy instruction by home and parents. Other children enter school unprepared for the mysterious world of writing and books and the printed, as opposed to the spoken, word. For these children, their fate is often frustration and early failure. The solution, Hecht claims, resides in the preschool years, beginning with the kindergarten. Teachers must identify literacy problems, demystify the world of the printed word, and compensate for the lack of children's literacy readiness.

Hecht describes some promising experiments in teaching literacy to children. In one, starting with conversation, small-group interaction, and the creation of "spoken texts," the teacher moves gradually to written texts, with the children always active in the process of revision and editing their own "texts." Hecht concludes that "When the goal of the classroom is genuine communication and exchange of information between teachers and students rather than recitation and drill," the classroom will become a successful language learning environment, and the goal of excellence and equity for all will become a more realistic goal.

James S. Catterall and Harry Handler place the discussion of the politics of school reform firmly in the context of post–1950 school reform movements. They point out that these post-Sputnik educational reform movements occurred at a time of economic expansion. They describe several problems these reform movements faced that bear on our current educational situation: for example, the "issue attention cycle" of the public tends to be short-lived, and school reformers pay too little attention to "implementation politics." That the current school reform movement has been so long-lived they attribute to "key bargains" struck over critical issues of accountability, assessment, and funding among the chief parties to educational reform, particularly the public school system's leaders at the district and state levels and the state legislatures and state governors.

Catterall and Handler caution against projecting sweeping reform expectations, not only for the reasons cited above but also because ultimately school reform has to do with choices among values; because such choice involves allocation of public resources; and because allocation of public resources occurs in the context of public debate and "politics," with results that are unforeseeable. They do venture to predict, however, that the American political scene at the national and state levels will be agitated in the near future by at least three educational issues: (1) the allocation of public resources between the low-achieving and "at risk" and the collegebound student populations; (2) the allocation of public resources to enhance "choice" between public schools or between public and private schooling; and (3) " . . . the lengths to which we are willing to experiment more radically with the structure, organization, and funding of our public schools" in order to achieve excellence and equity.

In the final chapter, Val D. Rust underscores the school reform movement's seeming lack of knowledge of or familiarity with relevant educational debates in Western Europe and the provincialism of our public debates over educational issues. He points out that issues of local control, parental choice, national curriculum, and national assessment have been, and still are being, debated in Europe. On the emergent (in the United States) issue of parental "choice," Rust observes that in England and Norway, democratic polities like our own, the decision has been made to provide some mix of control between parent and state over where a child or youth goes to school and what he or she should study, with the state in both these democracies providing some measure of financial support to enhance parental choice, even if the choice is a private, religiously oriented school.

Rust's depiction of the educational experience of England and Norway emphasizes the virtue of candid and informed public debate, and political negotiation and compromise, over appealing to the courts as a means of settling controversies in education. Rust cautions, however, against any temptation to indiscriminate borrowing or indiscriminate drawing of lessons from other countries. He observes that the "school struggle" continues in England and Norway, as both countries reassess the role of the school in reconciling the tension between egalitarian goals and excellence, and between encouraging the expression of cultural and religious diversity while discouraging divisive ethnocentric and exclusivist tendencies.

The editors of this volume are aware that the following chapters do not provide the last word on the school reform movement. Our authors make recommendations, offer suggestions, and urge courses of action, but we realize that there are few answers to our educational problems here. The educational problems of our time are complex, and many issues of great import for the future remain to be debated. Our hope is that our colleagues on faculties in schools of education around the nation will join us in the debate and that our readers will be better prepared to participate in that debate.

NOTES

1. Solmon, L. C. (1985), Quality of education and economic growth, *Economics of Education Review*, *4*, 280–85.

2. Solmon, L. C. & LaPorte, M. A. (1987), The educational implications of the high technology revolution, in A. Kleingartner & C. S. Anderson (Eds.), *Human resource management in high technology firms* (Lexington, MA: Lexington Books).

3. The National Commission on Excellence (1983), *A nation at risk: The imperative for educational reform*. (Washington, DC: U.S. Government Printing Office), p. 5. Actually, with appendices the report is sixty-four pages long.

4. Honig, B. (1985), *Last chance for our children* (Menlo Park, CA: Addison-Wesley), pp. 185–87.

5. The education profession "is not the only obstacle to the attainment of excellence," Finn continues. But the implication the passage leaves is that of course it is. Finn, C. E., Jr. (1985), The challenges of educational excellence, in C. E. Finn, Jr., D. Ravitch, & P. H. Roberts, *Challenges to the humanities* (New York: Holmes-Meier), pp. 193–94. A similar point is made in Adelson, J. (1985), Four surprises, or why the schools may not improve much, in J. H. Bunzel (Ed.), *Challenge to American schools: The case for standards and values* (New York: Oxford University Press).

6. Finn, C. E., Jr. (1988, January/February), What ails education research, *Educational Researcher*, *17*, 5–8. This is followed by an angry reply to Finn by educationists R. J. Shavelson and D. C. Berliner, which in turn is followed by Finn's equally hostile response.

7. Solmon, L. C. (1988, April 18), *The future demographics of higher education in the U.S.: Prospects for traditional students*, p. 9. Paper prepared for the Ford Foundation Symposium on Demographics, New York.

8. Solmon, L. C. (1988, April), *California higher education, labor market requirements, and social equity: Are the goals conflicting?* p. 15. Paper prepared for the Institute of Industrial Relations, UCLA, conference "Can California Be Both Competitive and Caring?"

9. Palmer, E. L. (1988), *Television and America's children: A crisis of neglect* (New York: Oxford University Press).

10. The Rand Corporation does useful research here. See, e.g., Sedlak, M. & Schlossman, S. (1986), *Who will teach?* (Santa Monica, CA: Rand Corp.).

11. Clark, D. L., & Astuto, T. A. (1986, October), The significance and permanence of change in federal education policy, *Educational Researcher*, *15*, 5–8; Timar, T. B., & Kirp, D. L. (1988), *Managing educational excellence* (New York: The Falmer Press), Chap. 1. Also important here is Finn's "The challenges of educational excellence" (note 5). See also Finn, C. E., Jr., & Ravitch, D. (1984), Conclusions and recommendations: High expectations and disciplined effort, in C. E. Finn, Jr., D. Ravitch, & R. T. Fancher (Eds.), *Against mediocrity: The humanities in America's high schools* (New York: Holmes-Meier).

12. Good examples are Goodlad, J. I. (1984), *A place called school* (New York:

McGraw-Hill); and Sizer, T. R. (1984), *Horace's compromise* (Boston: Houghton Mifflin). Some deans of schools of education are involved in that phase of the school reform movement having to do with teacher training, teacher status, and conditions of work, through the so-called Holmes Group. And the school practitioner's voice has been heard via the National Education Association and the American Federation of Teachers. The 1988 *Harvard Educational Review* special issue, *Educators on Excellence: Steps Toward Real Reform*, is a collection of four articles and a lengthy book review, all culled from the *Review* between 1986 and 1988 and is a good example of educationists writing to and for other educationists.

13. This problem is not limited to the field of education. As Jacques Barzun has pointed out, the glut of research is a problem that afflicts all of academe. (1987, February), Doing Research—should the sport be regulated? *Columbia Magazine*, pp. 18–22.

14. Some readers may recall the "Rockefeller Report on Education." The Rockefeller Brothers Fund (1958), *The pursuit of excellence: Education and the future of America* (New York: Doubleday). The following from a 1964 reformist tract should also provide cause for reflection: "New ideas are routing traditional ideas and are beginning to transform every aspect of school practice, from curriculum to architecture, from the structure of the grades to the purpose of learning, from the training of teachers to the motivating of students." Gross, R., & Murphy, J. (Eds.) (1964), *The revolution in the schools* (New York: Harcourt, Brace), p. 1. For the context, we recommend Ravitch, D. (1983), *The troubled crusade: American education, 1945–1980* (New York: Basic Books).

15. This problem is epitomized by the recent passage of Proposition 98, the school funding initiative, in California. Although earmarking a fixed percentage of the state's budget and any budget surpluses for education, Proposition 98 gives no guidance on how such new funds are to be spent. Skirmishes have already broken out about whether new funds can/should be used to increase teacher salaries, or whether they should be used to achieve smaller class sizes, purchase new textbooks, and so on.

16. For example, U.S. Department of Education (1986), *What works: Research about teaching and learning* (Washington, D.C.: U.S. Government Printing Office). This is painfully thin gruel and illustrates just how much the school reform movement needs help in the area of pedagogy.

17. We would like to call attention to the work of M. C. Wittrock, especially his (1986), Students' thought processes, in M. C. Wittrock (Ed.), *The handbook of research on teaching*, 3rd ed. (New York: Macmillan), pp. 297–313; (1987), Models of heuristic teaching, in M. J. Dunkin (Ed.), *International encyclopedia of teaching and teacher education* (Oxford: Pergamon Press), 68–76; and, a constructive review of research on learning strategies, in E. Goetz & C. Weinstein (Eds.), *Learning and study strategies* (New York: Academic Press). We also recommend Lee S. Shulman (1986, Spring), Those who understand: A conception of teacher knowledge, *American Educator*, pp. 9–15, 43–44. For the more specific subject of the teaching of history, so dear to the school reform movement, there is much to learn from Weinberg, S., & Wilson, S. M. (1989), Subject matter knowledge in the teaching of history, in J. E. Brophy (Ed.), *Advances in research on teaching*, (Greenwich, CT: JAI). The chapters by Professors Valadez and Hecht in our volume also contain concrete suggestions for improving padagogy.

18. After describing professional educators as "wary, suspicious and a bit resentful" toward the school reform or excellence movement, Finn goes on to observe that if the education profession turns its wariness and jealousy into massive resistance, the excellence

movement will not achieve much. Such resistance, he warns, in the long run will play into the hands of more radical school reformers of both right and left, with unpredictable consequences for the survival of public education in anything resembling its familiar form. Finn, C. E., Jr. (1984, Summer), "Gee, Officer Krupke" and other barriers to excellence in the schoolroom, *Policy Review*, p. 73.

1 Every School a Clinic: A Historical Perspective on Modern American Education

Sol Cohen

It is a commonplace that American public schools are in a state of crisis. The list of ailments is long, and so is that of the proposed remedies. But what, exactly, is the nature of the crisis? And what can a historian of education contribute to our understanding of it?

We are currently in the throes of another school reform movement. Reformers call for dramatic improvement in the quality of education in our public elementary and secondary schools as the nation's number one domestic priority. Excellence is their watchword. Excellence is to be achieved through a rigorous curriculum in the "basics" or the "new basics," tougher promotion and graduation standards, frequent achievement testing for students, competency testing for teachers, and lengthening the school day and the school year, along with a restoration of discipline and an orderly learning environment.[1] The tide of public opinion seems to be running with the reform movement for now. But it remains to be seen how far the reformers' proclaimed objective of excellence will be translated into public school policy and practice. That the issues at stake in the school reform movement are philosophical or, in the broad sense, ideological has been pointed out by several commentators.[2] In their attempts to identify the chain of ideas undergirding contemporary American education, variously depicted as progressive, modernist, or secularist, they so far have overlooked an essential link in that chain. Current school practice and policies are supported and sustained by a conception of education or an orientation to education that can be called by the shorthand term "therapeutic," and that reformers will have to contest if they are to have any fundamental or long-term impact on the public school.

By the "therapeutic conception of education" I mean a set of ideas about education embodying a mixture of psychiatric and essentially psychoanalytic norms, concepts, and language of discourse that stresses the centrality of the emotions in human behavior; views parents and the family as a seedbed of neurosis and maladjustment, children and youth as exquisitely vulnerable or predisposed to maladjustment, the school as a kind of psychiatric clinic, and the teacher as a kind of therapist; and that holds that the overriding concern of the entire educational enterprise is to work for the prevention and cure of psychological maladjustment—or, more positively, to foster students' mental health and psychological adjustment. The source of ideas for and the inspiration behind the therapeutic conception of schooling, and the driving force behind the diffusion of psychiatric and psychoanalytic or therapeutic values, concepts, and language throughout American education, was the mental hygiene movement. Few intellectual and social movements of this century have had a more widespread influence on the theory and practice of American education than what can be subsumed under the heading of the mental hygiene movement.

American education has been far more influenced by psychiatry and psychoanalysis than has heretofore been realized. In 1920 hygienist or therapeutic concepts of education were the possession of a small community of avant-garde psychiatrists, psychologists, and social workers. By 1950, when the Mid-century White House Conference on Children and Youth adopted as its theme "For Every Child a Healthy Personality," concern for students' mental health and emotional adjustment had been integrated into progressive education and was becoming pervasive in American educational discourse more generally. In 1955 mental health as an educational objective, by then fused with progressive education, could be depicted as "a cliché of the times."[3] Hygienist or therapeutic concepts remain potent to this day, occupying a significant place in the mental world of educational practitioners as well as of the general public. Yet the influence of psychiatry and the mental hygiene movement in American education is today largely forgotten. But the purpose of this chapter is not simply to fill this gap in our memory of our educational past, but also to point out the direct relevance of hygienist concepts for the current school reform movement. The past, as Faulkner remarked, is not dead, it is not even past. "The culture of the past," Northrop Frye observed, "is not only the memory of mankind, but of our own buried life." And study of it, he continued, "leads to a recognition scene, a discovery in which we see, not our past lives but the total cultural form of our own present life." This chapter presents some recognition scenes. My belief is that what we recognize in them is a compelling part not only of our own buried educational past but of our present educational situation as well.

Finally, this chapter depicts an episode in the broader story of the assumption by the school of ever-expanding surrogate functions, one of the major themes of twentieth-century educational development in the United States. From many quarters today the public school is criticized for taking on responsibilities of parents and family, and of health and other social agencies, while neglecting those educational or instructional functions it alone can best accomplish.[4] The public school is vulnerable to such criticism. The question to ask is how it has happened that we have come to expect the school to assume ever-expanding responsibility for the care of children and youth, as if it had some omnipotent power. Two things are certain: the public school did not acquire its characteristic biases in an intellectual vacuum, and it did not acquire them overnight.

One can date the beginning of the mental hygiene movement from 1909 and the organization of the National Committee for Mental Hygiene (NCMH). Among the lay persons active at the birth or in the early years of the NCMH were William James, Julia Lathrop, and Charles W. Eliot, as well as Clifford W. Beers, author of the path-breaking memoir *A Mind That Found Itself* (1908). A small group of progressive psychiatrists, including Drs. Adolf Meyer, August Hoch, C. Macfie Campbell, William Alanson White, and Thomas W. Salmon, provided the NCMH's early medical leadership.

Before World War I the NCMH was content with a modest program aimed at improving the condition and the treatment of the institutionalized mentally ill and mentally defective. By the 1920s, however, its scope had expanded from an essentially meliorative program into a crusade for the prevention of all forms of maladjustment while attempting to extend its province into the nation's schools. The theoretical basis for the crusading zeal that came to characterize the mental hygiene movement in education in the 1920s was fashioned out of psychoanalytic concepts extrapolated from Freud (as well as, in lesser degree, from Jung and Adler), added to Dr. Adolf Meyer's "psychiatry of the whole person," with psychoanalysis as the catalyst.

The optimistic and even utopian hopes of the mental hygiene movement in education rested on a new conception of the cause of mental illness that placed the emphasis on psychological and environmental factors and on the possibility of treatment and cure while minimizing the then-dominant hereditarian and organic or neurological emphasis in American psychiatry with its therapeutic pessimism. The psychiatrist leaders of the NCMH and the architects of what was christened the New Psychiatry held that a large proportion of mental illness was not some form of "insanity" but a form of psychological maladjustment acquired or learned for which a remedy was not impossible or even difficult. The new view held that maladjustment did not strike suddenly or from out of the blue, but had its origins in early childhood. Instinctive tendencies or emotional patterns acquired or learned in the early years of childhood (Freud's emphasis on the first five years was gradually expanded to include all of preadolescence and then adolescence) tended to persist in the unconscious and were the principal determinants of later psychological maladjustment. The emotions were the essential core of personality, penetrating the mental life of all of us, the normal as well as the pathological; indeed, they were the most determining aspect of human behavior, more decisive than intelligence or rationality or will.

This notion of the dominant role of the emotions is central to the hygienist model of personality from which everything else followed. Thus, the child's behavior was neither good nor bad, but "purposive," motivated by the search for satisfaction of emotional "needs," and largely unconscious. Maladjustment and mental illness resulted from the frustration or prohibition or suppression of emotional "needs," leading to inner conflict and repression, the scourge of mental health and wholesome personality development. The repressed or unsatisfied needs continued to operate on an unconscious level, influencing thought and surfacing later in maladjustment and psychological disorders of all sorts.

The reformulation of the cause and course of mental illness opened up a vast new field for psychiatry, for the mental hygiene movement, and ultimately for public education. Psychiatrists and hygienists were led to a radically new approach not only to problems of mental illness but also to problems like dependency, delinquency, and crime. In the new view the latter were to be regarded as medical or psychiatric problems; "symptoms" of underlying psychological maladjustment or faulty personality development; forms of mental illness. That is, faulty personality development could lead either to neurosis (or more serious mental illness) *or* to antisocial behavior such as delinquency and crime. The implications of the new view were quickly drawn by hygienists. To correct or prevent the basic factors causing the "symptoms" would be to strike at the root not only of mental illness but also of many social problems. And prevention was feasible because—and here we come to the core belief of the mental hygiene movement—the chief source of its optimism, personality development was in large measure dependent upon environmental factors that were in society's power to modify. Belief in environmentalism made hygienist intervention in childhood and adolescence theoretically possible, practically feasible, and even morally imperative.

The pieces for a mental hygiene movement with the focus on the public school were almost in place. Even before World War I NCMH officials, led by Dr. Thomas W. Salmon, the first medical director, were eager to steer the NCMH into a program of prevention with the focus on children and the public school, but the NCMH lacked the financial resources to make such an idea operative. In the postwar period, the Commonwealth Fund (CF), created in 1919 by the Harkness family with the vague mandate "to do something for the welfare of mankind," had a huge sum of money at its disposal and was actively soliciting ideas on how to dispense it. Inevitably the fate or the fortunes of the CF intersected with those of the NCMH.

In early 1921 Dr. Salmon proposed a joint NCMH-CF program aimed at the prevention of juvenile delinquency. His proposal was quickly acted upon. In December 1921 the Commonwealth Fund launched its momentous "Program for the Prevention of Delinquency." The program provided the main financial support of the NCMH and the mental hygiene movement in the 1920s, and constituted the dynamic core of the mental hygiene movement in this decade. Under the direction of NCMH psychiatrists, the program launched the child guidance movement and greatly stimulated the development of child psychiatry as well as psychiatric social work in this country. And, finally, the program became the spearhead of the mental hygiene movement in education.

The initial aim of the Program for the Prevention of Delinquency was the early identification and treatment of "predelinquent" or "problem" children; its locus of activity, the juvenile court and the child guidance clinic. But program leaders soon concluded that preventive work had to be started before problems arose, that the goal of the program should be prevention of maladjustment in general, and that the locus of activity should be the public school.

Actually, given the hygienist emphasis on the importance of early experience, the primary site for preventive efforts should have been parents and the family, not the school. In fact, hygienists turned their attention to parents only to give them short shrift. One of the main themes of mental hygiene literature of the 1920s is parent-blaming. Hygienists made a direct causal connection between parents' treatment of children and all subsequent psychological or behavioral disorders. The seeds of maladjustment were sown in childhood. No child escaped the home unscarred. The faults of parents were many. Regardless of good intentions, parents did harm. "There is no such thing as a 'bad' child," declared one hygienist—in a phrase that would echo through the decades—only sick or maladjusted children and bad parents.[5] The parents were bad because they were ignorant of the emotional needs of children, were rigidly moralistic, and relied on excessively harsh restraints, prohibitions, and punishments in raising children. Hygienists turned to the public school and the teacher to accomplish everything that parents had bungled.

It was not so much that hygienists thought teachers were any less rigid or authoritarian than parents, but that teachers seemed more accessible and—thanks to compulsory education—the public school provided a huge captive audience. Children and youth were compelled to attend school; the school had jurisdiction over them during the formative years. The compulsory education laws made the public school an irresistible target for hygienists: "If we are going to prevent dependency, delinquency, insanity, and general inadequacy, the school should be the focus of our attack."[6] The ultimate goal of the mental hygiene movement in education was stated succinctly by another program staffer: "Every School a Clinic."[7]

The influence of the mental hygiene movement in American public education has been essentially of two kinds: first, its influence has been felt by way of a general orientation to education; and second, its influence has been felt through specific concepts and policies it helped promote. In general, hygienists sought a radical shift in the public school's priorities. It is the kind of shift implied in a leading hygienist's assertion that "Education has been . . . too much confined to teaching; it needs to be developed as a scheme for assisting and guiding the developing personality."[8] This was fundamental; the person who made the statement, Dr. William Alanson White, one of the founding fathers of the NCMH, was articulating the central plank of the mental hygiene movement in education. How was the public school's transformation into an agency for guiding personality development to be achieved? By psychologizing the total school environment, by converting every aspect of school life into psychiatric phenomena, by putting all school procedures to the test of whether they passed mental hygiene muster. This meant, on the negative side, removing all obstacles to wholesome personality development—that is, the elimination, so far as possible, of all sources of frustration or pressure or stress in school. And, more positively, it meant requiring the teacher to assume the functions of a hygienist or therapist.

When hygienists viewed the public school, they saw not the benign and uplifting little red school house of American folklore but a site where stress, anxiety, and repression reigned, a uniquely stressful and psychologically harmful milieu responsible for untold cases of emotional disorder and nervous breakdown as well as juvenile delinquency and crime. The main sources of stress and anxiety in school were identified as four: the school's intellectual and subject matter emphasis, its grading policy, its patterns of discipline and classroom management, and the training, attitude, and personality makeup of its teaching staff.

Hygienists denounced the intellectualist emphasis in public education as, in the first place, misdirected; our lives are ruled by emotion, not intellect. The school's emphasis on the acquisition of knowledge, on subject matter content and achievement, was antisocial, starved the emotions, and led to a compulsive striving that left the personality scarred. In the second place, and most significant, hygienists denounced the content and achievement emphasis in education because, in their view, the latter condemned many children and youth to failure; to hygienists that was *the* cardinal sin against wholesome personality development.

There was nothing new in the hygienists' downgrading of the intellectual; one could even find such tendencies among the ranks of professional educationists. The contribution of the mental hygiene movement to American education was to interject psychiatric values, concepts, and terminology into American educational discourse about school failure. The mental hygiene movement was preoccupied with the psychological costs of school failure. Hygienists focused on school failure as exclusively a psychological problem (as opposed to an instructional or educational problem implicating knowledge, skill, or teaching method). Hygienists held that failure had traumatic and enduring effects on students' self-esteem.

Hygienists directly connected failure, psychic trauma, and personality maladjustment. Failure led to feelings of inadequacy and inferiority, then to undesirable defense mechanisms like fearfulness, shyness, and withdrawal, and then to neurosis or even more serious mental disorder: the development of a "shut-in personality." Or failure led to antisocial compensations like truancy, delinquency, and crime. And that large numbers of students were bound to fail, given the fact of compulsory education and the public school's emphasis on mastery of academic subject matter, was to hygienists axiomatic. On the other hand, success led to feelings of self-confidence and a positive approach to reality. Hygienists were not interested in why Mary or John failed. All they knew was that the practice was intolerable and had to be abolished.

How could all students be shielded from failure? How could every student achieve success? To hygienists, the practical corollaries seemed self-evident: the easing of competitive pressures, the deemphasis of examinations and grades, and the devaluation of the academic curriculum. Hygienists supported the activity- and project-based curriculum that progressives in education were then calling for. They urged the elimination of tests and grades. And they proposed that the public school adopt a new criterion of success, one that had no relation to academic achievement. The real success of public education had to be measured not in terms of the development of intellect but in the degree to which the student progressed in his or her personality adjustment. By this new standard, it was hoped, even while their "needs" were being met, the least academically able students might be spared the trauma of failure and nonpromotion. The policy in many American public school systems of no failure, of passing all students, and of disregarding standards of scholastic achievement as a condition of promotion found initial justification in a seminal 1909 study of the connections among failure, pupil retardation, and early school leaving (and the twin evils of waste and school efficiency).[9] The teachings of mental hygiene regarding the harmful effects of failure on students' mental health and personality development made the case for no-failure policies much more persuasive.

If stress and pressure in school were to be alleviated and the classroom transformed into a therapeutic environment, not only would failure and fear of failure have to be eliminated but entrenched pedagogical ideas about discipline, misbehavior, and classroom management would have to be repudiated and overthrown. What mental hygiene theory required of the public school in the area of discipline was momentous: that the revolutionary new concepts and theories that psychiatry in the early 1920s was beginning to apply to the understanding and treatment of delinquents and criminals be applied by teachers to the misbehavior of students in the classroom. A specific set of concepts can be identified. First and most important, hygienists advocated that misbehavior in school be redefined or reconceptualized as a medical problem rather than a moral problem; misbehavior was an illness mandating some type of psychological intervention or treatment rather than a "sin" requiring punishment.

We will briefly sketch some other corollaries. Misbehavior in the classroom was aimed at satisfying an emotional "need," largely determined by experience during the childhood years; the student had little rational control over it and could not be held responsible. The student who broke rules, defied order, and otherwise misbehaved was not bad or naughty, but sick or maladjusted; in need of treatment rather than punishment. A student's misbehavior in class was a symptom of frustration; the child was not having his or her "fundamental" or "basic" needs met; the proper response was therapeutic rather than punitive; punishment or reprimand only increased the severity of the underlying problem.

Radical ideas, if repeated long enough, become commonplace ideas, even clichés. Eventually it takes an effort of memory to remember how novel such ideas once were, or where and whence they originated. There was a long tradition of hostility to discipline and of advocacy of permissiveness in American education. What the mental hygiene movement provided was a medical or psychiatric understanding and language of discourse that gave scientific legitimation to such sentiments and eventually came to occupy a central place in the discourse of American education. Hygienists were not oblivious to the imperatives of discipline or classroom management, but they were convinced they were offering teachers a more scientific and effective way to control student behavior than punishment and threat of punishment—the psychiatric management of the school milieu and of the students' emotional "needs." This comes out clearly in hygienist discussions of the "problem child" in school.

In still another radical break from educational tradition, the mental hygiene perspective defined students' expression of aggressive feelings in the classroom, the traditional bane of the teacher, as hardly a problem at all; repression of aggression was the problem. To hygienists, introversion, inhibition, shyness, too much suppression of feelings, and excessive self-control were more serious problems than aggressive behavior and overt violation of rules.

It was once thought that the child was endowed with dangerous impulses that had to be curbed. Now those impulses were seen as dangerous only if curbed and harmless if expressed: repression was dangerous; the discharge of emotions, healthy. Hygienist theory held that the shy, quiet, introverted student who caused no trouble for the teacher in class was the real "problem child," more in need of help than the aggressively misbehaving student because the price of suppressed aggression might be neurosis and even more serious mental illness in the future.[10] To hygienists, the kind of student whom generations of public school teachers had looked upon as a "good" or model student was a repressed and maladjusted student who had to be drawn out of his or her shell. From this viewpoint, the teacher who was strict or censorious and perceived as a feared authority figure contributed to students' inhibition and repression. Hygienists called upon teachers to be more sympathetic to or tolerant of aggressive behavior in the classroom, assuring them that "sublimation" or "catharsis" could provide the happy ending, that in a therapeutic environment all classroom discipline problems would disappear and students' personalities would be freed to develop in wholesome directions.

Hygienists pinpointed teachers as the critical link between hygienist theory and reformed classroom practice, and placed the major burden of responsibility for converting the school into a clinic on the shoulders of the teacher. The mental hygiene movement enormously extended the teacher's field of operation, providing the profession of education with a new ideal of the teacher: the teacher-as-therapist. The teacher-therapist was expected to heal rather than to instruct: to be an expert in the mental hygiene of children and youth, to detect and treat symptoms of maladjustment among students, to go beyond the students' overt behavior and get to know their intimate hopes and fears, to inquire into their relations with parents and siblings in order to undo or correct faulty patterns of emotional development acquired at home or established during the early parent-child relationship. Finally, the teacher-therapist was expected to foster students' personality "adjustment"—the passive, shy, and uninhibited as well as, or more than, the aggressive.

Given their conception of the school as a clinic and the teacher as therapist, it was natural for hygienists to turn their attention to the reform of teacher training. Hygienist goals could not be achieved with teachers who were preoccupied with marks or discipline or the subject matter curriculum. Far more important was knowledge of mental hygiene and personality development. Hygienists urged a complete reversal in teacher training: a shift from preoccupation with knowledge of subject matter to knowledge of mental hygiene and the laws of personality development, a shift in emphasis from the subject to be taught to the person to be taught, a shift as one prominent hygienist put it, "from the teaching of subjects to the development of . . . the whole child."[11]

Such, sketched in its general aspects, are the essential components of the "school as clinic." The main thrust of the mental hygiene movement in education was captured by William I. and Dorothy S. Thomas in their important 1928 study, *The Child in America*. The authors refer confidently to the "increasing helplessness of the family" and the subsequent necessity for the expansion of the public school's functions. "The school," they observe, "is taking over from the court, the clinic, and other social agencies a large share of that responsibility which the increasing helplessness of the family had thrust upon them." At present, they continue, the sentiment that the school is the logical place from which to work for the prevention of social problems has taken the form of a demand that the school shall take over "the responsibility for the 'whole child' . . . the development of his whole personality."[12]

Any reform movement possesses not only a goal or program and an ideology but also a change strategy, implicit or explicit. The goal of the mental hygiene movement in education was not to increase the number of mental health professionals in the schools, nor was its goal the introduction of curricula and courses in mental hygiene. The mental hygiene movement sought something more permanent and fundamental: to alter the school practitioners' orientation, their frame of reference, their "attitude" toward students, teaching methods, the curriculum, classroom procedures, and the ends of education. The objective of the mental hygiene movement in education, to quote a key program document, was to "establish the mental hygiene point of view as a pervading educational philosophy."[13] Hygienist leaders realized that deeply rooted educational traditions stood in the way; hygienists frequently expressed concern about overcoming teacher resistance. To overcome such resistance, they adopted a long-term strategy of developing "awareness—interest" in the mental hygiene view of education and language of discourse among an audience of community influentials, progressive parents, and professionals who would facilitate the acceptance of hygienist beliefs and values by the education practitioners. Here we can indicate only briefly the intellectual routes by which the mental hygiene point of view of education was disseminated. In the 1920s the major responsibility for disseminating the mental hygiene point of view of education was assumed by the Program for the Prevention of Delinquency.

The program's efforts to advance the mental hygiene view of education were extraordinary for its time. The program made a systematic effort throughout the 1920s to reach child study groups, church groups, civic organizations, parents' associations, college and university groups, physicians, social workers, judges, probation officers, writers and editors, and leaders of opinion in the fields of higher education, public health, and child welfare. There was also a huge literature aimed at public opinion more generally; the program distributed tens of thousands of free reprints of articles and pamphlets. In addition, the CF had its own book publishing arm, which allowed the program to publish a score of books and pamphlets on mental hygiene and education. The program was thus able to disseminate a vast amount of literature on the implications of mental hygiene for the school that reached community leaders and opinion makers in government, universities, foundations, and major national civic and religious groups.

Gradually, hygienist ideas about schooling, the mental hygiene perspective on parents, children, and youth, filtered into the consciousness of policymakers and influential publics. By the end of the 1920s, the mental hygiene point of view, hygienist concepts and language, and the hygienist view of parents, children, and education were gaining ascendancy. In the 1930s the Progressive Education Association (PEA) adopted hygienist language, rhetoric, and concepts and in fact replaced the Program for the Prevention of Delinquency as the main conduit for the dissemination of hygienist or therapeutic concepts of education. The relation between the mental hygiene movement and the progressive education movement is important and requires further discussion.

The PEA developed independently of the mental hygiene movement in the 1920s, but clearly on a parallel track. Originally concerned mainly with children and the reform of public grade school education, by the late 1920s the PEA was ready to extend its reach into the public high schools but needed some new ideas in order to approach philanthropic foundations for financial support. The PEA found what it needed in the mental hygiene movement: ideas that were more scientifically up to date than its too familiar child-centered rhetoric, and that at the same time not only complemented but also extended and deepened its own educational ideology.

Personal contacts were made between hygienists and progressives in education at the 1930 White House Conference on Child Health and Protection.[14] The alliance between hygienists and educational progressives developed rapidly; mental hygiene ideas quickly became integrated into progressive education. By the late 1930s the mental hygiene point of view was firmly entrenched in PEA thinking, and hygienist conceptions, rhetoric, and vocabulary had become part of the linguistic currency of progressive education. For example, the oft-cited pedagogical slogan "meeting the needs of adolescence" was borrowed from the mental hygiene movement and made famous by the PEA.[15] The PEA's various commissions with their innumerable publications, conferences, and workshops introduced thousands of parents, teachers, and school administrators to the mental hygiene point of view in the 1930s and 1940s.

Textbooks provided the other main channel through which therapeutic concepts of education were disseminated among the education profession before World War II. The early literature of the mental hygiene movement was not written with the teacher in mind. The idea of the public school's responsibility for the mental hygiene of children began to filter into textbooks for teachers in training only in the mid–1920s, then slowly and steadily gained force. In the 1930s and through the 1940s, a flood of textbooks on mental hygiene and the school appeared. They reveal which hygienist beliefs were being disseminated and the specific vocabulary in which these beliefs were embedded. They displaced or dislodged traditional views. A new educational climate is revealed by the language and tone in which the following rhetorical question is posed in *Emotion and the Educative Process*, an influential 1938 textbook: "The issue must be made clear. Is it more important that children develop adjusted, integrated personalities, or that they fulfill some other traditional academic objectives?"[16]

Collectively, textbooks like these functioned on the national level as a communication network for the diffusion of hygienist beliefs about the school among aspiring entrants to the field of education, initiating future professors of education as well as future public school teachers and school administrators in the therapeutic conception of education. Gradually, through the provision of a framework of conceptions, an orientation, a vocabulary—hygienist ideas, the hygienist way of looking at the public school—the hygienist language of discourse filtered into the consciousness of future teachers, school administrators, and educational policymakers. It is here, in the cumulative process of the dissemination of hygienist language, that we can trace the influence of the mental hygiene movement in public education. Finally, beginning in the late 1930s, mental hygiene concepts and nomenclature begin to figure prominently in the publications of the major national professional education organizations: the National Education Association, the American Council on Education, the Association for Supervision and Curriculum Development, and the Educational Policies Commission.

After World War II the climate of public opinion in the United States was especially favorable to mental hygiene concerns. The postwar period was one of enormous national concern about the mental health of Americans, as shown by the passage by Congress of the National Mental Health Act in 1946. Mental hygiene concepts and language of education became deeply embedded in the consciousness of the nation, part of the common stock of knowledge, and part of the emergence of what Philip Rieff calls "the triumph of the therapeutic" and what Christopher Lasch refers to as the "medicalization" of American culture.[17] By this time, neither the NCMH nor the Commonwealth Fund was very active in educational reform. The CF had begun to phase out the Program for the Prevention of Delinquency and its support of the NCMH in the early

1930s, and to concentrate its resources in medical education and medical research. Without CF support, the NCMH withered; by the late 1940s it was almost moribund. But, by then, neither the NCMH nor the program was needed. The school reform movement that the NCMH had started and the Program for the Prevention of Delinquency it had steered through almost three decades had developed a momentum of its own. The ''medicalization'' of American public education went forward without it.

The culmination of the hygienist drive to make therapeutic concerns the guiding principle of American public education was reached in 1950, at the Mid-century White House Conference on Children and Youth. The mental hygiene approach to education is summed up in the conference's slogan, ''For Every Child a Healthy Personality.'' The 1950 White House conference, so far as the schools were concerned, charted no new path. It stressed the decades-old hygienist contention that the public school is basically an institution to foster students' personality adjustment, with everything else secondary. By 1950 therapeutic concepts of education enjoyed a broad base of public support; the professional leadership of the public schools was receptive. Without controversy or debate, the conference ratified the therapeutic conception of schooling as a new sphere of educational orthodoxy.

The widespread publicity enjoyed by the conference reverberated through the 1950s and into the 1960s, producing another round of textbooks on mental hygiene and education. And now hygienist concepts began to penetrate not only into textbooks in educational psychology but also into textbooks in administration, principles and methods of education, and foundations of education as well as the burgeoning field of curriculum theory, helping to initiate a new generation of teachers and school administrators in therapeutic concepts of education and the mental hygiene view of the school. By the end of the 1950s, mental hygiene language, concepts, and nomenclature had been incorporated into prevailing educational thought; had become a ''cliché of the times,'' part of the consciousness of all those concerned with education, and celebrated or satirized in movies, novels, and musicals.[18]

Some concluding observations about the mental hygiene movement in education, the current situation in American education, and the reform movement are in order.

The mental hygiene movement in education is an example of the uniquely American faith in the omnicompetence of the public school. Whatever the problem, we are seriously assured that our salvation depends on the public school. Pressure is put on the public school to adopt ever widening responsibility for surrogate functions. It is as though neither parents and the family, nor religious or health agencies, nor any other social agency has any function to perform for the young. But once family and parents and social agencies are dismissed, there can be no conception of a division of labor between school and home and other social agencies. Children and youth are gathered in the public school. The public school must tend to them in every aspect of their lives; the school must be responsible for the education of "the whole child."[19]

In the name of prevention of neurosis and other mental disorders, the mental hygiene movement called upon the public school to assume responsibility for the psychological adjustment of children and youth. Teachers were encouraged to believe that it was in their power to preserve the coming generations from maladjustment or to heal the afflicted. There is too little space here to say much by way of criticism of the mental hygiene movement. Suffice it to say for now that although there was no limit to the pretensions of the mental hygiene movement in education, hygienists lacked any serious appreciation of the difficulties of implementing their ideas in the school, let alone of the tenuous research base in personality theory on which their school reform activities were founded. There was no attempt to differentiate the ordinary unhappiness, conflicts, and pains of growing up from pathological problems.

From time to time an insider would raise his or her voice to warn against overzealous school reformers in the mental hygiene movement. In 1932 Adolf Meyer, one of the founding fathers of the NCMH, expressed serious reservations about turning the school into a clinic and the teacher into a psychiatrist. "We must look to the school to attend to things that it can do," he warned. "I am very skeptical about the wisdom of introducing too much pathology into the school. . . . We have to cultivate in the school interest in the things which are of the school and for the school."[20]

Few hygienists were willing to listen to words of caution. The problem was urgent. Maladjustment and mental illness seemed to be ubiquitous, afflicting the nation like a modern plague. The situation called for action. Hygienists turned to the school-as-clinic as the panacea. The school would counterbalance unhealthy personality traits acquired in the family environment while fortifying the personality of all children and youth, but only if it ceased to be a source of maladjustment and instead become a haven where all children and youth would experience success, build up self-esteem, and develop their whole personality.

One cannot discount the humanitarian impulse, the impulse to do good, that animated the mental hygiene movement in education and that helped account for the enormous appeal and widespread acceptance of therapeutic concepts of education. No doubt, thanks in part to the mental hygiene movement, teachers have taken a more sympathetic approach to the "needs" of their students, and many children and youth have been spared the shame, humiliation, and self-doubt of failure and nonpromotion as well as harsh or uncompromising discipline. There were unanticipated consequences, however. Good intentions sometimes exacerbated problems that were supposed to be prevented, as Fred Hechinger pointed out about the "no failure" policy. The "concept was humane, and yet the consequences were often cruel." Students who lacked basic skills and knowledge were exposed to daily frustration and humiliation.[21] Furthermore, teachers were overburdened with conflicting and incompatible messages.

Teachers were not to fail or discipline students, yet they could not ignore or forget that they had to be concerned with their students' behavior and academic performance. They were still supposed to achieve certain instructional objectives and to maintain order and discipline. How could they cope with all these expectations? Teachers tried to have it all ways: therapist, social worker, and surrogate parent in the morning, authority figure, instructor, and upholder of standards in the afternoon—or all simultaneously. Education in this country is distinguished by the broad, almost unlimited responsibilities placed on the public school.[22] School reformers are exaggerating only a little when they complain that "our schools are confused about their educational mission and have no shared sense of what their major goals should be or how they can achieve them."[23]

Here is where this chapter may have some direct implication for the current wave of school reform. Although the school reform movement may at present have the initiative, therapeutic concepts of education still command passionate loyalty in the profession and remain firmly entrenched in the public's thinking. Of course, the words "hygienist," "therapeutic," and "progressive" are no longer attached to them; they function as largely tacit convictions, thus attesting to their deep-rooted nature. So long as therapeutic concepts of schooling remain unexamined, they pose an unresolved dilemma for the reform movement.

Let us mention one or two of the most obvious examples. The reformers' drive for educational excellence necessarily involves the setting of standards of academic achievement, much higher standards than have been in place. Some students, perhaps a large number, will fail to meet those standards. The school reform movement has not yet seriously addressed the problem of school failure. Chester Finn, one of the key figures in the school reform movement, takes an almost cavalier approach to the problem. "The excellence movement," he says, "has a higher tolerance for failure than does the education profession. Though it is not yet clear, as a matter of practice or politics, how much failure the excellence movement can endure without weakening its populist base."[24]

But the notion of failure as psychologically damaging is deeply embedded in the consciousness of parents and the education profession. Will the public be able to display such tolerance toward school failure? Will public school teachers and administrators be able or permitted to fail students? One should recall the opposition of parents to the efforts of the Minneapolis public schools to use tests as the basis of promoting children from K to first grade or holding back those who fail, or their opposition to the recent attempts to hold back children in Chicago's elementary schools because of poor reading scores.

Achievement and classroom discipline are closely intertwined. Nevertheless, the reform movement has yet to seriously confront the problem of discipline in school. That youths' misbehavior and even violence in school is a symptom of frustration and unmet needs, and that it calls for understanding of causes and not "discipline," also has a strong hold in the public's and the profession's consciousness. Recall the furor attending President Reagan's call for restoration of "good, old-fashioned discipline" in the fall of 1984, or the furor attending

the activities of Joe Clark, the tough principal of Eastside High School in Pa-
terson, New Jersey.[25] Will educational practitioners be able or allowed to enforce
standards of behavior, impose sanctions, prevent students from receiving diplomas, suspend, or even expel them?

It follows, if this analysis is corrrect, that if the reform movement is to have
any deep and lasting impact on American education, it will have, in the first
place, not only to aggressively disseminate its own educational values, concepts,
and language of education but also to explicitly challenge entrenched therapeutic
values, concepts, and language of education. And in the second place, the reform
movement will have to place the idea of the school-as-clinic on the agenda for
public discussion and open for debate the entire question of the meaning of the
schools' responsibility for the psychological adjustment and mental health of
students, what has merit in this idea and what has not, and the relative responsibilities of parents, teachers, schools, and other agencies for the well-being of
children and youth. A public debate over just what the primary function of the
public school is and what the public school can or cannot reasonably be expected
to achieve is overdue. Without such a debate, the current school reform movement
will be as ineffectual and ephemeral as other post–1950 reform movements in
American education whose watchword also has been "excellence."

NOTES

1. Some authoritative statements are Finn, C. E., Jr. (1985), The challenges of
educational excellence, in C. E. Finn, Jr., D. Ravitch, & P. H. Roberts (Eds.), *Challenges
to the humanities* (New York: Holmes and Meier); Finn, C. E. Jr., & Ravitch, D. (1984),
Conclusions and recommendations: High expectations and disciplined effort, in C. E.
Finn, Jr., D. Ravitch, & R. T. Fancher (Eds.), *Against mediocrity: The humanities in
America's schools* (New York: Holmes and Meier); and Sewall, G. T. (1983), *Necessary
lessons: Decline and renewal in American schools* (New York: The Free Press), esp.
Chap. 10.

2. E.g., Adelson, J. (1981, March), What happened to the schools, *Commentary*,
pp. 36–41, (1985), Four surprises, or why the schools may not improve much, in J. H.
Bunzel (Ed.), *Challenge to American schools: The case for standards and values* (New
York: Oxford University Press). See also Oldenquist, A. (1983, May 18), The decline
of American education, *American Education, 19*, 12–18.

3. Kotinsky, R., & Coleman, J. V. (1955), Mental health as an educational goal,
Teachers College Record, 56, 267.

4. See in this connection Goodlad, J. I. (1984), *A place called school* (New York:
McGraw-Hill), esp. Chap. 2; and Powell, A. G., Farrar, E., & Cohen, D. K. (Eds.)
(1986), *The shopping mall high school* (Boston: Houghton Mifflin), esp. the discussion
of the "services curriculum."

5. Bassett, C. (1927), *The school and mental health* (New York: Commonwealth
Fund), pp. 9–10. This was originally a series of lectures before the National Education
Association.

6. Truitt, R. P. (1927), Mental hygiene and the public school. *Mental Hygiene*,
p. 270. *Mental Hygiene* was the journal of the NCMH.

7. Woods, E. L. (1929), The school and delinquency: Every school a clinic. *National Conference of Social Work, Proceedings*, pp. 213–21. Hygienists published frequently in social work journals in the 1920s.

8. White, W. A. (1920), Childhood: The golden period for mental hygiene, *Mental Hygiene, 4*, 262.

9. Ayres, L. P. (1909), *Laggards in our schools: A study of retardation and elimination in city school systems* (New York: Russell Sage Foundation).

10. This was the message of a study destined to have enormous influence on the teaching profession. Wickman, E. D. (1928), *Children's behavior and teachers' attitudes* (New York: The Commonwealth Fund).

11. Bassett, *The school and mental health*, p. 60.

12. Thomas, W. I., and Thomas, D. S., *The Child in America* (New York: Alfred A. Knopf), pp. 222–23.

13. Commonwealth Fund (1922), *Annual Report*, p. 7.

14. By then a small but influential cadre of educational progressives—E. Irwin, W. C. Ryan, Jr., V. T. Thayer, C. Zachry, and L. K. Frank—had become adherents of the mental hygiene point of view. An influential group of psychologists at Teachers College, Columbia University, committed to mental hygiene concepts—including G. Watson, P. Symonds, and R. Strang—had emerged in the late 1920s and early 1930s. And even earlier, a group of child and education psychologists trained at Clark University, including L. Terman, J. E. W. Wallin, and W. H. Burnham, had become converts to the mental hygiene movement.

15. The merging of the progressive education movement and the mental hygiene movement is revealed in the reports of several commissions set up by the PEA in the 1930s: the Commission on the Relation of School and College, the Commission on Human Relations, and the Commission on Secondary School Curriculum. An example of how close progressive education and mental hygiene had become in the 1930s is the following, from the report of the PEA's Commission on Secondary School Curriculum: "The mental hygiene point of view . . . must come to pervade every department, activity, relationship of the school . . . the distinctions commonly drawn between education on the one hand and guidance and therapy on the other are not so fundamental as they seem." Thayer, V. T., Zachry, C. B., & Kotinsky, R. (1939), *Re-organizing secondary education* (New York: D. Appleton-Century), pp. 364–65, 367.

16. Prescott, D. (1938), *Emotion and the educative process* (Washington, DC: American Council on Education), p. 137.

17. In *Life*'s 1950 survey of public attitudes toward education, 90 percent of those polled accepted "the whole child" as the proper object of school concern. Cited in Clifford, G. J. (1975), *The shape of American education* (Englewood Cliffs, NJ: Prentice-Hall), p. 144.

18. E.g., the "Gee, Officer Krupke" number from *West Side Story*—or the following from Shulman, Max (1957), *Rally round the flag, boys* (Garden City, NY: Doubleday), p. 7:

Maggie: Guido, do you know what a teacher's job is? . . . A teacher's job—no, a teacher's sacred obligation—is to repair the trauma that children incur at home! . . . Action is what we need—and right now! A massive re-education program! Mental health for parents! . . . But it will take years to get a mental health program started. . . . Meanwhile, somebody has to try to repair the damage that parents are doing to their children at home. And that's where we come in—we, the teachers.

19. American education did not discover the school's responsibility to the "whole child" solely through the medium of the mental hygiene movement. Even before 1917

the school was called upon to appropriate functions of parents, the family, and health and social work agencies, and to assume responsibilities in the areas of health, hygiene, vocation, nutrition, and recreation—to become, in Cremin's apt phrase, a "legatee" institution. Cremin, L. A. (1961), p. 117. *The transformation of the school* (New York: Random House). All such tendencies were accelerated in the 1920s by the mental hygiene movement. To demand that the school assume primary responsibility for the psychological adjustment of children and youth may be veiwed as another step in this progression.

20. Quoted in (1932), *American Journal of Orthopsychiatry*, 2, 229.

21. (1984, June 5), *New York Times*, p. 19.

22. John I. Goodlad refers to this as the school's "we can have it all" complex. (1984), *A place called school* (New York: McGraw-Hill).

23. Bunzel, J. Introduction, in Bunzel, *Challenge to American schools*, p. 4.

24. Finn, The challenges of educational excellence, 194–95.

25. (1988, February 1). *Time*, pp. 52–58. The cover story, "Is getting tough the answer," is devoted to the controversy over the views of Principal Joe Clark and the problem of school discipline, a story in which what we have called therapeutic concepts of discipline played a significant role.

2

Neo-Humanism and Educational Reform

Carl Weinberg

The reform movement in education conceives its objectives in terms of pursuing excellence and reestablishing for the United States a community of scholars and workers who are competent enough to compete with people of other nations over a wide range of skills. As a populist movement of sorts, the school reform movement has goals that, while meritorious, are not particularly informative about the method or process by which educational excellence is to be attained. The recommendations of various prestigious commissions, well digested five years after *A Nation at Risk*, have still not resulted in any particularly transforming programs on a grand scale. Most recommendations, as a matter of fact, were already in place before the commissions met. High school standards were being raised, students were being held accountable for more and better achievements, universities were enforcing stiffer entrance requirements, and teacher candidates were being expected to major in subject matter areas.

It is true that our high schools have not been producing as many top-quality graduates in proportion to our population as secondary schools in Japan, for instance, but that has more to do with certain issues the school reform movement did *not* deal with rather than with those it did. Centrally these are issues of (1) how to ensure social justice in education (the ideal of equality) while upgrading achievement (the ideal of excellence); (2) the relationship of expressive goals to the goals of cognitive achievement; and (3) how to individualize instruction while holding all students accountable to the same criteria of evaluation.

The reports that spurred the reform movement, while dealing with program goals and what should be taught, have paid next to no attention to how they should be taught. The kinds of curricular programs that can most successfully accommodate the diverse student population that our public high schools contain have never been confronted. Surely the assumption that all students can achieve excellence under the same conditions through the same teaching strategies must be suspect. What, in the reformers' program, is going to compensate for the absence of homogeneity in the student population in high school, and the emergence of the idea in many youth subcultures that education may not be the surest path to success? How are we going to inspire the thinning stream of students who come to school prepared to achieve excellence? What are we going to do about the masses of high school students turned off by what they perceive to be the boredom of classroom work?

The answers the humanistic educator would provide to these questions are specifically oriented to those educational issues mentioned above, which the school reform movement has yet to confront. The humanist educator insists these are not only relevant issues but, given the realities of social and cultural change, they are fundamental to achieving a national standard of excellence in education. What has to be done involves examining how the goals of equality and excellence may be compatible, how expressive processes can help to achieve cognitive goals, and how it involves ensuring that "at risk" students are not sacrificed in the hope of salvaging an "at risk" society.

Much of this chapter is devoted to offering the neo-humanistic point of view on these three issues, within the context of the general history and principles that ground the contemporary humanistic position in education. I have chosen the expression "neo-humanism" to represent the contemporary perspective on schooling most radically opposed to the implication that public schools are failing because of inherent flabbiness of standards and expectations related to student achievement. The broad base of criticism in which this perspective is located is the tradition that points schooling away from purely cognitive skills and universalistic standards of evaluation. The neo-humanist, while not particularly loyal to the past practices of humanistic schooling, is nonetheless highly committed to the values embodied in past models of humanistic education. These values, brought to bear on the current controversy over school reform, can best be understood in light of the contrasting values against which the ideological struggle must occur.

The controversy that followed the appearance of the several reports on the state of American education has run the gamut of educational ideology. Without reference to traditional political labels such as "right" or "left," "conservative" or "liberal," we are left with some basic dichotomies of opinion centering, for the most part, on issues of (1) standards; (2) types of goals for students; and (3) the processing of students. The humanist position on these issues is frequently at odds with both the general public sentiment and a community of scholars who have sought to rationalize that sentiment in an ongoing intellectual debate. I will begin my presentation of what I have called the "new age" humanistic perspective by setting it in the context of that debate.

The works I have drawn from in order to establish the ideological lines of the debate are, on one side of the debate, furthest from the humanist position: Mortimer Adler's *The Paideia Proposal*, Finn, Ravitch, and Fancher's *Against*

Mediocrity, and Finn, Ravitch, and Roberts' *Challenges to the Humanities*. On the side most representative of the humanist position are John Goodlad's *A Place Called School*, Theodore Sizer's *Horace's Compromise*, and Ann Bastian, Marilyn Gittell, Colin Greer, Ken Haskins and Norm Fruchter's *Choosing Equality*. What follows is a summary of the point of view that neo-humanists feel they must confront, vis-à-vis the questions of standards, goals, and processing of students.

Standards, in the language of those who are pushing for a return to the emphasis on achievement that characterized an early period of educational history (before the presumed decay set in), have descended into mediocrity. The cause of this fall was a systemwide loss of faith in the achievement ethic, followed by a steady decline in the level and the kind of standards that buttressed that ethic. These standards relate not only to the actual achievement levels of students but also to a number of values and attitudes associated with excellence, such as the work ethic, decorum in school and classroom, accountability of teachers and students, and tolerance for failure. The position to which the neo-humanists are opposed is that these standards must be raised and adhered to. This includes the assumption that educators must decide what is good for students to know and rigorously go about holding them to learning it.

The goals of public schooling, say the advocates of rigorous standards rigidly applied, must be cognitive in nature. These cognitive goals relate particularly to the learning of historically validated subject matter areas or disciplines, but also are relevant to the acquisition by the student of sound values and correct behavior. The goals must be universally adhered to across school districts. That is, we do not have different goals for students based on racial or ethnic characteristics or social circumstance. The means of achieving excellence, argue the advocates of higher standards and unidimensional (cognitive) universal goals, is not particularly at issue, as long as educators are loyal to knowledge and hold high expectations for students. If the means by which excellence is sought does in fact produce knowledge at acceptable levels, those means are thereby validated.

On the issue of excellence vs. equality, those who support high standards for all take the position that these are not opposites, that we can achieve both. It is my opinion that the questions of what is or is not an opposite is not a matter of language analysis but of predictable outcome. Social welfare and defense are not opposites, but we find it very difficult to find adequate money for both simultaneously. But the thrust of the reformers' argument here against which humanists are most strongly in opposition is that differentiation of students, leading to individualized goals and processes, is somehow antagonistic to excellence and often to equality as well. The fact, they argue, that high school teachers have to deal with so many unprepared students should be treated as a problem of prior education, not of race or social class. To work on the reading problems of the disadvantaged while providing instruction in literature and history to the advantaged is indeed giving unequal treatment based upon social characteristics. But there is a historical as well as a cultural explanation for the differences in preparedness, and probably there always will be. It seems, to the humanists viewing the dilemma, that it is misconceived at best and abandonment at worst to proceed as if the realities of socioeconomic and cultural differences can somehow, in the time it takes to transform the schools, become a difference that doesn't make (educationally speaking) a difference.

Having established the context within which the balance of the chapter is located, I move now to present the neo-humanistic perspective and its theoretical roots, with the intent of showing that higher standards for student achievement (as well as teacher competence), exclusive emphasis in the curriculum on cognitive goals, and undifferentiated processing of different students are not the solution that advocates in the reform movement believe it to be.

In the history of educational controversy we soon forget the losers. Sometimes those programs competing for success in the public schools emerge victorious only in the lexicon of educational historians. To be labeled a "movement" does not imply that that movement is enjoying wide success in the everyday work place of education.

Such was the case with the "free school" or "humanistic" education movement of the mid–1960s and 1970s. Summerhill had become a recognized name in progressive educational reform, but recognition, while giving impetus to criticism on a grand scale, was responsible for reform only in microcosm. A genuine concern for the holistic development of the individual, while reasonably well articulated by reformers and implanted in the consciousness of the average educator, could not sever the knot of mass educational programs in this country. The link of schools to the limitations of economics and the security of tradition was too formidable an opponent. At the same time, Sputnik reform had not had the impact its supporters had hoped for, in the sense of upgrading academic standards and performances; but educators still had in mind the old accomplishments and believed they had the proper structure for the old version of excellence in place. Unfortunately for their goals, they had neither the population of the past nor the trend of modern history on their side.

In the mid–1960s humanistic education was represented culturally by the "free school" movement and its concern for the whole person, and politically by the struggle of disadvantaged minorities for equal opportunities and equal accomplishments. The humanistic-equality movement found a broad base of support in the actions of university students who attempted to hold universities hostage to its demands of "relevance" and access—access for minorities whose high school academic records and achievement test scores, along with the curriculum of the schools they attended, did not allow them to compete successfully for entrance to the university. For many years the combined efforts of radical white students and ethnic minorities (both students and nonstudents) had a major impact upon broadening the base of college admissions and opening up the curriculum of the university to issue courses that dealt with the social concerns of minorities and women.

The humanistic-equality movement spread into the public schools at all levels.

Integration activities, facilitated by busing, both mandated and voluntary, combined with a number of programs (e.g., Head Start) oriented to overcoming disadvantages, were presumed to be located primarily in the areas concerning education of poor minorities, the lack of academic skills needed to enter school at a competitive level, and the inferior education that was received in segregated schools.

At the same time graduates of teacher education programs had been taught to honor the individual. This was not the first time this attitude was emphasized, but the idea that all behavior was motivated and could be changed struck many new teachers as a proper place to begin orienting to the classroom. Academic subject matter goals were, however, often submerged under stress teachers faced in dealing with unique and often disruptive individual students. Meanwhile, although expectations for traditional achievement on the part of public school teachers and administrators were dropping and average basic skills scores were showing downward trends, the call for help did not go out to representatives of the movement that accompanied these changes, the new breed of humanistic educators. It went, rather, to those representing an unwavering faith in the old ways, those who saw basic skills as the sine qua non of the classrooms and the new technology as the handmaiden of a return to skill training and systematic instruction, later to be facilitated by minimum competency programs and tests.

In the 1970s, in the face of emerging concerns for basic competencies on the part of educators and parents, accompanied by wholesale social and personal disorganization on the part of teachers and students who could not settle upon a viable curriculum, the humanistic or "free school" influence started disappearing from the educational scene. It was replaced by a general concern for "holding the fort" through strong discipline and a minimum competency, basic skills emphasis.

Where the humanistic experiment had the greatest visible impact on the structure of the school and the curriculum was in the "alternative" school. Alternative schools were of three sorts: (1) the "free school," which was a privately supported learning environment; (2) the alternative public school, which was tax supported but theoretically operated on many of the precepts of the humanistic movement; and (3) the school within a school, tracks or programs created within existing public schools but administered and run separately.

The philosophical foundation for these alternative schools was a mélange of principles for personal development, for the most part intuitively derived from the experiences and events of the cultural changes of the 1960s. Among these principles were the notions that (a) members of the school community—teachers, students, and parents—would collectively decide upon the curriculum and the rules by which the school is governed; (b) the child's educational development must incorporate both expressive and cognitive abilities; (c) the child's mental health is of maximum concern, and teachers must make every effort to remain sensitive to his/her psychological development; (d) interpersonal relations are the business of the school, and the development of interpersonal skills is essential for the harmonious operation of the school and for the developing character of the child; (e) moral education in the form of value clarification and development is a priority; (f) sensory awareness, awareness of body, and the ability to learn from kinesthetic experiences are valuable goals; (g) evaluation of progress is individual, nonstandardized, and noninvidious, and should be directed primarily to the student's goals for him/herself.

To varying degrees these assumptions guided the programs of alternative schooling in America. But, like a candle, the alternative school movement burned brightly, flickered, and then died. The causes were varied but primarily were two: the economics of support and the dilemmas of curriculum-making.

While economics played a part, as we shall undoubtedly see it playing a part in severely handicapping the current reform movement, perhaps, had the advocates of the alternative school movement found a way to accommodate the curriculum to the real needs of children in a rapidly changing world, alternative education might have survived.

Unfortunately for the movement, and no doubt for education in general, the concept "free" in the "free" school movement was never well understood. In the absence of conceptual clarity on the part of teachers and parents who hastened the "free" school movement to its disappearance, either as failure or as transformation into college preparatory schools, the notion of freedom was lost as a curriculum structuring idea. A curriculum of "freedom" turned out to be no curriculum at all. Children, left to their own devices to generate activities, either did nothing at all or returned to earlier modes of interest for which the "free" environment provided no challenge. Freedom, it seems, has little value apart from challenge. Rather than emphasize the child's right to do anything he/she wants to do, freedom, in order to structure development, must be the freedom to challenge existing structures and ideas; but in order to challenge, structures must exist and ideas must be presented.

The educational principles associated with the radical humanism of the 1960s and 1970s, rendered moribund by the "back to basics" movement of the 1970s and early 1980s, appear to be surfacing again under the impetus of what can be called a "new age" cultural renaissance. In part social criticism, in part development in the arts, and in part a potpourri of accommodations or reconciliations with opposite beliefs and lifestyles, the "new age" movement appears to be under way. Any major program of school reform for the 1980s and 1990s will have to come to grips with some of the fallout.

Perhaps the reemergence of some of the strains of the earlier cultural humanism as a viable educational alternative can be accounted for by social forces outside the school that impinge upon the current introspective posture we as a society have taken with respect to our problems. The concern for quality products, for example, in order to compete in foreign markets, raises questions about the kinds of skills, commitments, and talents that a society needs to build things better— or, more to the point, more competitively. This kind of concern opens the door for a consideration of the role of creativity in economic development and what the public schools might do to improve their record of ignoring creativity goals in the interest of teaching for minimum competencies.

We might further speculate that humanistic assumptions and influence from the 1960s and 1970s come from the baby boomers who now have school age children. While not committed to radical alternatives, as perhaps many of their parents were, they are sensitive to the need for a balance in the schools between academic and personal development.

Within the educational community itself, it seems the gate that admits this current resurgence of humanistic ideas in education was, ironically, left open by the failure of the minimum competency movement. This movement, already beleaguered by critics from within (concerns about the arbitrariness of cutoff scores, racist implications of using competency tests for high school diplomas, and the exclusive preoccupation of teachers with goals that can be measured on a competency test) will now have to be justified from without, from the current climate of concern about mediocrity. One thing we know about schools and students is that when you define the minimum expectations, you may define the norm. Mediocrity is the logical outcome.

In response to both internal and external criticism, public school practitioners, sensitive to talk about reform, may be more receptive to ideas about alternative schooling. Many of these ideas are gaining a foothold in mainstream schooling, and experimental programs are under way in many places.

Critics of conventional schooling are once again beginning to take up their pens to ask for a renewed consideration of old ideas in new clothes. Moral education, cooperative learning, critical pedagogy, community schooling, aesthetic eye programs, and updated versions of democratic schooling are emerging as the "new age" educational humanism of the 1980s. Waiting in the wings, it can be presumed, are programs for the 1990s that accommodate a wide range of "new age" interests. What these interests might be, how they reflect some of the basic principles of earlier humanism, and how they might interact with the current reform movement in education are questions answered in the remainder of this chapter.

In its most pedagogically relevant form, "new age" humanism seems to refer to, if not invoke, what might be seen as an updated cultural epistemology. There is an assumption implicit in the use of the term "new age," as it applies to learning, that we as a culture have arrived at a point where traditional models of knowing, those oriented to cognitive-analytical development, are distinctly incomplete.

The spreading acceptance by educators of the notion of "right brain" learning is an example of how the whole person concept is represented in contemporary humanistic thought. This notion presumes that people learn differently, depending upon which hemisphere of the brain they favor, the verbal-analytic (left) or the impressionistic-visual (right). In many ways this thrust, while perhaps leaning too heavily upon uncertain applications of scientific knowledge, serves to lend support to the confluent learning models of the earlier age of humanistic education. Other examples of humanistic updating are the emphasis in reading curriculum on personal meaning, the growing implementation of aesthetic development programs sponsored by the Getty Foundation, the recognition of broader conceptions of intelligence emerging from the psychological studies of Howard Gardner, and the moral education programs based on the models developed by Kohlberg and his associates at Harvard.

While earlier humanistic models swung from cognitive to personal development, partly to compensate for past neglect and partly to extend the conception of the role of the school, "new age" humanism appears to have learned its lesson from the past. The lesson is that the society will, at best, accept a balance between expressive and cognitive development. Those reformers who purport to return schooling to the time-honored training of the intellectual faculties are naive in not recognizing that a large segment of the informed public is sympathetic to having expressive and interpersonal goals for the classroom.

While centering upon the concept of the individual as a multidimensional being, the real power of 1960s humanism lay in the belief in community. Individuals could feel the power of community in their own sense of loyalty and commitment to the enterprise. Studies of effective schools have shown again and again that schools most harmonious in the sense of operating like a total community (incorporating parents and aides from the community) are those which help students succeed, especially those who are most likely to fail and drop out. The conclusion of the research efforts of James Coleman and some of his colleagues at the University of Chicago strongly support the community school model. The cooperative learning thrust to which new and in-service teachers are being exposed takes humanist assumptions about community directly into the classroom.

If "new age" humanism could be reduced to one informing concept, that concept might well be multidimensionalism. Most of what is emphasized in schools requires students to exhibit a very limited range of abilities. These abilities are almost always cognitive-analytic and are grounded in what has always been referred to as the basic skills: reading, writing, computing. Expressive, aesthetic, and interpersonal skills never seem to count for much. As long as students can read and write correctly (not necessarily interestingly or with interest), teachers and administrators seem quite satisfied.

The point here is that school evaluations occur along a wide range of subject matters but a very narrow range of abilities. The evaluations that "count," those which predict mobility and success generally, are competence in those skills which contribute to scores on standardized tests.

The conventional pattern of school evaluations has always been antithetical to the humanistic view because students are invidiously compared with each other along some standard of performance. As a reaction to this pattern, a new emphasis on cooperative learning and aesthetic development has emerged, and specific programs are in place in many schools. We are beginning to make an active commitment to creativity and the kinds of skills, not all "basic," that creativity requires. Creative work is activity that involves persons attending to their own subjectivity (feelings, preferences, associations to stimuli, unique perspectives on what things mean) and choosing things to do that uniquely reflect them. This is what it means to be original. In the classroom we often find students willing to be compliant, to please teachers or not to annoy them. Or we may find just the opposite: students doing everything in their power to displease teachers, to annoy them, to distract them from their tasks. The humanist would see both adaptations as springing from the same source, a reaction to the requirement of compliance to an educational program that denies the student access to him/herself and the freedom to perform along a broad range of acceptable achievements.

The humanistic assumption, both new and old, is that all students are potentially creative. Originality, rather than being a unique talent, is simply a matter of being reflective and making choices. All humans who are not acting self-consciously—that is, are complying exclusively with others' expectations for their lives—can be reflective and make critical choices. A critical choice is one that results from the opportunity to reproduce our best sense of ourselves in the world of everyday action. What is in my best interest? What process do I enjoy working with? What skills do I need to do what I want to do, what resources? "New age" humanists find themselves aligned politically with the proponents of "critical pedagogy." "Critical pedagogy," while viewing change from the perspective of issues of equity and equality, supports an educational program similar to the early models of humanistic education, particularly in the area of viewing learning as a dialogue between the learner and his/her social and psychological world. The goal here is to push meaningful learning beyond mechanical skills to those understandings which help persons make sense of the relationship between the social world and themselves in such a way as to direct their life choices and commitments.

The question the humanist educator, who wishes a role for the humanistic perspective in the educational reform movement, must answer is how excellence is possible if we retreat from unidimensionalism and standardization to a position of reflective critical choice and creativity. The humanist's best answer to this question is represented in an aesthetic development model of school curriculum, based upon a set of humanistic principles. These principles are oriented to the issue of how people learn and the kinds of things they need to learn in order to engage in creative work. What follows is a brief discussion of the major conceptions of a humanistic pedagogy, brought up to date and made relevant to the current goals and concerns of the reform movement in education.

One of the most prominent social-philosophical assumptions that characterize humanistic thought as well as critical pedagogy is that social beings are in an endless struggle to liberate themselves from mythologies that imprison them.

"Otherness," a concept applied by R. D. Laing, a British psychiatrist interested in the way social consciousness bears upon mental illness, is a state of consciousness that sees the meaning of things and events in our lives as personal and changeable. Cultural arrangements, despite one's commitment to them, must be seen as historical developments with multifaceted interpretations. Things and events in the world of the child must be seen as related to some personally felt need or purpose, any other needs and purposes lead to depersonalizing the meaning of achievement.

A curriculum of "otherness" promotes greater creativity than curricula with fixed meanings and standards. Children, in the context of learning how things are, can be encouraged to imagine how they might be other than they are. Perspectives on art and literature are models for the development and maintenance of "otherness." The humanist is in considerable agreement with those who seek the attainment of universal cultural values for students. The disagreement is primarily in the process by which such wisdom is gained. Literature and history may well contain these lessons, but they are not the only way for children to discover them. The humanist's view is that the everyday life of the classroom oriented to aesthetic development (emphasis on individual expression) brings these lessons home more forcefully and in ways the student can best understand. From the earliest school age children can learn that you can color a tree red or a sky purple, and in the world of the classroom all can lead and all can follow.

What is the concept of person embodied in the "excellence" that current school reformers seek? The humanist views this question as relevant to the kind of excellence the public schools can produce, as well as whether it can be produced at all.

When the public schools undertook the task of turning a nation of immigrants into a nation of highly competent workers, they held the view that a person was no more and no less than a prospective contributor to the industrial development we as a society desired. As an orienting concept of the individual to be trained or educated, this view of person was not incompatible with the view the new twentieth-century individual had of himself. He (almost always a man) saw himself as someone who was in this country to learn the skills of success, thereby elevating himself as a social being to a position of economic security and esteem.

This challenge worked for both the individual and society from the turn of the century through the post-World War II period, when a second generation of socially mobile workers, now striving for professionalism in place of the bare tools for economic survival, emerged out of war. It was a time of explosive ambitions. Opportunities, made available by educational benefits for ex-soldiers as well as vastly expanded industrial development, abounded. Success in school was seen by all to be closely tied to opportunities. School life was competitive life, with the rewards of the new open occupational structure at stake.

American culture, however, no longer can instill a delayed gratification, Protestant ethic consciousness, nor is the desire to achieve educationally being inspired by culture heroes, those who are most likely to influence the masses of students in the public schools. If we can barely keep our youth away from drugs or alcohol, how do we propose to make them believe in sacrifice, industriousness, and conventional paths of ambition? The humanist's answer is that we cannot.

We must have a different conception of what a person (student) is, and we must organize an educational environment according to that model. The key concept in the humanist's conception of person, as this might direct educational practice, is subjectivity.

At other periods of our history when educational excellence was emphasized, the educator's sense of the person was that of an object, someone eminently amenable to manipulation, since the goals of the institution were the same as the goals of the individual. A factory model of advancement and allocation was efficacious to both the society and the individuals who cast their lot with the success goals of that society. With cultural change in the 1960s and 1970s came a broader conception of the individual. Persons were viewed, and were viewing themselves, as reflective, unique human beings and not just as a configuration of social roles that had to be liberated in order for the individual to take charge of his/her own choices and directions. What an individual was as a woman, a student, a Black, a worker, a husband or wife had to be brought into greater congruence with one's sense of self and one's aspirations.

To the humanist viewing the conception of the student implicit in the reform movement, the emphasis has to be toward greater individualization, toward taking into account unique combinations of influence in the student's life, as well as his/her particular learning style. We have to teach to the student's subjectivity, help him/her understand the world through his/her particular view of it, treating him/her as a special individual. It is only this perspective that leads to the development of creativity, since creativity must originate with, as well as represent, the person. And, the humanist would claim, excellence can be achieved only by linking itself to the student's creative imagination. That is how he/she will learn to read and write and how he/she will be motivated to use these skills in the future.

Another perspective from which "new age" humanism views the current effort to reform the public schools is the humanistic perspective on what it means to be a human being. Education, humanistic pedagogues insist, should begin with the nature of human qualities waiting to be developed, in a metaphorical sense longing to be developed, not with the nature of the subject matter to be taught.

The quality most central to pedagogy is the human being's nature as a confluent being. The educational idea is that we can understand them confluently, and we can develop our capacity to know the world by opening our senses to the awareness of how things in the world differ.

"Confluence" refers to an assumption that human beings experience the world both cognitively and affectively. There is head knowledge and there is heart knowledge. It requires both to engage a full-fledged understanding. The question is how they might work together to achieve excellence—or is excellence in the reformers' view to be taken exclusively as head knowledge? If so, what are the dangers? The danger in treating learning exclusively as the nourishing and developing of cognitive problem-solving ability is that, for a great many students, imagination is linked to the ability to feel what others are experiencing. For most of these students the way to feel something is to experience it within the context of their central experience, their location in the world of people, social structures, and events. The humanist views the classroom as a place where students are "turned on" by experiencing things that trigger their imagination. Great works of literature, as valuable as they may be intrinsically, do not stimulate either understanding or imagining if the content is removed from the student's feeling, and thereby from his/her understanding. Teachers, say those who want a return to the old ideal of excellence, need to be more proficient in their subject matter areas. The neo-humanist would lean more strongly toward familiarizing teachers with teaching models that help students personally experience the lessons of literature, history, and social science.

Respect for the individual's capacity to look inward and bring forth from that sense of self (feelings, intuitions, senses) a quality product is an image of excellence that reformers would do well to incorporate in formal education. Training the individual to use his/her feelings and senses was an enterprise that characterized much of alternative education in the 1960s and 1970s. The idea was to employ that sense of self in combination with more analytic capabilities to make each learning encounter complete.

Another assumption that informs and coheres both humanistic and aesthetic activity is the notion that the process of learning has its own integrity apart from any products that emerge from it. What educators need to be concerned with, the humanist would argue, is how well the learning activities themselves are conceived and experienced rather than how well the student scored on tests that may not reflect any long-range or important understandings.

Most of the comparisons of test scores across nations that led eager American reformers to push for upgrading of standards in U.S. public schools, aside from misrepresenting the issue (academic students in other countries were compared with a normative sample in the United States), did not deal with any of the deep or personally significant outcomes of education that humanists seek. Pointing students toward tests by which we can assess immediate observable progress skews the educational task toward those tests and not toward the long-range development of the individual. Only by concentration on the process by which individuals take the most from their educational experience can we assure lasting and important achievement.

The highest aspiration of the humanistic model is a learning process that assumes the development of a creative, self-directing individual. The humanist views as a categorical mistake the attempt to link excellence to scores on standardized tests. Excellence is either achieved or not achieved in the process of educating, and it is here, in the process, not in standardized product achievements, that the reform movement must look for it.

Let us turn now to the ways in which these humanistic principles relate to the prospects for educational reform.

The major commissions assessing the state of educational quality in the United States have made it particularly clear that excellence was not to be achieved through elitist programs. The goal was the upgrading of all students. Here they left it. Since 1983, when the excellence challenge was uttered, something must have gone wrong in the translation, since both educators and the public have become polarized over issues of excellence and equality. Those most concerned with equality see the school reform issue as a grave threat to the educational progress of ethnic minorities since *Brown v. Board of Education*. Old humanists and new egalitarians, willing to sacrifice some versions of excellence for a broad base of equal achievement, stand opposed to any interpretation of excellence as retrenchment from a commitment to ideals of equity in the public schools.

On the other hand, there are those who view what they take to be the disaster in educational quality as springing from the accommodation of the schools to the pressures of civil rights organizations, translated into government policy through a stream of laws, regulations, and court decisions. These policies, they believe, have diluted the educational program to such an extent that high-ability students have been stifled and reduced to mediocrity based upon lowered expectations and minimum challenge.

Most educators, however, given the charge to upgrade a very diverse population, recognize that there is only so much that can be done, given the constraints of time, money, and an incredible range of human and logistical limitations. Nonetheless, in the best spirit of reform they are looking for ways of upgrading where and how they can. It is to their benefit, the humanist would argue, to try to see how excellence of all must begin by overcoming social and economic disadvantages of many. There are two dimensions to this challenge: to see the relationship between equality and excellence, and to see ways of achieving it. The "new age" humanist believes he/she has the answer to both questions.

Cultural excellence, viewed as qualities, requires a nation of people who can produce it as well as recognize it. Equality as an educational goal will not emerge from a nation of elitist consumers and think tank managers. Quality inheres in work and commitment to excellence. Equality, in these terms, means upgrading the skills and competence, cognitive and affective, aesthetic as well as mechanical, of all members of a consuming, producing society. Knowing facts or developing skills to the level of succeeding on achievement tests does not guarantee either the ability to discriminate quality or the interest in having it in one's life. The humanistic goals of awareness of quality and commitment to producing quality and possessing quality make sense only within an equality framework, if the social purpose is upgrading a nation, rather than servicing an elite cadre of consumers.

The answer to the question of how we achieve both excellence and equality resides in some of the basic assumptions of contemporary humanism. Most significant of these is the belief that all students, regardless of social experience, have a potential for achievement; that as human beings they all possess the inclination to understand and the capacity to be creative and contributing members of society. The reason they do not realize their potential has to do with the way they are treated (or taught) as students and in other realms of their daily life. Instead of being pushed to upgrade themselves as learning objects of an impersonal educational conglomerate, they should be educated as subjects containing all the unique attributes of their subjective natures, interests, styles, and experiences.

Many educators and school programs are achieving excellence with the equality model well in mind. While it is certainly likely that well-to-do students will outdistance their poorer classmates in the race for maximum computer and scientific literacy as long as we allow unequal resources to determine success or failure in achievement competition, the contribution of private industry to the resources of many public schools in disadvantaged communities puts a lot of poor kids back in the game. In states such as New Jersey, Massachusetts, and California, new programs are in place to upgrade the achievement of kids in the inner-city public schools.

In the experience of most educators who have made it their business to survey the world of schools and schooling, it is unequivocally their conclusion that despite resources, equal or unequal, the best indicator of how well a school is upgrading the quality of learning in its students is the quality of atmosphere. It is a recognition that achievement, for working-class kids as well as the middle class, is a function of morale, concern, vitality, community, and even love. In schools that have been so designated, interest is high, students are engaged, and creativity is actively pursued. This brings us to our penultimate issue, the relationship between expressive activities and cognitive goals that reformers seek.

School retrenchment (the more conservative interpretation of what the reformers were after in the original commission reports) seems to imply that the important goals of scientific and technological knowledge, as well as excellence in academic subjects in general, were sabotaged in part by the expressive, human relations role that schooling assumed in the 1960s and 1970s. The neo-humanists' response to this assumption is that the failure of the schools is not due to the fact that the expressive-human encounter movement was taken too far, but that it wasn't taken far enough.

In too many places, the humanist would argue, the expressive functions were treated more as tokens than as core activities and were kept separate from the main thrust of schooling. In order to demonstrate that aesthetic development is a high priority, we would need to see two things in particular: an integration of the arts (i.e., creative writing, dramatic expression, visual arts) in the central body of the public school curriculum and a conscious effort to build such a curriculum and evaluate it in a systematic, developmental way. The incorporation of the Getty Aesthetic Eye program in California school curricula is an example of that commitment.

In the humanistic view, the development of cognitive abilities is tied to creativity in the sense of having students recognize that in order to express themselves, skills are necessary. Commitment to basic skill competence is more likely to emerge from a recognition by the student that skills will help him/her do what he/she wants to do, better, than from the abstract goals of future success, which many educators futilely invoke in an attempt to motivate underachieving students.

Second, the relationship between expressive or affective activities and cognitive development is represented in the thrust of confluent education programs, also discussed earlier. Students, it is presumed, will better understand subject matter that can be integrated into their experiential base and expressive needs. To establish curricular strategies that achieve such an integration, it would take a more imaginative and creative teacher than those who are trained to be satisfied with presenting knowledge as abstract and detached pieces of information.

As Goodlad pointed out in his national survey of schools, 95 percent of classroom time is dominated by teacher talk. It is my opinion that the major problem of teaching is that the orientation of teachers toward learners has never shifted much beyond the obsolete goal of so-called excellence. The way children of the present generation of students learn is not the way any generation of teachers teaches. In Eleanor Duckworth's book *The Having of Wonderful Ideas*, the argument she persuasively makes (at least persuasive to humanists) is that teachers can probably teach subject matter they only marginally understand better than disciplines they know well and probably love. It is the process of mutual dynamic encountering of ideas, knowledge, and feelings, students interacting with teachers in a community of inquiry, that will achieve excellence of understanding, not unilaterally raising expectations and standards.

The final question for those who seek a humanistic solution to the problem of upgrading quality in the public schools is to determine how we can salvage the vast population of students who are at risk of failing while upgrading standards that, logically, we would have to assume will produce a higher proportion of school failures.

The humanistic view is not that these students are failing the schools but that the schools are failing them. We have not found a way to interest them in what the schools have to offer, and because we (school people) believe we are the proper judges of what students should learn, we do not see the value of helping them learn what they would like to learn. When we accuse students of being unmotivated, we never look at the full extension of that charge. That is, we do not say they are unmotivated to learn what we want them to learn. We heap the responsibility for lack of motivation upon their confused shoulders. We try to motivate them by challenges to their futures, but they are unmoved. The tedium of unexciting classroom processes might well be overcome by promises of specific extrinsic rewards for enduring what for them is unpleasant and difficult, but we have nothing to offer except abstract banalities about the long-range value of education.

The solution to the problem of "at risk" students requires a war on failure along two fronts, the public school programs themselves and viable, visible opportunities for those who succeed in those programs to put that success to use. The humanistic programs discussed throughout deal with the first issue, the type of curriculum that would succeed with "at risk" students. The second line of attack must be associated, in some creative way, with the resources of the private sector of the society. Jobs must be guaranteed, scholarships must be made available, vocational education must be upgraded with respect to counseling, training, and connection with private industry. In this way the most important resource of a society demanding quality might be retrieved, that is, those human beings who could make a contribution but will not, as long as school programs cannot be experienced as personally and directly relevant to the needs and unique capacities of the individual student. The battle against all of the "at risk" categories, from dropouts to substance abusers, from suicide risks to those suffering from a range of mental illnesses or some form of social maladjustment, must, the humanist would claim, be engaged at the human level.

It should be a fundamental human right of all students to be given an engaging quality public education. A society that wants quality in the products of the schools has an obligation to produce quality in the schools. The humanistic view of quality in schooling is grounded in the recognition that students are multidimensional, expressive, confluent beings who would love to know and appreciate the world, if only it weren't made so unpleasant for them to do so.

SUGGESTED READINGS

Bastian, A., Fruchter, N., Gittell, M., Greer, C., & Haskins, K. (1986). *Choosing equality*. Philadelphia: Temple University Press.

Boyer, E. L. (1983). *High school: A report on secondary education in America*. New York: Harper & Row.

Duckworth, E. (1987). *The having of wonderful ideas*. New York: Teachers College Press.

Getty Foundation. (1987). *The aesthetic eye—A curriculum for aesthetic education*. Los Angeles: Getty Center for Education.

Goodlad, J. I. (1984). *A place called school*. New York: McGraw-Hill.

Gross, B., & Gross, R. (1985). *The great school debate*. New York: Simon & Schuster.

Rogers, C. (1983). *Freedom to learn for the 80s*. Columbus, OH: Charles E. Merrill.

Shor, I., & Friere, P. (1987). *A pedagogy for liberation*. South Hadley, MA: Bergin & Garvey.

Sizer, T. (1984). *Horace's compromise*. Boston: Houghton Mifflin.

3 A Vocational Educator's Perspective on the School Reform Movement

Harry F. Silberman and John E. Coulson

Since 1983 numerous commissions and reports have declared that our public schools are not performing adequately. Criticisms of education are a common occurrence in the United States, but this latest outburst has been the most intensive and prolonged since the Sputnik era. The authors of *A Nation at Risk* were primarily alarmed over the possibility that this nation's position of economic preeminence would be forfeited unless dramatic school reforms were initiated. The ensuing school reform efforts have continued to be driven at least in part by concerns about the American labor force's declining competitiveness, as evidenced by the frequent comparisons of the quality of our public schools with those of our major industrial competitors.

The problem is amplified by the growing proportion of the population that is at risk for school failure, including, among others, disadvantaged and minority populations, teenage parents, groups for whom English is not their primary language, and individuals who are involved with drugs and urban gangs. The need for educational reform has been intensified not only by the projected changes in the composition of the labor force but also by changes in the age distribution of the population. There is a declining number of young labor market entrants due to the "baby bust," and we can thus expect a tighter labor market with increased demand for education and training as employers are forced to use people with limited skills who were previously bypassed in the presence of a surplus labor supply.

Adding to the difficulty is the increasing volatility of job requirements. Some jobs are experiencing rapid upgrading while others are being downgraded. Educational deficiencies are being highlighted at a time when the need for adaptable workers is accelerating. The changing job market increases the demand for a flexible labor force. Furthermore, the growth in the number of service jobs, which are typically found in smaller firms with higher turnover rates, will produce more frequent job changes. Employees must be flexible and able to learn on their own.

As the title of the volume in which this chapter appears implies, the school reform movement can be viewed from a number of different perspectives, and a brief explanation of the authors' perspective seems appropriate at this point, since it guides the chapter's analysis of strengths and weaknesses in the current school reform movement.

In relation to the above-mentioned economic concerns that generated the latest school reform movement, our perspective is that of researchers interested in the transition from school to work. We are interested in how well or "excellently" the education process in America prepares youth to enter the job market and to find employment that will satisfy their financial needs and provide lasting job satisfaction. For a large segment of the population, this transition process is a difficult one, yet it heavily shapes their economic future.

When the school-to-work transition process is discussed, attention is too often focused only on the last few years of schooling—whether those years be in high school or in some postsecondary institution—and on the first year or two of work. Such a viewpoint seems to imply that all of the earlier grades are somehow dealing with information and skills too primitive or abstract to affect job performance, and that only the later years are directly relevant. Furthermore, it suggests that the step from school to work is a one-time, one-way process. We believe that this viewpoint is misguided. Indeed, we feel that this basic misconception has to a considerable extent created the conditions leading to public education's perceived inability to prepare youths for job success or excellence in an increasingly competitive international marketplace.

From the authors' viewpoint, the entire process of work preparation must be much more closely integrated with formal education and with other important aspects of life, including the crucial influences of family, peers, and other social forces that operate so strongly on every individual. Preparing for a job is not something you do in the last year or two of school. It is, or at least it should be, something that underlies and guides the entire process of education from the earliest years. There should be no sharply drawn distinction, as there often is these days, between academic courses and job preparation. This is especially important because different students leave the formal school system at different grade levels. One implication of this approach is that all courses, regardless of grade level, should contain work-relevant practical applications as well as more basic principles and theories. This view of the close relationship between work and education should apply, we believe, whether the job ultimately involved is that of a clerk, a plumber, or a nuclear physicist. Just as job preparation should begin during the earliest years of education, so should education continue after an individual obtains a job. Job requirements change, and continued learning after a person enters the job market is essential.

Another facet of our perspective on the contemporary school reform movement is that students are a very diverse group, varying in background, ability, and aspirations. A wide variety of educational approaches is needed to deal with a very heterogeneous population of students, differing in fundamental readiness, in cognitive and social skills, and in cultural viewpoints at the time they enter school. Simply setting higher academic standards for those students will not ensure that they will attain the necessary skills. Without careful and sensitive planning of alternative instructional strategies to meet individual needs, higher standards may simply result in larger numbers of students failing to meet those standards.

As might be inferred from our perspective on job preparation as an integral and continuing part of the entire education process for a very heterogeneous population of individuals, we view any attempt to improve the country's economic competitiveness through changes in the educational system as a long-term effort. We are not optimistic about the lasting effects of any short-term educational efforts to cope with an emergency in which the nation's economy is perceived to be at risk. We believe that genuine reform requires fundamental improvements, not only in curriculum and instructional procedures but also in meeting the needs of the professionals—teachers, administrators, and researchers—involved in the enterprise. This will take a sustained effort and significantly increased resources at all levels. Simply requiring more of the same academic courses, without changing the way they are taught, will not increase the productivity or ingenuity of our workers.

Other chapters have described the major characteristics of the present reform movement, so we shall simply summarize some of its more salient features and then examine its positive and negative aspects from our perspective. First, many of the recommended reforms have focused on improving the quality of teachers. Second, most of the current reforms have emphasized changes in the curriculum. A third major feature of the school reform movement is its emphasis on tougher accountability standards. A fourth characteristic of the school reform movement is its insistence that excellence and equity can be achieved simultaneously.

The education reform movement has several valuable characteristics. It has called the public's attention to the importance of quality education and to the need for strong support for this country's educational efforts. Spokespersons at the highest levels of government, education, and industry have participated actively and visibly in discussions of the reform movement, and this has resulted in an almost unprecedented amount of media and public attention to America's educational problems and needs. In addition, there has been some recognition of the fact that education reform will require additional financial and other resources. However, this aspect has not been emphasized as much as some in the educational field might wish. For example, one leader of the reform movement, William Bennett, former secretary of education, has argued that educational excellence and level of funding are independent. On the other hand, Bill Honig, state superintendent of education in California, also in the reform camp, has made vigorous appeals for added funding.

Furthermore, key documents promoting the cause of the education reform movement, especially *A Nation at Risk*, have taken a generally positive tone. That is, they have expressed optimism that present problems can be solved, and they have focused on solutions rather than on lengthy discussions of presumed past culpability. Those supporting the current reform movement have made a number of specific action recommendations rather than simply expressing general philosophical positions. For example, Ernest Boyer recommends in *High School* that all students be given academic credit for community service activities. Such recommendations provide a valuable basis for discussion and debate.

Then, at a time when economic resources are limited and the public has grown leery of ever-increasing government expenditures, *A Nation at Risk* and other derivative documents make some explicit choices about what things are most important in public education today (e.g., English, mathematics, history) and what things are mere trimmings (e.g., physical education and personal development courses). E. D. Hirsch, in *Cultural Literacy*, even suggests long lists of information items, including names, dates, and places, that everyone should know. While there are likely to be disagreements about these particular choices, the important point is that the making of choices is essential. Finally, the education reform movement places strong emphasis on the importance of keeping government and school officials and the general public well informed regarding the successes and failures of public education. Without such feedback, there can be no continuing public pressure for educational improvement and no informed basis on which to achieve that improvement.

While the school reform movement has been commendable in these several regards, the movement also contains a number of questionable assumptions and features that bear closer scrutiny. These will be critically reviewed.

First, much of the school reform rhetoric suggests that public schools are primarily responsible for the state of our nation's economic well-being. It is assumed that the nation is at risk because of a "rising tide of mediocrity" in our educational system. Economic competitiveness is viewed as a schooling issue. But education is more than schooling. Education is a product of the total culture. Societal changes such as the advent of television, single-parent families, increasing levels of drug and alcohol abuse, two-working-parent families, and the increasing numbers of youth from low-income, minority, and non-English-speaking families all affect student achievement independently of the quality of schools themselves. In any event, school achievement may have less impact on the economy than such factors as excessive labor costs compared with the labor costs of some of our economic competitors, excessive consumption and unwillingness of the public to live within its means, the burden of U.S. global defense commitments, managerial decisions that place short-term profits and speculation ahead of needs for plant modernization and product quality, and compensation and promotion systems that favor managerial over technical personnel.

A second questionable assumption underlying the current school reform movement is that requiring more of the same academic courses will promote greater transfer of learning to a rapidly changing work place. More difficult academic course requirements have been mandated to strengthen the minds of students, to improve their reasoning skills, to prepare them for a rapidly changing economy, and to make the economy more competitive. The school reform movement prescribes a "core" or "new basics" curriculum with rigorous academic standards for all students. The baccalaureate degree is replacing the high school diploma as the new standard level of schooling for a majority of the population. The school reform movement considers a broad liberal arts education the best preparation for all students, regardless of their occupational aspirations. Critics of the school reform movement point out that the homogeneity of teaching methods in academic courses, with teachers lecturing and students taking notes and preparing for tests, may not be the best way to promote flexibility and adaptability in the future labor force. Although conventional teaching approaches will raise test scores, such school-type skills may not transfer very well to work settings. Adding more academic courses, without changing the passive way they are taught, is not likely to improve our educational system.

Many of the tough-talking articles that prescribe more difficult courses for students imply a belief in the old "mental discipline" theory, which postulates that the mind is like a muscle that gets stronger when exposed to painful exercise. Many studies on mental discipline have found this theory wanting. Difficult subjects, believed to discipline the mind, not only do not alter students' reasoning ability but often put students off new learning. Making demands that exceed the capacities of students (because, for example, underlying prerequisite skills have not been mastered) may simply create anxiety and failure, and lower the students' self-esteem. Many students learn more from doing things that interest them, working on practical projects, than from formal academic instruction. Some researchers have found reasoning to be context-specific. That is, learning doesn't automatically transfer from school-like settings to applied settings. Transfer depends on the similarity between the context in which learning occurs and that in which the learning is to be applied. The provision of a wide variety of practical experiences that require students to apply principles in real-world contexts is more likely to enhance transfer. Unfortunately, the passive instructional methods used in most public school classrooms do not facilitate such transfer.

A third assumption that appears to be an implicit part of the current school reform movement, and with which we have a problem, is that general education and specific skills training are mutually exclusive. A broad general education is assumed to be more useful in a rapidly changing economy; consequently the reform movement has ignored specific vocational education. In this respect, however, employers' statements of need and their actual behavior are often not consistent. Many employers say that they want generalists and ask the schools to prepare students with a broad general education, but they then hire people with specialized training who are experienced and already productive, who will "hit the floor running." A financial firm prefers the MBA to the history major. An engineering firm chooses the engineering student over the humanities major.

Recent reports on the progress of school reform are critical of vocational education for substituting overly specialized job skills for basic education. Although this perception that academic education and specific skills training are mutually exclusive has prompted the reform movement to be critical of vocational education, there is no evidence that vocational courses necessarily or inevitably provide inferior education. It is true that vocational education majors are more likely to have below-average scores on standardized tests, but that difference cannot be reasonably attributed to their lack of academic courses, since they take an average of only two fewer academic courses than other students. Vocational programs, in fact, appeal to a cross section of the student population. National statistics show than 97 percent of all high school students take at least one course designated as vocational. Indeed, studies reveal that students who take a vocational concentration accrue as much gain on basic competencies during the last three years of high school as students who remain in the general curriculum. It is important to distinguish between the quality of instruction and the effects of self-selection factors that result in different kinds of students enrolling in different programs. Some programs appear to be of high quality because of the superior capability of the students who are enrolled in them. Other programs are of high quality in spite of the composition of the student body. Quality of instruction, ability, and motivation of students affect achievement outcomes.

The heavy emphasis of school reformers on general education, in any event, totally ignores the educational value of specific skills training. Many students are motivated by the sense of career direction afforded by vocational education. Well-designed vocational programs can promote excellence and human development along many dimensions. Students who master specific skills acquire a sense of personal competence and are better able to adapt when faced with new skill requirements. They can also derive aesthetic satisfaction from doing a job well. They can learn the discipline and integrity of craftmanship. In working on cooperative projects, they can learn team skills. They can acquire a heightened sense of altruism through providing others with products and services. When specific skills are mastered to the point that they are virtually automatic, it frees students to function at higher levels. For example, when keyboarding is automatic, the students can think about what they are putting into the computer. In short, specific skills training may contribute to the growth of students' personal qualities, which, in the long run, may be vital to the attainment not only of economic benefits but also of the cultural benefits so dear to the school reform movement. There is nothing inherently contradictory between early skills training and intellectual development. Biographies of outstanding individuals reveal a strong tendency toward early skill development.

A fourth questionable assumption underlying the current school reform movement is that increased accountability will improve the efficiency and effectiveness of the education and training system. Bureaucratic controls and regulations have been increased. Greater emphasis has been placed on such quality indicators as achievement test scores, number of academic courses taken, college admissions, job placements, and earnings of graduates. Summary reports of individual school performance, with state and national comparisons of performance indicators, are driving forces in the current reform movement. Unfortunately, checklist accountability schemes often result in states' monitoring compliance with global indicators such as average SAT scores or average job placement rates, which do not reflect either the instructional nature of classroom practices or actual job performance requirements. Many of the top-down management systems may create more problems than they solve. Top-down accountability systems encourage teachers to be accountable rather than responsible and diminish the professionalism of teaching.

More relevant for this chapter, job placement and earnings, commonly used as accountability criteria for vocational programs, may not be valid indicators of program quality for a variety of reasons over which the programs have little or no control. For example, students who enroll in different programs are not comparable. Then, cyclic changes in the economy and in the size of the labor force combine to determine the availability of jobs. In addition, wages, working conditions, and the availability of more attractive job options determine whether a graduate will accept a training-related position, and job discrimination and geographic barriers may prevent some graduates from finding employment in the area in which they prepared. Finally, the proliferation of training programs and the escalation of credentialing requirements create an inflationary devaluation of training programs at the lower levels. The emphasis of the school reform movement on accountability stems from a legitimate concern, but educational programs should be evaluated with a variety of measures of immediate outcomes or competencies over which those programs have some control. With such data, the programs can be redesigned to be more effective. Excessive emphasis on accountability indicators that are heavily influenced by extraneous economic factors beyond the influence of the instructors takes away the flexibility and sense of responsibility of those professionals who operate the system.

A fifth questionable aspect of the school reform movement is that when the latter occasionally does acknowledge the importance of education for work or occupational preparation, it fails to differentiate between the long-term and short-term needs of students. School reformers tend to blur the distinction between long-term vocational educational programs and short-term job training programs. The underlying assumption seems to be that the different needs of these programs can be dealt with in the same manner. Short-term programs often attempt to achieve outcomes that will require long-term preparation, or vice versa. Unfortunately, most of the important personal qualities that will raise the competitiveness of the labor force—such as adaptability, responsibility, and cooperativeness—take a long time to develop. Short-term crash training programs have little impact on such qualities.

Educational reformers and policymakers must recognize the importance of giving priority to long-term preservice education and training processes in raising the economic competitiveness of the labor force. They should make a clear distinction between long-term vocational education programs that are intended to prevent future unemployment and are normally an integral part of the comprehensive curriculum available to all students, and remedial, second-chance, and short-term training programs for the hard-to-employ. A series of political events had gradually blurred the distinction between these short-term and long-term types of programs. Although the policy of targeting funds on short-term training of hard-to-employ populations is well intended, such programs tend to become stigmatized and their educational quality suffers. Any serious effort to improve vocational education will require a clear distinction between long-term, articulated vocational education programs and short-term training programs for at-risk populations.

The community colleges and various technical institutes have typically offered preservice training programs leading to the associate of arts degree or to a certificate of achievement. Recently, however, these institutions have increasingly been providing short-term customized training for specific companies to upgrade employee skills and to retrain displaced workers in these firms, or to train the economically disadvantaged, using Joint Training Partnership Act (JTPA) funds. It is estimated that a large portion of the vocational students in postsecondary institutions are taking such short-term in-service training rather than long-term preservice preparation. Regional occupational centers also participate in contracting short-term training services to meet company-specific needs of industry in some areas. The financial benefits of this shift toward short-term training may have distracted educational policymakers from their responsibility to provide students with a longer-term general vocational preparation. One solution to this problem is to ensure that education for work at the baccalaureate level includes a strong component of instruction stressing practical application of principles and theory, that it not become so general and conceptual, so academic, as to remove the trainee from the potential client, product, or job. In addition, the technical and professional curricula should be articulated to provide a career ladder for those students who wish to advance.

The last assumption underlying the current school reform movement that we wish to question is the movement's claim that a commitment to excellence need not be at the expense of equitable treatment of our diverse public school population. The school reform movement has emphasized quality or ''excellence'' as a primary goal, but asserts it stands for equality as well. During the 1960s and early 1970s the emphasis clearly was on equity. In the face of limited resources, we may see a shift in emphasis toward short-term efficiency as a goal in future decades. There are trade-offs among these three competing goals. These trade-offs are more or less apparent, depending on how the goals are defined. Quality or excellence is often defined by test scores or other numerical indices, and it is normally judged by making comparisons with other schools, states, or nations. The group with the greatest mean score, or the greatest net gain when summed over all cases, is judged to have the highest quality. Assuming there is no ceiling effect (that the test has items whose difficulty level is beyond the reach of the most able members of the group), the most effective strategy for maximizing the mean is to invest the greatest share of resources in those who are likely to benefit the most and score the highest, that is, the more able and motivated students. Thus, from a quality standpoint, priority is given to the most talented students at the highest education levels. This is also an efficient strategy, since the cost for an equivalent increase in students' performance at the lower end of the continuum would be much greater; but such "efficiency" is achieved at the expense of equity and caring.

Equity is often defined by the distribution of outcomes, and is normally judged by the variance of the distribution of scores: the smaller the variance, the greater the equity. The most effective strategy for minimizing the variance is to compensate for initial deficits by investing the greatest share of resources in those with the least ability and motivation. With this compensatory strategy, priority is given to the least talented students at the lowest education levels. But it promotes equity at the expense of excellence and short-term efficiency, since extra remediation is required to rectify deficiencies and fill the gaps in prerequisite skills of those at the low end of the continuum.

Efficiency is often defined as the minimization of costs in time and money for a given output. The strategy is to find the quickest and cheapest allowable way to provide the required education and training services. The emphasis is on scientific management with standardization of goals, tight accountability, avoidance of expensive equipment and facilities, and elimination of waste and unnecessary duplication. This is the frugal, penny-wise, lower-taxes strategy. Such options achieve high levels of short-term efficiency, sometimes at the expense of both excellence and equity. Most public policies seek compromises among these three values. The trade-offs are most apparent at the upper or lower limits in achieving any of these values. We would prefer to have it all, but the realistic challenge is to formulate policies that create a desired balance among these competing goals—policies that will have long-term cost effectiveness.

Allan Bloom wrote a best-selling book, *The Closing of the American Mind*, that emphasized these trade-offs. He traced the decline of American higher education to the emergence of equity over excellence. He saw the advent of liberal democracy, with its emphasis on acceptance of differences and openness to different values (value relativism), all in the name of equity, as undermining the demand for hard moral choices and commitment to excellence. Bloom is also very disturbed by the rampant careerism among students, who are so preoccupied with preparing themselves for a specific occupation that they have closed their minds to all else—their material goals tether their intellects. Bloom does not seem to appreciate the educational value, or the contribution to personal and moral development, of students' practical efforts to prepare themselves for work or for a career. He is convinced that vocational and academic pursuits are mutually exclusive. Bloom's message seems to be that equity ought to be sacrificed at the altar of excellence.

A major conclusion from the above discussion is that the school reform movement has ignored or deprecated the role of vocational education in promoting excellence and equity in education. In December 1984, the National Commission on Secondary Vocational Education addressed this neglect and attempted to obtain some attention for school programs that enroll close to a third of American youth. The commission published a report, *The Unfinished Agenda: The Role of Vocational Education in the High School*, that identified a number of problems still in need of attention if the goals of the school reform movement are to be achieved. We would like to call them to readers' attention.

The Unfinished Agenda attempted to make the case for vocational education in the name of excellence and equity. It argued that all students, whether collegebound or not, need a mix of both academic and vocational courses and enough elective options to match their interests and learning styles. The report listed the virtues of vocational education as an alternative to the traditional passive instructional process. For example, it pointed out that vocational education is by nature an active process of learning by doing. Students learn to solve practical problems when they create products and provide services. Furthermore, vocational education is a cooperative process in which students learn to work together and help each other on group projects. Finally, vocational education motivates students and gives them a sense of direction.

The Unfinished Agenda observed that the school reform movement created a problem for vocational education because one effect of increased academic course requirements is to limit access to elective vocational courses. The commission recommended the use of cross credit for comparable courses as one solution to this problem. Another problem identified by the commission was the poor image of vocational education that is conveyed in the school reform literature. To alter negative stereotypes and improve its status, the commission urged that vocational courses be altered to appeal to a wider range of students, including the collegebound. In some countries, the commission observed, where vocational programs serve as a path to higher-level occupations, those programs enjoy high status and the best universities recognize them in their admission requirements. To ensure that all students are treated fairly, regardless of who they are or what handicaps they may have, or whether they plan to go to college, the commission recommended that each student should receive sufficient guidance to establish an individual employability plan.

The Unfinished Agenda also recommended raising the quality of learning experiences in vocational programs to improve the basic skills and problem-solving abilities of students. Since this would require the articulation of academic and vocational curricula, the commission recommended that academic and vocational teachers work together to help students see the connection between theory and practice. Another issue raised by the commission, one consistent with the school reform agenda, was the need to raise the quality of vocational teachers.

The report recommended more competitive salaries and other incentives to attract and retain effective teachers, and called for more effective leadership in the professional development of staff. In addition, the report called for vocational teachers to constantly update their occupational skills and to acquire the same level of education and same teaching skills as their academic colleagues.

What has happened to vocational education since the school reform movement was initiated in 1983? In preparing this chapter, the senior author asked all the state directors of vocational education to send him information about the changes that have occurred in their regions. The twenty-seven lengthy replies to the request indicate that the school reform movement has had some impact on vocational education. Although their observations were not in total agreement, directors' letters and associated materials contain some common trends.

1. Increased quality control standards. Most changes since 1983 have resulted from new state bills that have increased academic course requirements. The emphasis has been on basic skills. Quality control has also focused on improving the teaching profession with new teacher education and certification standards. Most states also have planned to strengthen the academic foundations of vocational education. They have asked special committees to review policies for vocational education, prepare model curriculum standards, and define criteria for evaluating programs. Some states have improved program quality by establishing new occupational learning centers and by appropriating funds for the purchase and maintenance of equipment.

States, then, are making changes in their vocational education programs that are consistent with the school reform movement's emphasis on excellence. For example, Virginia is developing an interesting vocational program for gifted elementary and middle school students. A "governor's school" in Fredericksburg provides summer courses for gifted children in laser technology, robotics, computer-assisted drafting, and artificial intelligence. It also provides leadership and decision-making experiences via internships in banks, architectural firms, and the Naval Weapons Lab to allow high school students to explore management and high-tech career options.

2. Cross credits. In response to the increased number of academic courses required for graduation, many states reported that vocational or "applied academic" courses may be used as alternatives to meet new graduation requirements. For example, in some school districts, business English will satisfy some English requirements. In other places, students who earn one unit in science and six units in a specific occupational service area may meet the science requirements for a high school diploma. Or a principles of technology course taught as an applied science course by a certified science teacher may be acceptable for credit in lieu of one science unit. Similarly, courses such as computer electronics and business mathematics may be acceptable for credit in lieu of a mathematics unit. At least fourteen states have made some provision for course substitutions or cross credits for vocational or applied academic courses. One reason for this policy was to avert the potential for new course requirements to increase dropout

rates. But another consideration was the concern for maintaining access to vocational education for those who need it and want it.

3. Strengthening basic skills instruction. In accord with the emphasis of the school reform movement on basic skills proficiency, some states have added "applied academic" classes to their programs to help blend vocational and academic education in math, science, and communications. They also have created new instructional procedures and curriculum materials to show vocational instructors how to teach basic skills through technical.content and practical experiences in an occupational field. In-service training of vocational teachers is being used to get them to require students to do more planning, thinking, reading, writing, and mathematics. In addition, the Southern Regional Education Board has formed a consortium of thirteen southeastern states to strengthen the development of the basic competencies of vocational students. Ten recommendations for improving vocational education have been initiated in a five-year pilot project with systematic plans for evaluation at test sites in each of the thirteen states.

4. Recruitment. Despite the efforts of the school reform movement to exclude, or even to denigrate, vocational education, some states have maintained or increased their vocational enrollment levels and report shortages of teachers in several technical program areas.

With the success of the school reform movement, however, most states have found it necessary to engage in vigorous recruiting efforts to maintain vocational enrollments of high quality. Most states prepare news releases that advertise the number and value of their vocational programs. Their public information offices have developed and distributed these materials to offset some of the commonly held misperceptions about vocational education. An impressive example of such material is a letter to an adviser of a high school vocational organization in Clarksburg, California, from a former student preparing to graduate from Harvard Law School, which was widely distributed. In the letter she attributed her academic success to the self-confidence and leadership skills that had been acquired from the responsibilities that she, as a fifteen-year-old, had been given by her high school vocational club (FHA-HERO). "That year," she testified, was "probably . . . the most valuable time in my educational career."

5. Coordination and articulation. With the heavy emphasis of the school reform movement on accountability and efficiency, most states cite efforts to increase coordination among providers of vocational education and to articulate programs across grade levels and between secondary and postsecondary institutions. Oklahoma, for example, reported an interesting partnership between the Public Service Company and the State Department of Vocational and Technical Education in providing low-interest loans and expertise in facilitating the construction of a dozen energy-efficient homes by vocational students who were directly involved in every step, including planning and site selection, air-conditioning, carpentry, masonry, plumbing, wiring, landscaping, interior decoration, sales, and accounting.

It is evident from the above activities that the vocational educators in the country *are* responding to the school reform movement—for instance, setting higher standards, recruiting qualified students, arranging for cross credits, focusing on basic skills. But an even stronger case must be made by vocational educators if they are to be included in the reform movement. They should take a more proactive stance and argue that vocational education cannot be ignored by the school reform movement without jeopardizing the very values the movement intends to achieve: excellence *and* equity. Possible approaches to achieving greater excellence and equity are discussed below. Although we argue in this chapter that sharp distinctions between vocational education and general education should be eliminated in the long run, we refer in the following discussion to vocational education, because this is the terminology in current use.

We are making some progress in using vocational education to promote excellence and equity in education, but much remains to be done. The following recommendations need to be considered in regard to the promotion of excellence.

First, integrate general education and specific skills training. A prerequisite to achieving excellence in and with vocational education, one that is implicit in the recent increase in coordination and articulation activities of the states, is the need to increase our efforts to integrate general and specific forms of work preparation. Contrary to the assumptions of some school reformers, both academic and vocational courses prepare people for work and life, and each includes both general and specialized, or specific, subject matter. In all fields, specific skills are prerequisites to general skills. Specific skills build confidence and free the learner to attend to higher-level tasks. In practice, however, academic and vocational courses may require different treatment. To accomplish the integration of specific and general forms of preparation, academic courses need to incorporate more application and practical experience. Vocational courses need to place greater stress on basic skills and on understanding the principles of technology, teaching *why* as well as *how*. This synthesis should begin in the earliest grades, where, for example, general study topics are tied to specific construction and art projects.

In reviewing what states have done to integrate general and specific forms of preparation since 1983, we believe it is time to question, and perhaps to go beyond the stage of merely reacting to the recommendations of the school reform movement. For example, we must be careful not to take the heart out of our vocational programs, not to remove their work-related component. We must guard against converting those courses into inexpensive fifty-minute survey courses. While it is important for all courses to strengthen academic skills, it is also necessary to protect the active, experiential, work-related character of vocational education. In some public schools, efforts to use vocational education to reinforce basic skills has led them to remove the laboratory projects and fieldwork from the program, converting it into a passive cognitive discipline. Students learn more from answering their own questions with ''hands-on'' technology projects than from memorizing facts from their textbooks in order to answer test questions. We must not convert vocational programs into watered-down survey courses in which students only talk about science, technology, or economics rather than doing it. That would eliminate the inherent value of vocational education as an educational process. John Dewey expressed it well when he said, "The ends are inherent in the means."

Second, concentrate on motivating students and developing team skills. American industry is moving in the direction of more participative forms of management, and reforms should help schools prepare workers for these new systems. Vocational programs should capitalize on their inherent ability to motivate students and to develop team skills.

All students must eventually learn to communicate, make decisions, plan, and work with others to create a variety of products and services. Yet, in a recent survey, responses to a question about what was wrong with school included such answers as the following: "We aren't allowed to work with our fellow students. I get in trouble when I help other people or when they help me." Students learn by doing—they learn to cooperate by doing teamwork. This process of developing cooperative skills is aided if their learning activities give students recognition and pleasure. Although some school reformers are concerned only with outcomes, and are uninterested in whether the youngsters feel good about themselves, without adequate motivation, significant learning is not likely to occur. At its best, the education process blurs the distinction between work and play. When adults are asked who had the most profound educational impact upon their lives, they seldom mention teachers who were outstanding transmitters of knowledge. They are more likely to speak of teachers who motivated them, provided them with personal support, and with whom they had trusting and friendly relationships. Teachers who had all the answers are not considered as helpful as those who worked with students to find the answers.

As indicated in some of the materials we received from the state directors of vocational education, vocational programs can best do their part to promote excellence by increasing students' motivation to learn and by contributing to students' participative skills. School programs that provide personal support and challenge students to make full use of their talents are more likely to build student motivation. For example, a popular instructor in a film animation program at Rowland High School in southern California regularly gets students involved in international film competitions. Another popular instructor, who teaches graphic communications at Don Bosco Tech in Rosemead, California, uses a collaborative learning approach in which students work in small, mixed-ability teams and help each other complete projects. Companies that are shifting to more participative production systems to increase their productivity can use the graduates of programs that have developed team skills. Such examples seldom appear in the school reform literature.

Third, raise the status of vocational, technical, and practical arts education. Vocational subjects are often stereotyped in school reform literature as providing narrow training for low-status jobs. Courses that teach students how to use a word processor, or how their cars, telephones, and television sets function, are viewed as too "narrow." But school reformers like E. D. Hirsch, in *Cultural Literacy*, says that teaching students about Torquemada, sang froid, magma, Giotto, and Dürer will "prepare them for the future." Hirsch prescribes his "broad" curriculum as an antidote to the country's problems. There is no question that every person must have general information if he or she is to comprehend what is read and to communicate with others. But cultural literacy comes from experience and interaction as well as from the great books. The need for cultural literacy should not be used as an excuse to denigrate applied courses. Vocational courses and courses in the performing arts, for example, represent alternative ways of achieving cultural literacy. These applied courses can help to bridge the gap that separates students who come from different social strata.

The school reform movement has ignored vocational education and made it more difficult to raise its status. By increasing academic graduation requirements, it has diverted the ablest students away from the practical and applied subjects. A program's status depends on the quality of its students. Vocational education should be more accessible and attractive to collegebound students. The practical arts should not be stigmatized as the exclusive preserve of less able students. There is nothing inherently inferior about technical and applied subjects. In Norway, for example, vocational education has high status and is a prerequisite for college admission.

The school reform movement has spurred the drive to raise the academic requirements for instructors of vocational education, a reform that, however, has made it more difficult to find qualified vocational teachers, who must have a substantial record of successful work experience in their field in addition to their academic background. A more reasonable method of increasing the quality of vocational instructors would be to pay them more competitive salaries. That would increase the supply of applicants and allow greater selectivity. The perception of any program depends on the image, status, and reputation of its instructors. The school reform movement has increased funds for staff development through in-service courses, and such courses are helpful, but only if technically talented people are available to start with. The quality of the teacher makes all the difference. Students learn by observation. They need outstanding role models whom they trust and to whom they can personally relate. On the other hand, the school reform movement has done nothing to upgrade the equipment and facilities for technical and applied programs. We must pay the price if we want excellence in preparing a more competitive labor force. The status of our technical programs suffers when the equipment is obsolete or not sufficient to convey the principles of technology that represent the occupational domains being taught.

What must be done to promote equity? There was a consensus in the materials we received from most state vocational educators about the value of vocational education in promoting equity. It is abundantly clear to vocational practitioners that calls for vocational education as a separate track for special-need populations, without adequate equipment, modern curriculum, or well-qualified instructors, will not promote excellence or efficiency or equity. Indeed, the prospects for achieving the equity goals of school reform are not very bright with the present emphasis on a single, unidimensional academic school curriculum for all students. A broader agenda is necessary. The school reform movement may have too narrow a platform on which to erect a structure that is capable of supporting its lofty objective of educational excellence and equity. We have four recommendations.

First, pay more attention to parenting and early child care. Education is more than schooling. One addition to the school reform agenda is that more emphasis must be placed on the quality of parenting and early child care. The key attributes of adaptability, cooperativeness, and responsibility are established quite early in the home and take a lifetime to develop. Parenting that conveys a sense of the child's importance and an expectation of success prepares the child to benefit from school programs and, in the long run, is necessary to create a more competitive future labor force. Parent education must be an integral part of educational reform.

The quality of parenting is also influenced by how people are treated at work. For example, it has been found that blue-collar workers stress obedience and conformity in their children, while white-collar workers are more likely to stress achievement and independence. The work culture affects parents' ideas about desired adult qualities and shapes child rearing patterns.

Second, pay more attention to work place education and training. The work place is the dominant educational influence in preparing the labor force through on-the-job learning experience. We must give workers better learning opportunities on the job and be more responsive to their needs for personal growth and educational development. In the long run, the overall quality and sophistication of work experience available in the work place is the most important factor in determining both the excellence or international competitiveness of our labor force and the equitable expansion of opportunity for those who are most at risk.

In the era of scarcity of skilled craftsmen, job training and retraining must be given higher priority if the equity goals of the present school reform movement are to be achieved. We must give adult workers more learning opportunities as a regular, ongoing part of their work routine, rather than the short-term crash training efforts that are often foisted upon them at the brink of plant closure. Workers who experience the value of learning in their own lives are likely to transmit that value to their children, making them more receptive to school reforms.

Third, pay more attention to housing policies and community problems. A topic that is seldom mentioned in the school reform literature is that segregation of students by ability occurs not only within public schools or in curricula tracks, but also among public schools. To achieve educational equity, we not only must end curriculum tracking within public schools but also must address the problem of segregation among public schools. This involves housing and employment policies. A district has no chance of creating more integrated schools with heterogeneous classrooms if disadvantaged parents cannot find housing or jobs in the district's community.

Unfortunately, in spite of all the good intentions of the school reform movement to enhance educational equity, schools exist in communities whose employment and housing policies greatly affect their ability to promote equity. Thus, any meaningful reform proposals must seek to have an impact on the entire community environment, not just the schools. State and federal fiscal policies should be modified to reward communities' efforts to enhance the equity goals of the school reform movement. To accomplish this objective, these policies must influence business and housing practices as well as educational practices. For example, we can give tax relief to businesses in predominantly middle-class communities and neighborhoods that provide training for and actively seek to hire individuals from disadvantaged backgrounds, provide special financial assistance to communities with predominantly middle-class families that will actively promote low-cost housing for disadvantaged families, and give tax relief to housing developers and contractors who make low-cost housing available to disadvantaged families in more affluent suburbs.

To achieve the equity goals of the school reform movement, we must provide supplemental funding to districts that have schools with highly mixed student bodies. Such funding should be based on prior academic performance and/or family income. The funding should be long-term, not "seed money" that lasts for a year or two and then disappears. Experience shows clearly that motivation to maintain special conditions in a school or school system disappears rapidly when the special funding is gone.

Fourth, pay more attention to the needs of the ordinary wage earner. To achieve genuine educational equity, we must raise the status of ordinary workers. Much of the difficulty in improving the competitiveness of our labor force can be attributed to the low status of the ordinary wage earner in our society. Many policies convey messages to workers that have a negative effect on their productivity. Witness the recent example of the unwillingness of companies to provide advance notice of plant closures. The school reform literature contains elitist rhetoric equating vocationalism with such terms as "triviality" and "mediocrity." With all the emphasis of school reform on preparing everyone for higher education, it is not surprising that many high school students do not see the relevance of their school programs to their lives and choose to drop out before graduating.

In response to the popular perception of the desirability and preference for professional occupations, the high schools are driven by college entrance requirements. Yet, reform literature to the contrary notwithstanding, the need for technical skills and preparation of workers for ordinary occupations will not disappear. The question is not whether we will prepare the next generation to participate in the labor force, but how. To promote greater equity in education, we need a renewed commitment to the preparation of the ordinary worker in our society. At a University of Minnesota conference several years ago, a member of the audience captured the essence of the commitment of vocational teachers to their calling by quoting from a poem, "Those who can't hear the music, think the dancer mad—keep dancing."

SUGGESTED READINGS

Adler, M. J. (1982). *The paideia proposal*. New York: Macmillan.

Bloom, A. (1987). *The closing of the American mind*. New York: Simon & Schuster.

Boyer, E. L. (1983). *High school: A report on secondary education in America*. New York: Harper & Row.

Campbell, P. B., and Parnes, H. S. (1986, August). New findings on effectiveness. *Vocational Education Journal*, 21–28.

Choate, P., & Linger, J. K. (1986). *The high-flex society: Shaping America's future*. New York: Alfred A. Knopf.

Erickson, F. (1984, Winter). School literacy, reasoning, and civility: An anthropologist's perspective. *Review of Educational Research*, *54*(4), 525–46.

Finn, C. E., Jr., Ravitch, D., & Fancher, R. T. (Eds.). (1984). *Against mediocrity*. New York: Holmes-Meier.

Finn, C. E., Jr., Ravitch, D., Holley, P., & Roberts, H. M. (Eds.). (1985). *Challenges to the humanities*. New York: Holmes-Meier.

Gamoran, A., & Berends, M. (1987, Winter). The effects of stratification in secondary schools: Synthesis of survey and ethnographic research. *Review of Educational Research*, *57*(4), 415–35.

Goodlad, J. I. (1984). *A place called school*. New York: McGraw-Hill.

Hirsch, E. D. (1987). *Cultural literacy: What every American needs to know*. Boston: Houghton Mifflin.

Hudson Institute. (1987). *Workforce 2000*. Indianapolis: The Hudson Institute.

National Commission on Excellence in Education. (1983). *A nation at risk: The imperative for educational reform*. Washington, D.C.: U.S. Government Printing Office.

National Commission on Secondary Vocational Education. (1984). *The unfinished agenda: The role of vocational education in the high school*. Columbus: The National Center for Research in Vocational Education, Ohio State University.

Resnick, L. B. (1987, December). Learning in school and out. *Educational Researcher*, *16*(9), 13–20.

Webb, N. M. (1985). Student interaction and small-group learning. In R. Slavin et al. (Eds.), *Learning to cooperate, cooperating to learn*. New York and London: Plenum Press.

4 Testing and the School Reform Movement: In Need of a Thermostat Instead of a Thermometer

James E. Bruno

> The goals of our educational reform movement are to prepare all students to function as informed and effective citizens in a democratic society, to function effectively in the world of work and to realize personal fulfillment.
> —Bill Honig (foreword to *English Language Arts Framework* [Sacramento: California State Department of Education, 1987])

> We recommend that schools, colleges, and universities adopt more rigorous and measurable standards, . . . Grades should be indicators of academic achievement so they can be relied on as evidence of a student's readiness for further study. . . . Standardized tests of achievement . . . should be administered at major transition points from one level of schooling to another and particularly from high school to college or work.
> —The National Commission on Excellence in Education (*A Nation at Risk* [Washington, D.C.: U.S. Government Printing Office, 1983], pp. 27–28)

California Superintendent of Public Instruction Honig's statement nicely summarizes one of the main thrusts of the school reform movement. Honig's use of the word "informed" is particularly appropriate to the following discussion. The recommendations of *A Nation at Risk*, quoted above, capture another of the main thrusts of the school reform movement. *A Nation at Risk* recommends that standardized tests of achievement be administered at major transition points from one level of schooling to another, and that such tests be administered as part of a nationwide system of state and local standardized tests. While we subscribe to the goal of the school reform movement—excellence and an *informed* citizenry—the testing procedures the reform movement is employing to reach this goal and to assess its success in reaching this goal disturb us and should be the subject of spirited public debate.

One of the key tenets of the school reform movement is that student performance should be measurable, and public schools and teachers must be held accountable for the results. The school reform movement currently relies heavily upon standardized tests of achievement to assess student performance. The arguments presented here will be critical of such tests and attempt to describe some ways in which the school reform movement might better drive public school reform, and measure and evaluate its success in achieving its goal of educational excellence and an informed citizenry. The immediate stimulus for our arguments are to be found in the current demands for legislation to establish a system of national testing of student achievement, in the campaign for national competency tests for certifying teachers or prospective teachers, and in the widespread use of standardized tests as "gatekeepers" for assignment to special education or remedial programs or for admission to accelerated programs, for high school graduation, for merit pay for teachers, and for allocation of funds to schools or school systems.

It is revealing to juxtapose the reflections of Assistant Secretary of Education Chester Finn, a leading spokesperson for school reform, on the role and instruments of testing in the school reform, on the role and instruments of testing in the school reform movement with the recommendations of *A Nation at Risk*. According to Finn, the school reform movement "manifests an almost singleminded interest in cognitive outcomes, rather than in school inputs or processes . . . it seeks evidence of measurable improvements in cognitive skills and knowledge."[1] The school reform movement, he continues "holds that the principal way to assess educational performance . . . is in terms of student learning outcomes, preferably the measurable kind." And, "Consistent with its emphasis on measurable outcomes, the excellence movement has a keen sense of accountability: a firmly held belief that the child, the school, and even the individual teacher are fairly held to account for the educational results that they produce." The school reform movement, Finn goes on, "is devoted to measures of student performance as gauges of success, sometimes almost as ends in themselves." Yet at the present time, Finn concludes, "we have terribly primitive means of assessing student performance in the ways that policy-makers crave most, namely, in comparing achievement among schools, school systems, states, and whole nations."[2]

We share Finn's concern. We concur that one of the major problem areas of the school reform movement has to do with the measurement of student educational achievement, especially through the use of standardized achievement tests.

This discussion will be critical of current standardized tests of achievement, which the writer believes militate against both the learning process and the excellence and equity objectives of the school reform movement. This chapter examines how the testing instrumentation and the information needs of the instructional leadership triad (teachers-administrators-educational policymakers) are not being met, and cannot be met, with current standardized educational assessment instrumentation. Replacing current "summative" or "thermometer" testing, which tests mainly for selection, placement, and exclusion, with a "formative" or "thermostat" testing—a type of testing instrumentation that assesses mastery with direct feedback to students, teachers, and the instructional programs—can place school reform on the solid quality-control foundation needed to increase the educational attainment of all students.

There is vast literature on the subject of testing and evaluation in education, most of it written by specialists for specialists. In this chapter the author writes for the nonspecialist. The references at the end of this chapter were chosen to be helpful to nonspecialists who wish to inform themselves further.

In 1971, the *Handbook on Formative and Summative Evaluation of Student Learning* persuasively made the case for "formative" tests and "formative evaluation" as contrasted with "summative" tests and "summative evaluation."[3] No one seems to have been listening. Or, in the interval, we have forgotten the distinction. The following discussion is an attempt to restate the case for "formative evaluation," to which the writer adds his own touch: utilizing new computer technology for more efficient and economical use of teacher and school time in the administration of "formative" tests, and the concept of student "confidence in recognition" of test items. Since we must often use the concepts "summative evaluation" and "formative evaluation," we need to explain these before proceeding. No one has done a better job of describing these concepts than the editors of the *Handbook on Summative and Formative Evaluation*, and the author borrows liberally from them below.[4]

"Summative" tests are customarily used to grade and certify students, as in a final examination or as in a college or high school entrance examination, and are usually published and standardized tests; the best-known of them is the Scholastic Aptitude Test (SAT). The most prevalent uses of summative tests are assigning grades, certifying certain knowledge or skills, predicting success in subsequent courses or levels of schooling, and comparing outcomes between groups of students or between schools or school systems. One of the essential things to remember about summative evaluation is that a judgment is made about the student, the teacher, or the curriculum with regard to the effectiveness of learning or instruction *after* the learning or instruction has taken place. Summative tests provide some feedback to students and teachers, but this is usually minimal, given the customary timing of the administration of such tests (at the end of the course or unit), their content (usually multiple-choice), and their scoring (simply right or wrong).

Most summative-type tests are "norm-referenced" or "criterion-referenced." For the sake of brevity, a norm-referenced test (NRT) might be defined as a test that statistically compares the performance of one student with that of another student. By the careful design of test items in terms of difficulty, one can achieve a normal distribution of scores. Statistical measures such as percentile (percent of students scoring below this student), stanine (dividing a distribution of scores into ninths), scaled, and grade-equivalent scores are typically associated with

NRTs. The Comprehensive Test of Basic Skills and the SAT are examples of NRTs. A criterion-referenced test (CRT) is another classification of test that sets performance standards for a binary (yes–no) type of decision concerning student performance. Typically, a percentile correct score (say 70 percent) on the examination is used as a selection standard. Those meetings or exceeding this selection standard can advance to the next level of instruction. Placement examinations, end-of-year examinations, and school district grade-level exams are usually based on a CRT format.

On the other hand, "formative" tests are constructed and used to determine whether students have or have not mastered a task or given body of material. They may also be used for the evaluation of curriculum-making and teaching methods. Formative tests are called "formative" because such testing takes place, or should take place, during the formative stage or learning stage and are part of the learning process, as opposed to the judgment process. Formative tests pace students' learning and help motivate them. They help ensure that each set of learning tasks has been thoroughly mastered before subsequent tasks are started. Such tests are especially useful in the diagnosis of students' difficulties because they provide feedback that informs the student and the teacher of what has been learned and what still needs to be learned, thus leading to a prescription of remedial measures for those students who need them. Such tests, therefore, should be administered frequently.

For the student who lacks mastery, the formative test should reveal the particular points of difficulty and the knowledge or skills he or she still needs to work on. To repeat, formative tests are most helpful in diagnosis if accompanied by a very specific prescription of particular instructional materials or processes. Formative tests should not be assigned grades but marked to show mastery or nonmastery, and followed by diagnosis, prescription, and remediation. That is why it can be claimed that the formative test becomes part of the learning or instructional process, not part of the judgment process. Formative tests obviously provide invaluable feedback to the teacher, since they can be used not only to help individual students but also to identify particular points in the instructional process that need modification. They also can serve "quality control" purposes in comparing the cycles of a particular course of study or comparing different classes. Most important, their function is to enhance the individual student's learning and the classroom instructional program long before summative evaluation.

The position of this chapter is that the basic functions of classroom testing are two: selection and weeding out students or the development of the student, by helping him or her to reach the highest level of learning he or she is capable of. That is, we will assume that the basic functions of classroom testing are "summative evaluation," testing that is concerned with grading and classification (a thermometer), and "formative evaluation," testing that provides direct feedback to the student, teacher, and the instructional program (a thermostat). Again, in this chapter we will be critical of current standardized, summative, thermometer-type testing whose purpose, as most frequently used, is grading and classification of students. Such tests contribute little to the improvement of teaching and learning, and rarely serve to ensure that students are learning what the school regards as the important tasks and goals of the instructional process. Furthermore, we suspect that grave deficiencies in the area of educational achievement and testing for educational achievement are resulting from the school reform movement's dependence on "summative evaluation" and its neglect of the "formative evaluation" process, and that these deficiencies have impinged most severely on inner-city, minority, low-achieving students.

Despite Finn's lament about "primitive" means of assessing student achievement, the school reform movement is still dependent upon standardized achievement tests. While teachers, school principles, other school administrators, and, to some extent, state education policymakers are blamed for the poor educational achievement of students, the reform movement displays an almost complete disregard of the limitations in the tests employed to measure student achievement. Instead, through use of media-oriented crisis terminology like *A Nation at Risk*, the public is excited into a frenzy of suspicion and criticism, usually directed at teachers and school administrators instead of at the tests.

The school reform movement calls for higher academic standards, tougher courses, more qualified teachers. It is not so much the content of school reform about which we have reservations; rather, as we noted above, it is not higher academic attainment for all students, but the means of driving and measuring the success of school reform, that we suspect. To take an extreme analogy to make the point, during the Vietnam War era, military policies were set in Washington, D.C., using "body count" information as the prima facie evidence of military attainment and performance. Many military historians now use the term "managed war" (based on body counts) to describe this era in American history as illustrative of poor policy and worse management that should never be repeated.

Unfortunately, the school reform movement seems to be moving toward its own era of "body count" and "managed war" in its campaign to win the war against mediocrity in education and to prove to the public that it is winning that war. Test scores, like body counts, have in the past few years tended to become the prima facie evidence of successful school reform, and have tended to be used by many school districts to drive instructional programs and to formulate educational policies. While some school reform leaders, such as Finn, sense the urgency of the problem of testing and the need for better tests, everyone—reformer, professional educator, parent, interested citizen—concerned with the school crisis in America should question the efficacy of test-score-driven education.

The school reform movement sees no conflict between the goals of excellence and those of equity. All students are to be brought up to excellence. To address the question of how to achieve excellence and equity, that is, how to improve especially the low educational attainment of inner-city and minority students, we need to examine not only the basic foundations and assumptions upon which educational attainment is currently measured but also the instrumentation being used to promote and measure school reform. If these essential facets of school reform are left unattended, the reform of public education could proceed along a path that may, in the long term, be counterproductive to school reform objectives.

For the school reform movement to achieve its goals of excellence and equity, it must encourage the development of testing and assessment instruments for classroom "formative evaluation." Rather than using summative-type testing devices (that is, the kind of "thermometer" testing and assessment that is characteristic of standardized testing in the American public schools today and that the reform movement currently relies upon), the reform movement needs to develop a "formative evaluation," "thermostat" instrumentation with direct feedback to students, teachers, and the instructional program. We offer some additional general observations to illustrate how urgent the need is.

American public schools can generally be characterized as being influenced by powerful exogenous (political, legal, social, economic) and endogenous (teachers, administrators, state policymakers) forces. These forces sometimes achieve a type of static equilibrium between the centripetal pull toward greater school district centralization and local control and centrifugal pull toward greater school district decentralization and state control. Sometimes one force is greater than the other. The current educational reform movement, with its dependence on standardized testing to monitor educational programs, has provided the impetus for a growing tendency toward centralization of power at the state level.

This is one—but only one—of the reasons that the current emphasis on test-driven school reform has about it a strong air of permanence. We say this because, in the first place, some states have jumped on the education reform band wagon. Using legislation, as in Texas, California, and New Jersey, they have mandated school testing programs. A great deal of the recent state department of education influence in local school district policy, we might interject, results directly from the former's substantially increased share of school district expenditures. With increased expenditures for education—that is, with the school's heightened financial dependence upon the state—comes the demand for accountability, and with the demand for accountability comes standardized testing.

In the second place, the demands of international commerce have required that our public schools remain competitive in the marketplace, especially in scientific and technical areas, and testing seems to reassure us that we are staying competitive. Third, testing is an extremely big business. For example, during the 1986–1987 school year an estimated 100 million-plus standardized tests were administered to 39.8 million elementary and secondary public school students! In 1987, 1,134,000 collegebound high school seniors took the SAT.[5] The test-and-text publishing complex has extremely strong lobbies, and through their political action committees wield enormous influence over educational policy at the state level. Finally, Americans, in general, do not like to be taxed without knowing what (the quality of educational services) they are receiving for their tax dollar (accountability and testing).

Consequently, we assume that mass standardized testing is likely to remain part of the American public education scene for a long time. Since testing influences what is taught, how it is taught, what pupils study, how they study, what they learn, and more, testing is a practice that warrants the closest scrutiny. Although, as we observed above, some state legislatures caught up in the reform movement have mandated certain standardized testing measures, one cannot attain school reform based on summative-type, standardized testing. Instead, testing practices associated with formative evaluation or testing that provides diagnosis and prescription and that serves the needs of student improvement and development lie at the foundation of educational attainment, and that is the kind of testing that the school reform movement requires. Given these assumptions, we will now point out some further deficiencies in current testing practices, and then discuss how mass testing can be made more effective for achieving the objectives of the school reform movement.

The school reform movement sees no conflict between excellence and equity. It wishes to raise the educational achievement of all students. Enhancing the educational attainment of all students, especially of "at risk" students, can be realized only through more comprehensive and effective formative evaluation at the classroom level. Consequently, how to enhance the individual teacher's efficiency and the effectiveness of the classroom formative evaluation process should be made school reform's priority.

There is a triad of professionals intimately involved in the education process in the public schools: the teacher, the administrator, and state policymakers. The design of a testing system that would provide diagnosis and feedback for each component of the educational leadership triad is essential if resources are to be channeled to those most in need: minority, inner-city, low-achieving students. The medical community, like the education community, has diagnostic and information needs for its triad of professionals. Of course, medicine and education are different realms. Still, we might learn something by studying how the medical profession reacts to "crisis." The triad of doctor, hospital administrator, and policymakers in the state health departments is remarkably efficient and effective in meeting the challenges of medical diagnosis (and disseminating information) in a crisis. The key to the effectiveness of the medical profession in the face of medical crisis is its focus on improvements in the precision, reliability, and maintainability of its diagnostic procedures (CAT scans, ultrasound, NMR, blood testing). In addition, information generation from the bottom (patient-doctor) upward (state-federal health officials) is used to maximum effectiveness. The direct analogue for the public school and the education profession has to do with the instrumentation required for the diagnosis of student learning problems, and the key to education's ineffectiveness lies in its neglect of the instrumentation needed for classroom formative evaluation.

The breakdown in or the neglect of the formative evaluation process places minority, low-achieving students especially at risk because they are promoted through the grades independent of their skill levels in language arts, math, and science. Yet the school reform movement calls for more rigorous academic fare and higher standards for all. Requiring ill-prepared students to take more difficult courses for graduation seems unfair, since they will not be able to derive any real benefit from their education. Some, as has been well publicized, are even awarded diplomas or graduation certificates. It is as if one graduated from a music conservatory without being able to read music. We are back again to the challenge of developing tests that improve the diagnostic procedures that will lead to educational prescriptions that will lead to enhanced classroom learning.

With the need to develop tests for "formative evaluation" in mind, we will briefly examine some other problems with the testing instrumentation that is currently used to service the needs of the school reform movement. Since measuring the success of school reforms by using the results of multiple-choice standardized tests entails serious, perhaps insoluble, problems, it is important that these problems be recognized. First, the quality indicators of schooling currently most often used by school reformers and those public school systems influenced by the latter are typically based on the results of state- or local-school-district-developed "objective" criterion-referenced, multiple-choice standardized tests (CRT) and/or norm-referenced standardized tests (NRT) such as the SAT.

But these are not the best indicators to guide school reform. They cannot be used to direct or redirect the instructional process—especially in the area of classroom formative evaluation. Are they—and surely this is one of the reasons for their popularity—even "objective"? Regarding this latter point, it is interesting to note that it is the "objectivity" of standardized multiple-choice tests that seems to impress public school officials and parents, but for different reasons: School officials are impressed because of the tests' amenability to easy or cost-efficient scoring and the removal of teacher or examiner subjectivity in scoring; parents are impressed because they associate "objective" tests with "scientific" tests. School officials, parents, and the general lay public should be reminded, however, that such tests are called "objective" because they are a substitute for teacher's judgments, which are decreed to be too "subjective"—which is not to say the tests themselves are not "subjective."[6]

This caveat aside, one major limitation of the school reform movement's preoccupation with standardized testing for achievement has to do with its tendency to test for only a narrow band in the spectrum of school outputs—cognitive outputs in math, sciences, and history, for example, because they are easily quantifiable—at the expense of more elusive "higher-order thinking skills," which the school reform movement proclaims it seeks to promote, such as imagination, judgment, and creativity. The net result of limited test-driven practices is that they tend to undervalue some kinds of skills and knowledge and overvalue other kinds. Then there is the overlooked problem of the lack of cooperation among students in the testing and assessment process. Among other test-taking conditions that should be "equal" we would include, most importantly, that students employ a test-score-maximizing strategy (that is, all students want to get the highest possible score). In an important article James Raffini suggests that low-achieving students, in order to protect their self-esteem when taking tests, deliberately follow what might be best described as a "sabotaging" strategy: "Below-average students protect themselves against failure in an educational competition they cannot win. The common defense in avoiding a sense of academic failure is to stop trying."[7]

In essence, getting low-achieving students even to cooperate in a school or school district testing program by giving their best (or maximum) effort is a major, neglected problem in using testing to drive or measure school reform. Yet is is these low-achieving students that school reform is presumably committed to helping. Also, one would assume that directions for taking standardized tests would be constructive and helpful. Study for a moment the following test-taking directions given to a group of students in Los Angeles city schools in 1987:

- Answer the question even if you are not sure—you may get it right.
- If you cannot figure out the answer, guess.
- Do not leave any question blank.
- Answer every question.
- Don't spend too much time on one question.[8]

What are the implications for learning, or for evaluation of learning outcomes, in the kind of test directions given to students in the above example? What are the implications for diagnosis or feedback and remediation for low-achieving students? Standardized achievement tests with such directions, which are not atypical, become a guessing game, not a test of understanding, knowledge, or information.

Thus, we confront a situation in which the school reform movement's commitment to equity, as well as excellence, may be compromised by its reliance on standardized testing, since the group most directly in need of help—low-achieving, low-SES, inner-city students—actually provides the least cooperation with the testing and assessment programs currently associated with school reform. In addition, such students get the least information and feedback needed to help them learn. Correspondingly, their teachers get the least information on which to base any educational prescriptions that might help such students achieve better. Of course, such testing also affects the top end of the achievement distribution as well as the bottom end. Reducing the quality of testing to that of Trivial Pursuit or a guessing game trivializes all of education. In short, the lack of diagnosis and educational "feedback" information that characterizes present widely used summative, "thermometer" testing and assessment methods tends to make both teachers and students first suspect and then sabotage the entire testing and evaluation process. Which brings us to the phenomenon of "test wiseness."

Significantly, one major school organizational response to the reform movement's emphasis on mass standardized tests of achievement is to teach "test wiseness." Major ethical as well as practical problems for teachers and schools are, however, generated by the trend toward prepping students (and teachers) for tests. The testwiseness movement has generated its own industry and has made its presence felt not only in the high schools but also in the university. Consider the following letter to the editor of a student newspaper at a large West Coast university. Especially note how it illustrates some of the major professional and ethical concerns associated with standardized multiple-choice testing as well as the enormous impact multiple-choice testing has on some students. The student is in conference with her psychology professor during office hours.

> I just stared at my psychology professor and didn't know what to say. I couldn't believe she was asking me to purchase a $25 book on how to take multiple choice exams.
> The professor gave her this advice: "I think you'd better rethink your major. Are you sure you want to stick with psychology knowing that 90% of the exams are multiple choice and you do not do well on these types of exams?"[9]

Testwiseness is anti-teacher-as-professional. Think, for example, of the amount of time teachers devote to teaching testwiseness, or teaching to the test, or even teaching the test itself—time that is taken away from instruction in the classroom. I doubt that teachers enter their profession to teach students how to guess in order to pass tests. Furthermore, testwiseness can be purchased or acquired by those who can afford it, with the result that students with identical true educational attainment may have widely different scores on the same test, depending upon their testwiseness. This economic bias in testwiseness is prejudicial to students from low-income families, devastates student morale, and greatly impedes real learning. Most significantly, testwiseness prevents minority and low-achieving students (indeed, all students) from receiving the proper diagnosis and assessment of their learning difficulties and problems so that they can improve their educational performance. Unfortunately, after leaving high school or college, these same test-wise students may possess little real knowledge but do possess a test-wise skill they may never use again. Self-worth and self-esteem in children and youth are derived from the possession of confidence-enhancing knowledge and skills, not from testwiseness and test-wise scores on standardized multiple-choice exams.

Gerald Bracey, a former director of research, evaluation, and testing in the Virginia Department of Education, notes that some teachers in Virginia did not teach their students how to add and subtract fractions because the state's minimum competency test included questions on multiplication and division of fractions, but not on addition or subtraction.[10] Another example of the kind of miseducation almost inherent in testwiseness has come to our attention. Two forms of the same test were given to a group of high school students. One form asked a question having to do with converting Arabic numerals to Roman numerals, and in the other form the question was asked going from Roman to Arabic numerals. Students gave 40 percent more incorrect responses to the question that involved converting Roman to Arabic numerals because these students were "prepped" for the Arabic-to-Roman test item.

Finally, we offer into evidence a study of the Texas Teacher Test, a revealing example of test-driven reform. In March 1986, public school teachers and school administrators took the Texas Examination of Current Administrators and Teachers to see if they were qualified to keep their jobs. The results were a remarkable 96.7 percent pass rate. Also remarkable were the massive efforts geared to "teaching to the test," including review courses, study books, and workshops. Here are some examples of "teaching to the test," excerpted from workshop presentations:

You don't want to leave any empty spaces. There are no penalties for guessing on the test.

Remember, you only have to know it's wrong. You don't have to know why. You don't have to correct it. Just know that it's wrong.

It's better to paragraph in the wrong place than not to paragraph at all.[11]

These strategies, as the study's authors put it, have the effect of helping the "examinee 'hide his ignorance' " or "use the multiple choice format to 'pretend to know.' " What can such a test have measured? They conclude, "The widespread availability of 'test-taking tricks' has to be considered a partial explanation for the extremely high passing rates."[12] The cost to the taxpayer was over $35 million.

To summarize, mass standardized testing programs of the kind currently utilized and encouraged by the school reform movement to drive school reform affect all public school procedures. The education reform movement should seriously consider the potential unintended negative consequences of such testing programs, which fall in at least four major areas:

I. Local Control
  1. Tends to undermine local control of public schools because standardized tests determine what is taught in the classroom.
II. The Curriculum
  1. Tends to shift school educational objectives toward those which can be quantified and measured by standardized tests.
  2. Tends to narrow school curriculum in order to align it to standardized tests.
III. The Teacher
  1. Promotes teaching to the test and even cheating, which results in distortions in assessments.
  2. Takes time away from other goals to coach for tests.
  3. Undermines authority of teacher's judgments.

IV. The Student
  1. Promotes a false sense of mastery of skills, information, or content.
  2. Tends to under- or overestimate minority students' actual abilities.

Distortions in the entire educational process result when the school's concern shifts from the intrinsic value of the education program to the testing program. Current testing programs dictate the curriculum and teaching methods as well as the instructional objectives of schooling. The reform movement's support of mass standardization testing to narrow educational objectives drains major amounts of instructional resources from more valuable school objectives. Thus, widely used thermometer-type standardized tests of student achievement—and a faulty thermometer at that—are compromising the school reform movement. "It makes no sense," as John Weiss, executive director of the Massachusetts-based National Center for Fair and Open Testing put it, "to use a faulty thermometer to measure the nation's educational health."[13]

Furthermore, the leaders of the school reform movement might reflect on whether they wish to contribute to the enormous influence of what we estimate to be a multibillion-dollar education test-text publishing complex. Standardized tests are published and marketed as scientifically developed instruments that simply, objectively, and reliably measure student achievement, abilities, or skills. The fact is, as we have pointed out, that there are serious problems related to the construction, validation, reliability, administration, and interpretation of the most widely used standardized educational tests. Fortunately, the state courts and legal opinion have begun to scrutinize these tests. Issues of truth in testing, product liability, due process, and test validity, under a standard of "heightened scrutiny," are beginning to shape legal opinion regarding testing and, more important, how testing will be used in educational contexts. Some of the legal issues involving testing have been litigated in *Debra P.* v. *Turlington* (minimum-competency testing and test validity), *Peter W.* v. *San Francisco School District* (educational malpractice), *Hobsen* v. *Hansen* (ability grouping and tracking), and *Larry P.* v. *Riles* (IQ testing and cultural bias).[14]

To summarize, our major problem with the school reform movement is that the basic assessment instrumentation on which it is dependent is not sensitive to the demands of classroom formative evaluation—the foundation for driving educational attainment, especially for inner-city, minority, low-achieving students. School achievement can be enhanced by testing, but only by testing that meets the needs of the instructional leadership triad: diagnosis, prescription, and remediation. Present standardized summative-type testing, without feedback to the student, the teacher, and the instructional program, will in the long run prove counterproductive to the educational attainment aims of school reform. Better diagnostic tools for formative evaluation for classroom teachers need to be developed. Let public schools assess themselves in terms of what they (the schools) are attempting to accomplish. Examinations geared to actual curricula of schools are much more sensitive indicators of individual school performance and attainment than are conventional standardized norm- or criterion-referenced tests.

The situation may, however, be improving. Under the auspices of the Carnegie Foundation, Stanford Professor Lee S. Shulman is devising nonstandardized tests to certify teachers based on simulated performances and on portfolios of past accomplishments. In addition, the Carnegie Foundation has recommended that a new Student Achievement and Advisement Test (SAAT) should be developed. The advisement portion would be designed to help students make more informed choices. The task force of the Education Commission of the States has called for fair and effective programs of testing to monitor students' progress through periodic testing linked to carefully designed programs of remediation and enrichment for students who need special help. Theodore Sizer has called for flexible measures of student learning outcomes, including "exhibitions of mastery."[15]

Some public schools are breaking away from standardized testing programs and experimenting with "formative" testing. In his *Up from Excellence*, William W. Wayson describes how teachers in Stowe Middle School, St. Louis, are taking steps to ensure that students "were not just raising test scores by becoming more test-wise but by being genuinely better educated." And in Mullan Junior/Senior High School in Mullan, Idaho, and Marsalis Elementary School in Dallas, teachers make frequent use of teacher-made tests to monitor student progress and to identify instructional areas that need more attention.[16] Finally, a new testing procedure called Information Referenced Testing (IRT) is specifically designed for the formative evaluation process, and may hold promise for the reform movement.[17]

These are three critical elements usually associated with the design of a test: discriminant validity (does a test item separate high and low ability students) or criterion validity (does a test item match the instructional objective of the test); the way the test item is scored; and the response restrictions placed on the student in answering the test item. Most CRTs and NRTs are usually in a multiple-choice test format based on the simple and most restrictive right/wrong type of scoring system. The school reform movement is currently driven by assessment instrumentation based almost solely on a recognition type of multiple-choice testing. In such tests, the kind most commonly used to measure student achievement in our public school systems today, only the correct answer, not the confidence behind the recognition, is scored.

The school reform movement requires the kind of testing procedure that may involve recognition, but it must be recognition based on knowledge. To base educational reform on recognition testing alone, which is what current standardized mass testing practices amount to, rather than on recognition plus confidence in that recognition, is similar to basing an eye examination and subsequent prescription for eyeglasses on the basis of recognition of the letter on an eye chart and ignoring whether the patient is squinting and guessing at the letters. Clarity of recognition is important for the evaluation of a patient's visual acuity.

Confidence in recognition is as important for the assessment of a student's knowledge, skill, or information.

The information-referenced testing (IRT) procedure is based on a confidence-weighted, optically scannable response mode we call modified confidence weighted-admissible probability measurement. In one application of IRT testing, examinations were administered at one school site in the form of an instructional audit by the school staff at the end of the year to ensure that no student fell behind while advancing from grade to grade. In each grade teacher-designed IRT exams in each of the basic skill areas were given to students at the end of the year. The results were used to help teachers generate individual education plans for each student over the summer and to articulate the school instructional program to parents. The resulting detailed feedback to teachers, students, and parents highlighted any need for additional teacher in-service training, as well as specific areas in which special expertise or resources were needed to help students achieve mastery.

In another IRT application, this one at Martin Luther King Elementary School in the Los Angeles Unified School District, students were assigned to specific short-term instructional remedy classes (reeducation, review instruction, and enrichment) based on their educational needs as measured by IRT. Periodic information-referenced clustering or information-based tracking of students based on their educational needs provided feedback to teachers, and allowed them to provide intensive instruction directed at the specific needs of students. Other types of innovative, technologically sophisticated testing formats besides IRT are beginning to appear. We hope such tests will stimulate others to develop alternative, cost-efficient tests that simultaneously measure student achievement and provide diagnosis and feedback to teachers, students, and the instructional program.

Recent research literature on testing is beginning to demonstrate that learning is enhanced when formative tests are employed *and* when measures of confidence are included in the evaluation instrument. Darwin Hunt noted: "When self-assessment required the [learner] to indicate the degree of sureness in the correctness of each answer, acquisition [of learning] was expedited by as much as 25%."[18] Thus, other researchers besides the author are beginning to understand the importance of formative testing based on confidence in the certitude of knowledge.

To summarize, since World War II, in spite of enormous sums spent on public education, we have witnessed a decline in the educational achievement of students, which the current school reform movement hopes to redress. A reappraisal of the educational assessment instruments currently favored by the school reform movement is urgently needed if we are to meet the concerns about student achievement raised by the reform movement and to provide a framework for the implementation of its objectives of excellence and equity in education. The school reform movement has stimulated much testing activity aimed at measuring achievement.

Standardized multiple-choice tests are becoming the raison d'être of American public education. They not only have affected educational goals, curriculum, and teaching practices but also have created a new set of problems: such tests inadvertently serve as exclusionary devices disproportionately affecting the minority and low-SES student population. If we are to have mass testing, let us have testing for diagnosis and prescription and remediation—as feedback to the teacher, the student, the parent, and the instructional program—rather than testing for placement, selection, and exclusion. Let us strive to use testing programs as a means of formative evaluation, as a thermostat instead of as a thermometer.

NOTES

1. Finn, C. E., Jr. (1985). The challenges of educational excellence. In C. E. Finn, Jr., D. Ravitch, & P. H. Roberts (Eds.), *Challenges to the humanities* (New York: Holmes and Meier), pp. 192–94.

2. Ibid., pp. 196–97. An example of test-driven school reform may be found in California under State Superintendent of Schools Bill Honig. For example, in his *California's response to a nation at risk: A five year progress report* (Sacramento: California Department of Education, 1988), progress is measured in terms of standardized test scores, especially in SATs. For example, 15,000 more students are taking the SAT and "scores are going up" (p. 3).

3. Bloom, B. S., Hastings, J. T., & Madaus, G. F. (1971), *Handbook on formative and summative evaluation of student learning* (New York: McGraw-Hill). The *Handbook* was revised in 1981. All references here are to the 1971 edition.

4. Ibid., esp. sec. II, Chaps. 4–6.

5. Medina, N., & Neill, D. M. (1988). *Fallout from the testing explosion: Fair tests* (Cambridge, MA: National Center for Fair and Open Testing), pp. 3–6, (1988, October 16), *New York Times*, sec. III, p. 4.

6. *Fallout from the testing explosion*, pp. 11–12.

7. Raffini, J. P. (1986, September), Student apathy: A motivation dilemma, *Educational Leadership*, *44*, 53.

8. In possession of author.

9. Serrano, J. (1988, May 20), Multiple choice exams. Letter to editor, *UCLA Daily Bruin*.

10. *Fallout from the testing explosion*, p. 16.

11. Shepard, L. A., & Kreitzer, A. E. (1987). The Texas teacher test, *Educational Researcher*, *16*, 22–31.

12. Ibid., pp. 25–26.

13. (1986, February 21), *Los Angeles Times*, p. 4.

14. Some of these issues are discussed in Bruno, J. E. & Hogan, J. (1985), What public interest lawyers and educational policy-makers need to know about testing, *Whittiers Law Review*, *1*, 915–42. Other useful references are Kirp, D. L., & Yudoff, M. G. (1987), *Educational policy and the law* (Berkeley, CA: McCutchan Publishing Corp.); and Madaus, G. F. (1983), *The courts, validity, and minimum competency testing* (Boston: Kluwer-Nijhoff).

15. Sizer observes, "The requirement for exhibitions of mastery forces both students and teachers to focus on the substance of schooling. . . . To be fair, they need to be flexible: not all students show themselves off well in the same way. They cannot, then,

merely be standardized, machine-graded, paper-and-pencil tests.'' Sizer, T. (1985), *Horace's compromise: The dilemma of the American high school* (Boston: Houghton Mifflin), p. 216.

16. Wayson, W. W. (1988), *Up from excellence: The impact of the excellence movement on the schools* (Bloomington, IN: Phi Delta Kappa Educational Foundation), pp. 163–64.

17. Bruno, J. E. (1986), Assessing the knowledge base of students: An information theoretic approach to testing, *Measurement and Evaluation in Counseling and Development, 19*, 116–30.

18. Hunt, D. P. (1982), Effects of human self assessment responding on learning, *Journal of Applied Psychology, 67*, 75. One of America's leading experts on classroom teaching observes that the teacher must focus on students' output, which validates acquisition of the latter's knowledge or skill: "That output must be perceivable so you know (not hope) that students have achieved and are ready to move on to the next learning or whether you must reteach. . . . Also student output must validate that learning has been accomplished. Output can't be such that students can bluff, guess, or be lucky in their demonstration of accomplishment." Hunter, M. (1985), *Mastery teaching* (El Segundo, CA: TIP Publications), p. 5.

SUGGESTED READINGS

Bloom, B. (1981). *All our children learning*. New York: McGraw-Hill.

Epley, B. G. (1985). Educational malpractice: The threat and challenge. *The Educational Forum, 50*, 57–65.

Haney, W. (1984). Test reasoning and reasoning about testing. *Review of Educational Research, 54*, 628.

Hunt, D. P. (1982). Effects of human self assessment responding on learning. *Journal of Applied Psychology, 67*, 75–82.

Medina, N., & Neill, D. M. (1988). *Fallout from the testing explosion: Fair tests*. Cambridge, MA: National Center for Fair and Open Testing.

Pipho, C. (1985, May 25). Tracking the reforms: Part 5—Testing. *Education Week*, p. 19.

Raffini, J. P. (1986, September). Student apathy: A motivation dilemma. *Educational Leadership, 44*, 53–55.

Ravitch, D., & Finn, C. E., Jr. (1987). *What do our seventeen year olds know: A report on the first national assessment of history and literature*. New York: Harper & Row.

Salganic, L. H. (1985). Why testing reforms are so popular and how they are changing education. *Phi Delta Kappan, 67*, 607–10.

5 Reform in Special and Regular Education: An Interface

Frank M. Hewett and Virginia de R. Wagner

Raise the standards for academic excellence yet provide for the broad range of intellectual and academic abilities and motivational problems among students served. Set and enforce more rigorous standards for conduct and discipline yet maintain students with severe behavior problems who are a threat to themselves and others. Satisfy the expectations of parents of nonhandicapped children along with those of parents of the handicapped even though their expectations may be incompatible.

Sound contradictory? It is. For while efforts to bring about educational reform in regular education in the United States has been going on, equally serious efforts have been taking place in special education. Regular education reformers want more emphasis on academics and the quality of instruction in the classroom. They do not dwell on matters of individualization and flexibility. American public education must toughen its stance if it is to keep pace with such nations as Japan in preparing young people for the increasingly competitive future. Special education reformers do dwell on matters of individualization and flexibility. In the years immediately following Sputnik, this conflict of priorities was of little consequence. Quality was quality; competence was competence; and while special education existed, any concern about the effects of regular education reform on the handicapped was nonexistent and vice versa.

This chapter is about the turn of events in the late 1980s, when special education not only exists but exerts a great deal of influence socially, politically, and educationally. We shall begin our discussion with the turn of events involving special education since 1975 and then relate them to the present regular education reform movement.

REFORM IN SPECIAL EDUCATION

Special education has developed over the years in the United States to provide the "something extra" that handicapped children may need in order to receive the benefits of an education. These extras may be related to instructional modalities (e.g., Braille) or instructional plans (e.g., self-contained special classes). A long-term goal that has been realized in large measure is the provision of these extras for all handicapped children in the country. This has come about through federal legislation, particularly the Education for All Handicapped Act of 1975, Public Law 94–142.

In the 1970s it was estimated that of 8 million handicapped school age children in the United States, 3 million were receiving an inadequate education and 1 million no education at all. After a century or more of neglect, exclusion, and isolation, handicapped individuals were given the right to a free and appropriate public school education on a mandatory basis by Public Law 94–142.

Public Law 94–142 sent the states scurrying to locate the neglected millions of handicapped students. It also set in motion myriad administrative and instructional procedures that were specified by the law to increase the adequacy of the educational opportunities afforded the handicapped. In determining the extent and nature of an individual's handicap, tests and methods were to be utilized that took unique characteristics into account (e.g., mode of communication, cultural and language background) and did not penalize any individual because of that uniqueness. The law specified that the education provided for handicapped individuals must be individualized and appropriate. In an attempt to guarantee this, it was further specified that a written plan or individual education program (IEP) would be prepared by school personnel for each handicapped student. This plan was to include the following: a statement of the child's present levels of educational performance; a statement of annual goals, including short-term instructional objectives; a statement of the specific special education and related services to be provided to the child and the extent to which the child will be able to participate in regular educational programs (in other words, how far "mainstreaming" shall go or exactly what is the "least restrictive environment" for the handicapped child); and, finally, a schedule for review, at least annually, of the degree of achievement of the short-term objectives.[1]

The IEP was to be formulated with input from the parents and, when appropriate, the handicapped individual. This input included due-process rights. Parents could legally challenge public school districts if IEP goals and later efforts toward implementation of these goals were not to their liking. Parent power was clearly established. Beleaguered parents of handicapped children who in the past had been turned away by school districts with comments such as "We do not have a program for children like your child" now had the upper hand. They could counter with "If you don't have a program for my child, then start one or pay his tuition in a private school that does." In addition, even though the child was enrolled in what the district considered an appropriate program, if the parents did not agree, "due process" allowed them to challenge the schools for a more suitable placement. Parent participation and power, and a free and appropriate public school education for all handicapped children, are two of the three most significant special education reform elements of Public Law 94–142.

The third element, and perhaps the most relevant to our discussion of the interface between regular and special education reform, is that having to do with "least restrictive environment" or mainstreaming. As presented earlier in the statement of goals for the IEP, Public Law 94–142 is concerned with placing handicapped children in as normal a learning environment as possible. It requires that the amount of time appropriate for a given handicapped child to be integrated or mainstreamed into regular classroom activities be considered at the time the IEP is written.

According to the law, mainstreaming was never intended as a full-time requirement for every handicapped individual. It was recommended whenever "appropriate." However, a reform movement has begun in special education that aims at eliminating special education and other "second" education systems for mildly handicapped and disadvantaged children altogether. It has been labeled the "general education initiative," and has even more relevance to the goals of the regular education reformers that we shall discuss in detail shortly.

THE GENERAL EDUCATION INITIATIVE

In 1986, Madeline C. Will, the U.S. Education Department's assistant secretary for special education and rehabilitative services, issued a "white paper" calling for an increased "shared responsibility" among all educators. This challenge to the long-standing practice of second systems in education for children with special learning needs was supported by Mary Jean Le Tendre, the director of compensatory education programs in the U.S. Education Department.

Margaret C. Wang also has been prominent among educational psychologists and special educators urging implementation of the general education initiative. Basically, Wang would like to see regular classroom teachers and special educators work side by side in developing and utilizing strategies for teaching all students—regular and special—all of the time in the regular classroom. Her rationale for this is based on the failure of special education to adequately identify and program special students for special education assistance. Wang estimates that 15,000 children in the United States are referred each week for possible special education placement because they demonstrate poor social skills or a lack of progress in learning to read, write, or do mathematical calculations.[2] In the course of being evaluated, school psychologists and other so-called experts organize them into three basic groups: the learning disabled, the mildly retarded, and the behaviorally or emotionally disturbed. Once they are classified, it is assumed by some that an instructional plan unique to each of these groupings will logically emerge.

But such is not the case, according to those favoring the general education initiative. The classifications are considered highly unreliable, and the so-called unique characteristics each child is supposed to represent have not been shown to call for unique teaching strategies distinctly different from what any well-qualified, well-trained, and well-supported regular classroom teacher might provide. The procedures by which children are tested and diagnosed in an effort to put them into one of the classifications have been challenged. Scientifically invalid diagnostic approaches and unreliable classification systems are not likely to help children with special learning problems, assert proponents of the initiative. The disproportionate number of minority children and males who have been placed in one or more of these basic classifications for the mildly handicapped since the late 1960s provide additional testimony for questioning their fairness or usefulness. In California the celebrated Larry P. case (*Larry P*. v. *Riles*) challenged the appropriateness of using an individual IQ test standardized on white, middle-class children for purposes of classifying children of all races and socioeconomic statuses in terms of mental retardation. It resulted in outlawing the use of such tests for such purposes in the state. Given these shortcomings in operating a second system of special education in the schools, should colleges and universities continue to prepare teachers, classified by the same labels as the children, for special teaching assignments? Wang says ''no,'' since she views basic differences among these classifications as ''illusory.''[3]

What about research support for the general education initiative? Haven't we established by now that handicapped children are better off, feel better about themselves, and learn more when they are removed from regular education classes and taught in small, self-contained classes with homogeneous populations, specially trained teachers and teacher aides, specialized teaching materials, and a full range of supportive services (e.g., speech therapy, adaptive physical education, counseling)? Unfortunately, we have not. Between 1950 and 1980 some fifty studies were conducted to examine the efficacy of placing exceptional children in special versus regular classes. Overall, it was not determined that special class placement led to superior academic achievement, although being left in a regular classroom did appear to result in lowered social acceptance.

The general education initiative has been challenged by a number of special educators concerned with the welfare of children with behavior disorders. They do not agree that such children can be appropriately lumped together with the mildly retarded and the learning disabled or that they are adequately served in the regular classroom. They argue that behavior disordered children often require special classes and other special education environments. Successful teachers of behavior disordered students are seen as needing highly specialized skills and special attitudes toward teaching that are different from those required for most teachers. Finally, the behavior disordered are viewed as seriously underserved at present and the general education initiative is considered a real threat to the already meager special services now in existence.

However, advocates of the general education initiative claim an individualized and appropriate education can be provided for *all* children by making the proper adjustments in the classroom learning environment. One approach to such adjustments has been formulated by Margaret Wang.[4] She has designed the Adaptive Learning Environments Model (ALEM), conceived as a core general education program, a special education program, and a compensatory education program.

The overall goal of the ALEM is to maximize each student's acquisition of basic academic skills, social competencies, positive self-perceptions, and a sense of responsibility for school and the broader social community. Mainstreaming is a full-time affair for the mildly handicapped, and instruction based on individual needs is the norm rather than the exception. It is claimed that in such a setting handicapped individuals are less likely to perceive themselves as outsiders or failures. The need for remedial education and special schools, special classes, and other "pull out" strategies is sharply reduced, if not eliminated. How does the ALEM work? It begins by assessing each student's entering level of skills and knowledge, using assessments that can be directly translated to specific educational tasks. The curriculum of the ALEM consists of two complementary components. The first is a highly structured, prescriptive program in academic subject areas. The second consists of exploratory activities that encourage students' social and personal development through the planning and management of their own learning. The assignment and management of the curriculum activities relies on a self-schedule system. Students are trained to take an active role in their education. The ALEM counts on such self-direction and management to free the teacher from many routines.

In implementation of the ALEM, special education teachers become consultants to general education teachers as well as providers of direct instruction for special education students in the classroom. The regular education teacher is the primary instructor for all students. School principals function as instructional as well as administrative leaders. They design instructional strategies, participate in in-service activities, conduct staff development programs, observe in classrooms, and provide regular feedback to teachers.

The ALEM uses multiage groupings and instructional teaming. Multiage grouping provides flexibility for decelerating or accelerating students without the usual social consequences of repeating or skipping grades. Opportunities for spontaneous and planned peer modeling and tutoring are also provided. Finally, the ALEM encourages an active program of family involvement. Parents receive frequent reports of their children's progress, participate in designing and modifying educational programs, provide home instruction in consultation with teachers, and work as volunteers in the ALEM classroom.

Evaluations of the ALEM are reported to have found the plan feasible for both regular and special students. In ALEM classrooms both regular and special students increased interactions with teachers, and spent greater amounts of time on tasks and in self-initiated activities. They also made gains in math and reading achievement, and demonstrated feelings of competence and self-responsibility for learning as well as appropriate classroom behavior. In comparison with handicapped students receiving part-time instruction in special education resource rooms, ALEM handicapped students generally evidenced better achievement and attitudinal gains. The evaluation data confirmed the necessity for adequate administrative and organizational support if the ALEM is to be successfully implemented. This generally positive evaluation of ALEM has been challenged by others who claim a truly valid evaluation based on an independent, systematic, and comprehensive review of empirical evidence has not been done.

We have reviewed reform in special education as it has emerged since 1975 and Public Law 94–142. What are the likely outcomes of challenging the existence of special education as a second or separate educational system and integrating large numbers of mildly handicapped students full-time into regular public school education programs? What are the likely outcomes in relation to the goals of present-day school reformers? Recent history has provided some interesting clues to answer these questions.

In 1968 Lloyd Dunn, a highly respected special educator, sounded an alarm much as the proponents of the general education initiative were to do in the late 1980s.[5] His extremely influential article "Special Education for the Mildly Retarded: Is Much of It Justifiable?" resulted in school superintendents across the United States examining and reevaluating their special education programs for the mildly handicapped. It provided impetus for a national reassessment of the definition of mild mental retardation and in the state of California played a part in the overnight, wholesale dumping of thousands of students previously labeled retarded and assigned to special education classrooms back into regular classroom programs.

Dunn was particularly concerned with the classification of disadvantaged and minority children as retarded, and their subsequent placement in special education classes. He cited all the reasons presented by the general education initiative advocates for his concerns: efficacy studies, labeling effects, and diagnostic and classification limitations. In the late 1960s, what Dunn called the "American Revolution in Education" was in progress, and it bore remarkable similarity to the educational reform movement of today. Dunn saw this revolution as resulting in regular school programs being better able to deal with individual differences among pupils and concluded:

Although the impact of the American Revolution in Education is just beginning to be felt and is still more an ideal than a reality, special education should begin moving now to fit into a changing general education program to assist in achieving the program's goals.[6]

As a means of accomplishing this goal, Dunn suggested many of the features of what was to become the ALEM program: changes in school organization (more team teaching, upgraded programs, flexible groups), curricular changes (programmed texts, computerized teaching), personnel changes (teachers, consultants, teacher aides), and availability of psychologists, guidance workers, and remedial educators. He also advocated more reliance on the clinical expertise and teaching of regular classroom teachers than on the scores and evaluative data of traditional diagnostic approaches.

In 1970 the California state legislature began a series of actions based on concerns regarding the efficacy of special education, particularly for the mildly mentally retarded. These actions led to a reevaluation of all mildly retarded students in special education classes in the state. Students with IQs above 70 were immediately reassigned to regular classroom programs and state funds were provided to assist in their "transition" from special to regular education. Between 14,000 and 22,000 students were involved. Some 250 districts in California had formally approved transition programs between 1970 and 1974.[7] Here, then, was a mini version of the currently conceived general education initiative in operation in the early 1970s.

How successful were these previous special education students in regular classrooms? What about their academic achievement and social behavioral development? A large California school district in a major metropolitan area was examined. This district had a wide range of socioeconomic differences and an ethnic composition consistent with the total state. The eighteen junior high schools serving grades 7, 8, and 9 located in the district were used in the study.

Each of the previous special education students was matched with four regular classmates in his or her required English class. These regular class peers were matched to target pupils on the basis of sex and ethnicity and were selected on a random basis within each English class. The researchers also selected additional regular class control students to provide additional comparative data. These matched and control students protected the confidentiality of the students formerly classified as mildly retarded, for none of the regular teachers involved were told which of the students had been in special education programs.

The teachers in the study were asked to rate each student—previous special education, regular matches, and control—in relation to other students in the class. The results indicated that the students formerly labeled mildly retarded were consistently rated by the teachers as doing less well academically than their matches in the same classrooms. They also received lower grades and were rated as having significantly more social-behavioral difficulties and adjustment problems than their classmates. When normed test data was examined, the previous special education students again did significantly more poorly than their matched classmates.[8]

What can one say about these results? It appears that mere placement of mildly handicapped children into regular classrooms does not bring about any miraculous improvement in their academic or social functioning. It also appears that even without the "self-fulfilling prophecy" effect of labeling (i.e., teachers, when told a child is retarded, teach him or her as if this is so, and when no progress occurs, say, "What would you expect of a retarded child?"), mildly handicapped students do not fare well in regular classrooms. The ALEM supporters would undoubtedly argue that the English classes in this study were devoid of most of the special trappings and procedures that are a part of their model. Even so, seasoned special educators today may well be nodding their heads and thinking to themselves, "We've been there before, and it's no simple matter to place the mildly handicapped in regular classes and guarantee their progress and success."

So much for the issue of reform in the field of special education. Let us now consider the interface of the reforms discussed above with the reform movement in regular education.

THE INTERFACE

When one surveys the dozens of publications concerned with reform in education in the United States, an interesting observation can be made. Very few of these documents devoted to improving the quality of the educational experience provided children in this country mention handicapped students. *A Nation at Risk* allows that "additional time" should be allotted to meet the needs of "slow learners," but little else. *Action for Excellence: A Comprehensive Plan to Improve Our Nation's Schools* recommends including handicapped students in programs for "education and economic growth." The Task Force on Education for Economic Growth cautions that the quality of instruction must be improved "not just for an elite but for all." The Twentieth Century Fund Task Force has proposed extending compensatory education programs for "poor, low scoring, and handicapped" students. Other education experts joining in the outcry regarding the quality of American schooling—Ernest Boyer, John I. Goodlad, and Theodore Sizer, among others—have very little to say about special education's place in the school reform movement.

Dan Hallahan and James Kaufman of the University of Virginia suggest four reasons for the educational reformers' neglect of special education.[9] First, it may be that the reformers feel special education is fine just as it is and that it should not be changed. Second, the reformers may equate achieving excellence in the public schools with meeting the needs of only the most able students. Some reformers may not consider special education students worthy of educational attention. A third possibility is that spokespersons for the educational reform movement view special education strictly as a second system in education and one for which they lack the expertise to pass judgment. Finally, a fourth explanation holds great appeal for the most radical of the general education initiative proponents: perhaps special education as it is now conceived and implemented is so faulty and problematic that it is unacceptable in any "ideal" or "reformed" state of education.

Steve Lilly, a special educator, suggests that special education for the mildly handicapped with its "pull out" programs may be seen by school reformers as creating far more problems than solutions. Lilly challenges his fellow special educators—"the ball is in our court"—and adds, "Until we are willing to examine our flawed assumptions about children and teachers and become integral members of the general education community, one cannot expect either to be featured in [school] reform reports or to be involved in construction of the next era of public education in the United States."[10]

Chances are that there are elements of truth in all of the aforementioned reasons for the paucity of interest and focus on the handicapped in statements regarding educational reform at the present time. After almost 15 years of implementing Public Law 94–142, many educators are learning to live with IEPs and "mainstreaming" as a means of bridging regular and special education and meeting the educational needs of the mildly handicapped. The courts have dealt with unreasonable demands by parents and other advocates of the handicapped (e.g., *Hudson* v. *Rawley*, 1980) and established a precedent for "reasonable" and "adequate" rather than "optimal" and "perfect."

The second explanation or elitist position will always be with us. Residents of the exclusive Palos Verdes Estates area in southern California tried to be diplomatic and polite when they appeared on a 6 o'clock TV news program to protest a group home for high functioning autistic young adults being established in their neighborhood. "Of course we should be doing all we can for these poor people," stated one concerned resident, "and we have nothing against them personally. But what if one of them climbed a fence and drowned in one of our swimming pools!"

In addition, research has shown that regular classroom teachers often do not favor the integration of the handicapped in the classrooms because they feel very inadequate when it comes to understanding their special problems and what to do to help them. It may be that the possibility of having to deal with a child during an epileptic seizure creates resistance to working with the chronically ill; or having to deal with a blind child whose homework will be typed in Braille is anxiety provoking even though the work will be evaluated by a special education teacher; or worrying about always facing the deaf child so he or she can lip-read or monitoring whether the child's hearing aid is being worn or is turned on is seen as too much trouble. Then there are the mentally retarded. Can they really learn and remember even with a teacher's best efforts?

The final argument—that after all, there is no reason to articulate special education, compensatory education, or any other special system education, since there is only one kind of education that matters, and that is, good education— is very appealing but idealistic. Like so many idealistic positions, however, it must ultimately be put to the test of reality reasonableness. Let us now turn to that reality in the final portion of this chapter. Despite the neglect or denial of handicapped children by the school reform movement, their inclusion in regular education on a part-time or full-time basis in the future is a current reality. Public Law 94–142 has established this, and if proponents of the general education initiative have their way, the frequency and degree of integration will increase in the future. What does this mean to those concerned with, to mention just two obvious issues, academic excellence and school discipline?

Academic Excellence

Central to the goals of the educational reform movement is an increase of efficiency of instruction and quality of learning in academic subjects in the public schools. What are likely to be the effects on this goal of integrating three or four children who are three or four years below grade level in all subjects, one or two of whom probably don't have the ability to do much better and one or two of whom could do better but are so poorly motivated and have such a negative attitude toward school that they have given up trying? None of these children may handle stress or frustration well, and when they are bored or upset, they may make certain everyone knows about it. What do we know about the effects of such youngsters on everyone concerned: the classroom teacher, the nonhandicapped classmates, the so-called exceptional learners themselves, and the parents of both exceptional and nonexceptional students?

A study was done with almost a thousand regular teachers in the state of California who represented some fifty-five public schools in eighteen school districts that were representative of urban, suburban, and rural geographical areas.[11] The study focused on the teachers' perceptions of the possible effects of mainstreaming mildly handicapped children into the elementary grades. The teachers read short vignettes covering academic and behavioral backgrounds of six ten-year-old boys representing the mildly retarded (IQ 66), the learning disabled (normal IQ), and the emotionally disturbed (normal IQ). They then rated twenty-nine items that related to possible effects of these children being placed full-time into their classrooms. These ratings were based on a six-level "agree-disagree" response mode. The items referred to the following kinds of issues:

1. *The effects on the teacher.* With a child like this in your classroom, an excessive amount of time for curriculum planning will be necessary.
2. *The effects on the nonhandicapped children.* A child like this will adversely affect the other children's motivation to learn.
3. *The effects on the exceptional learner.* As a result of placement in your classroom, a child like this will develop a more positive attitude toward school.

The results of this survey indicated that teachers were indeed concerned about a major increase in curriculum planning time with the inclusion of these mildly handicapped children in their classrooms. They did, however, strongly indicate that problems that might occur with these youngsters in the classrooms were their responsibility, not the school principal's, the school psychologist's, or the special education consultant's. They were also mildly favorable to the item "Assignment of a child like this to your classroom was a wise administrative decision."

By and large no adverse effects on the nonhandicapped were anticipated by the regular classroom teachers. Expectations for the mildly handicapped children were also generally positive, except for the mildly retarded boy with an apparently valid IQ of 66. He was by far the least favorably perceived. The next most unfavorably perceived were an aggressive boy and one labeled "hyperactive." The teachers responded favorably to "The experience of being in your classroom will increase the chances of a child like this attaining a more productive and independent place in society" and very significantly rejected the item "A child like this will not respond even to your best teaching efforts," indicating a definite measure of optimism and teaching pride for all but the retarded boy. Several survey items relating to possible negative reactions of the parents of the non-handicapped toward integration of the handicapped were generally not supported by the teachers in the survey.

Subsequent studies of regular teacher attitudes toward mainstreaming of mildly handicapped children into classrooms have tended to be more negative, particularly for the mildly retarded. Regular teachers frequently report they feel inadequately prepared to teach retarded children and that they do not have access to the resource materials or consultant services necessary to assist them. School principals have some of the same reservations as teachers. One study found only 40 percent of the principals surveyed voiced positive attitudes, although 70 percent expressed general support for the idea of mainstreaming. The mentally retarded were rated as "least mainstreamable" by the principals. Other studies involving public school principals have found children with learning disabilities rated as far more likely to be successfully mainstreamed than the mildly retarded.

Will the presence of mildly handicapped individuals in the regular classroom adversely affect the academic progress of the nonhandicapped? The answers to this question have varied in the research literature. It has been found that both special education and regular teachers think that placing the mildly handicapped in the regular classroom would restrict the progress of other class members. In a study of K–12 teachers, approximately one-fourth felt mainstreaming had a negative effect on both the mainstreamed students and their nonhandicapped peers. In another study, experienced special education and regular teachers, counselors, and school psychologists did not view integration of the mildly handicapped as having a negative effect on the academic progress of their classmates.

Anita Johnson, a special education teacher and administrator, conducted a large-scale survey of a suburban school district in California that examined the relationship between mainstreaming and the academic progress of nonhandicapped elementary school children. The study focused on both the numbers of integrated mildly handicapped children in a given classroom and the amount of integration time involved. Twelve elementary schools participated and over 200 classrooms were examined. Including the mildly handicapped, some 5,500 students were involved. Briefly stated, the results found that in classrooms at every grade level the number of handicapped students and the time they spent mainstreamed into the regular classroom had no bearing on how well their nonhandicapped peers fared academically (based on fall versus spring districtwide group achievement testing).

A most interesting additional finding emerged, however, when the district's classrooms were examined on the basis of socioeconomic status (SES). This status was determined by the existence of Title I funding and high-cost housing geographical location—the funded schools were designated as low SES and the high-cost housing area schools as high SES. Within the low SES schools the reading achievement of nonhandicapped students had a positive relationship to the integration of mildly handicapped children. That is, the more handicapped students integrated in a classroom and the longer the time they spent there, the better the yearly reading achievement gains of the nonhandicapped. In explaining this finding one might use "the spread of effect." In the process of developing procedures and utilizing individualized materials to accommodate integrated mildly handicapped students, teachers may have found additional children who could profit from these even though the children had never been classified for special education.

Another experimental study concluded that the presence of handicapped or retarded children in a classroom may increase the confidence of nonhandicapped children in themselves and their abilities, and in turn this positive self-assessment may contribute to a more positive classroom performance. These conclusions are based on estimates made by the nonhandicapped of their own memory ability after viewing memory records of students labeled "mentally retarded" and "nonretarded." Another study found that there was no negative effect on the intellectual, communication, and social development of normal preschoolers when they were integrated on a ratio of one to two with mildly and moderately handicapped peers (i.e., one normal and two handicapped youngsters).

These last several studies vary in design, focus, and type of student, but they do suggest that those who automatically assume that nonhandicapped children will pay academically and otherwise if handicapped individuals are included in their classrooms may be premature in their judgments. Such drawing of premature conclusions—indeed, such inaccuracy—has a long history in attempts to mainstream or deinstitutionalize the handicapped, particularly the mentally retarded. In 1904, Walter Fernald was an outspoken opponent of allowing the mentally retarded to move freely in society. He predicted a high incidence of criminal and antisocial activity if the retarded were "placed out" of closed institutions. To his credit, he did study the outcomes of integrating the retarded into normal community settings; he and many others were proven dead wrong. With often only a modest degree of assistance, most retarded individuals became acceptable citizens in the community.

The interface of regular and special education reform will undoubtedly involve handicapped and normal children working and learning side by side in some manner. Our conclusion? We have no clear evidence that this will be a disservice to either.

School Discipline

Discipline is another area of potential conflict between regular and special education reformers. Unfortunately, we have no research that sheds light on such obvious questions as "Do students who are disruptive reduce the amount of effective learning time for other students?" and "Do nonhandicapped students model inappropriate language and behavior demonstrated by behavior disordered students?" Common sense tells us that interruptions in the classroom use up valuable time, and that some students not given to abusive language, disrespect for rules and authority, and negative behavior may very well be influenced "to test the limits" themselves when behavior problems continuously surface around them in the classroom.

What we do know is that regular classroom teachers are going to have to live with serious discipline problems until certain legal processes run their course and that on-the-spot, long-term suspensions and expulsions are no longer viable options. For example, in a 6–2 decision, the U.S. Supreme Court ruled that Public Law 94–142 was violated when the San Francisco schools indefinitely suspended and then attempted to expel two emotionally disturbed students considered dangerous by the district (*Honig* v. *Doe*). One of these students was charged with choking a classmate and breaking a window, and the other had been charged with stealing and extortion in school and with making sexual advances to female students in his classes.

According to the court decision, Public Law 94–142 authorized school officials to suspend handicapped children considered dangerous for a maximum of ten days. Longer suspension or actual expulsion could be carried out only if the child's parents consent to the action or if the school district can convince a federal district judge that the child poses a danger to himself or others. The court stated that it was upholding Congress' intention in formulating Public Law 94–142 to deny school officials the power to exclude handicapped children from schools on the basis of local policies and judgment. The court called attention to powers that officials still had for purposes of punishing dangerous students. These powers, authorized by the U.S. Education Department, included the use of "study carrels," time-outs, detentions, and restriction of privileges.

In terms of both academics and discipline, parents of nonhandicapped children have been found to be ambivalent toward mainstreaming. This ambivalence stems from concern with the alleged disruption of the educational system by focus on the handicapped, concern that normal children are now receiving less attention than previously (and hence are being shortchanged), and concern that the "rights" of the handicapped are overshadowing the "rights" of the nonhandicapped. A serious split may be developing between the parents of the handicapped and of the nonhandicapped, not unlike the split that developed between parents divided on the issue of busing to alleviate racial discrimination in the public schools.

How are we going to reconcile the "rights" of both the handicapped and the nonhandicapped? In addition, how are we going to move toward goals of academic excellence and improved classroom cooperation and motivation in light of increased diversity among students in the classroom? Let us review our discussion in this chapter and see where we stand with respect to answers to these questions.

To begin with, there is no question at present that all children in the United States have a right to a public school education. Children who are handicapped and need "something extra" in order to receive the benefits of that education are also, by law, entitled to considerations of individualization, appropriateness, and "least restrictive" placement. Are they entitled to these considerations at the expense of the nonhandicapped? Public Law 94–142 does not say that they are, and interpretations of the law tend to view handicapped children who are disruptive and who make inordinate demands on teacher time as inappropriately integrated into regular classrooms. From the evidence we have about the effects on the nonhandicapped of mainstreaming the handicapped, there is very little to suggest that the consequences are necessarily negative, although attitudes among administrators and teachers vary and the mentally retarded are rather uniformly rejected.

However, implementation of Public Law 94–142 is expensive. When President Gerald R. Ford signed the law in 1975, he did so reluctantly. He feared that the provisions of the law would raise the hopes and expectations of handicapped individuals and their families to an unrealistic level. But he also feared the wrath of the interest groups for the handicapped if he vetoed it. President Ford openly expressed his reservations about the availability of federal funds for the law's implementation in the future. In her call in 1986 for increased "shared responsibility" among all educators for the welfare of the handicapped, Madeline Will, the U.S. assistant secretary for special education, was undoubtedly reflecting the federal government's continued concern over the high cost of funding Public Law 94–142.[12] The emergence of the general education initiative and suggestions that the mildly handicapped be maintained in regular classrooms without the benefit of a second system of education unquestionably are related to that concern.

Accompanying the call for the general education initiative have been suggestions for making it work in the public schools. These suggestions are also applicable to accomplishing the goals of general educational reformers: increasing academic excellence and improving student functioning in the classroom. One set of specific guidelines in this regard is Margaret Wang's ALEM model. While the model has many commendable features, one cannot help but question the certainty with which it is presented by its author. Wang speaks of student self-direction and self-management as freeing the teacher from many routines; of school principals who "design instructional strategies, participate in in-service activities, conduct staff development programs, observe in classrooms, and provide regular feedback to teachers"; and of actively involved parents who provide instruction at home and work as volunteers in the classroom. They sound impressive, but are these realistic expectations for a majority of school districts, school programs, and school administrators throughout the United States?

There is certainly no consensus in either special or regular education that the general education initiative is clearly a step forward or a step backward when it comes to the welfare of either the handicapped or the nonhandicapped. No matter how flexible and individualized the approach, some children (e.g., the behaviorally disordered) are so atypical that they will require special classes or resource programs if they are to be educated in the public school. Public Law 94–142 has helped us recognize that the concept of least restrictive placement is viable, but it has not established that the majority of mildly handicapped children can be absorbed into regular classrooms full-time, no matter what the classroom instructional plan or how heroic the teacher.

Regular educational reformers may have overlooked handicapped children, and special education reformers may be overlooking nonhandicapped children. And both may be overlooking a vital factor in the midst of their reform rhetoric— the teacher—and a vital question—What is fair to expect of a regular classroom teacher? It seems that as instructional plans manifest their limitations and lofty societal goals for education fall short of accomplishment, we assume that some sort of teacher heroics will surface and save the day. The case can be made that this is implied in many of the statements made by both special and regular educational reformers. Teacher heroics are a precious, but not that rare, commodity in education. We are aware that some thoughtful observers, such as J. Myron Atkin, dean of the School of Education at Stanford University, disagree with us.[13] But when all is said and done, academic excellence increases when teachers put the extra effort into making it increase; discipline problems decrease when teachers put the extra effort into making them decrease; and mildly retarded, disturbed, and learning disabled students work and learn successfully in regular classrooms alongside normal peers when teachers provide the support, energy, creativity, and guidance to guarantee it happens.

Teacher heroics can and do exist, but both special and regular education reformers had better not take them for granted. They had better begin assembling the resources, supportive services, and funding necessary to nurture and develop extraordinary teacher motivation and effort. For no matter what research studies and program designs have to offer, teacher competence, dedication, and—yes— heroics will be the ultimate determiners of successful reform in special and regular education.

NOTES

1. Levine, C. L., & Wexler, E. M. (1981), *Public Law 94–142: An act of Congress* (New York: Macmillan), p. 127.

2. Wang, M. C. (1988, May 4), Weighing the regular education initiative, *Education Week*, 36–38.

3. Ibid.

4. Wang, M. C., Peverly, S. T., & Catalano, R. (1987), Integrating special needs students in regular classes: Programming, implementation, and policy, in J. Gottlieb & B. W. Gottlieb (Eds.), *Advances in special education* (Greenwich, CT: JAI Press), vol. 6, pp. 119–49.

5. Dunn, L. M. (1968), "Special education for the mildly retarded: Is much of it justifiable?" *Exceptional Children*, *35*, 5–22.

6. Ibid., p. 10.

7. Keogh, B. K., & Levitt, M. L. (1976), Special education in the mainstream: A confrontation of limitations, *Focus on Exceptional Children*, *8*(1), 1–10.

8. Ibid.

9. Hallahan, D. P., & Kauffman, J. M. (1988). *Exceptional children: Introduction to special education*, 4th ed. (Englewood Cliffs, N.J.: Prentice-Hall), p. 501.

10. Lilly, S. M. (1987). Lack of focus on special education in literature on educational reform, *Exceptional Children*, *53*, 325–26.

11. Watson, P. C., & Hewett, F. M. (1975), *Teacher attitudes toward mainstreaming: A preliminary report* (Los Angeles: University of California).

12. Will, M. C. (1986). Educating children with learning problems: A shared responsibility. *Exceptional Children*, *52*(5), 411–16.

13. Atkin, J. M. (1985), Changing our thinking about educational change, in J. H. Bunzel (Ed.), *Challenge to American schools: The case for standards and values* (New York: Oxford University Press), pp. 51–53.

SUGGESTED READINGS

Dunn, L. M. (1968). Special education for the mildly retarded: Is much of it justifiable? *Exceptional Children*, *35*, 5–22.

Fuchs, D., & Fuchs, L. S. (1988). Evaluation of the adaptive learning environments model. *Exceptional Children*, *55*, 115–27.

Hallahan, D. P., & Kauffman, J. M. (1988). *Exceptional children: Introduction to special education* (4th ed.). Englewood Cliffs, NJ: Prentice-Hall.

Hewett, F. M., & Forness, S. R. (1984). *Education of exceptional learners* (3rd ed.). Boston: Allyn & Bacon.

Keogh, B. K., & Levitt, M. L. (1976). Special education in the mainstream: A confrontation of limitations. *Focus on Exceptional Children*, *8*(1), 1–10.

Levine, C. L., & Wexler, E. M. (1981). *Public Law 94–142: An act of Congress*. New York: Macmillan.

Lilly, S. M. (1987). Lack of focus on special education in literature on educational reform. *Exceptional Children*, *53*, 325–26.

Mirga, T. (1988, January 27). Justices reject peril exception to Public Law 94–142. *Education Week*, pp. 1, 16.

Wang, M. C. (1988, May 4). Weighing the regular education initiative. *Education Week*, pp. 36–38.

Watson, P. C., & Hewett, F. M. (1975). *Teacher attitudes toward mainstreaming: A preliminary report*. Los Angeles: University of California.

Will, M. C. (1986). Educating children with learning problems: A shared responsibility. *Exceptional Children*, *52*(5), 411–16.

6 The "Distinctive" High School, Structural Change, and the School Reform Movement

Burton R. Clark

Americans need to evolve a new way of conceptualizing the organization of secondary education. Fortunately, spurred by questions raised in the school reform movement of the 1980s—though not yet effectively addressed by the mainstream of thought in that movement—this needed development is already under way in research and innovative practice. The evolution I have in mind moves schools from uniformity to diversity. It replaces official sameness with guided variety. It shifts operational control from the central bureaucracy of school districts to individual schools, thereby permitting the staff of each school to determine its character. Once widely effected, this change would cause upper secondary education to operate less like the elementary level and more like higher education. Most important, as I shall explain, it would replace the traditional ideal of the common school with a more modern ideal of "the distinctive school."

RECENT CRITICAL THOUGHT ON PUBLIC SCHOOL ORGANIZATION

Years before *A Nation at Risk*[1] gave the country a shock treatment on the "crisis" in American education, numerous analysts had raised the alarm about the growing bureaucratization and standardization of American public schooling. In the late 1960s David Rogers offered a devastating account of the dysfunctions of bureaucratic control in the New York City school system, in which he concluded that "nobody can make the system work if the bureaucratic structure is not radically altered"; and since that was not about to happen, "conditions will probably get worse before they improve."[2] Two decades later we can safely say he was dead right: the conditions did get worse.

In the mid–1970s, Dan Lortie's landmark study of American teachers reported in rich detail the organizational imperatives, bureaucratic in nature, that shaped the occupation of schoolteaching. Apropos of findings that have reemerged in a striking fashion in more recent research, Lortie pointed to a "dual captivity" in the relationship between teachers and students:

Students were assigned to particular schools by place of residence, and once in school they were allocated to specific teachers by school administrators. Teachers, having accepted employment in a given school district, were assigned to a school by the superintendent [or central staff] and to particular students by the principal. Thus neither student nor teacher had much to say about their relationship: each was forced to come to terms with an externally imposed requirement of cooperation.[3]

Then, in a brilliantly argued 1979 book, Arthur Wise insisted that the centralization and bureaucratization of control in such districts and state school systems had progressed to a point that frustrated the efforts of principals and teachers in the public schools and undermined the professional status of the teaching staff.[4] Management-by-the-numbers had replaced instructional leadership, and standardized teaching dominated professional discretion. In 1983—to take one more example—Rebecca Barr and Robert Dreeben showed in systematic detail how, in a top-down hierarchy of influence, school districts set the major parameters of organization for their constituent schools, and the schools in turn for their classrooms, and thereby shaped classroom learning.[5] By the early 1980s many other books and articles too numerous to mention here also helped construct a scholarly literature that could have directed reformers toward the tough problems of public school organization and school district control. By no means was the cupboard of ideas bare.

But the school reform movement set off in haste in 1983 and 1984, largely led by commission reports that were based on testimony and surface impressions rather than on in-depth study.[6] The movement acquired momentum in a way that dramatically caught public interest but then scattered that attention in every direction. Suddenly there seemed to be so much that was wrong, so many things to fix, and so little time in which to consider which changes might be most crucial. Hence the first wave of the reform movement was diffuse. If it had a central interest, it was in curricular efforts to require more work in various subjects, old and new, that were seen as basic: English, history, mathematics, science, geography, foreign languages, computer training. Various states set out to test students more often for subject mastery and to stiffen graduation requirements.

Then, in 1986, led by the Carnegie Forum's *A Nation Prepared: Teachers for the 21st Century* and the Holmes Group's *Tomorrow's Teachers*, attention shifted to the recruitment, training, and certification of teachers. That shift soon became known as the "second wave" in the reform movement, one that had a better center of gravity in its focus on the quality of school personnel. Prominent in this wave have been efforts to improve recruitment and training in schools of education, to test teachers for minimal competencies, to increase salaries, and to establish a National Board for Professional Teaching Standards that will certify master teachers.[7] The overall intent has been to reverse the downward slide in the "professionalization project" of schoolteaching by directly attempting to improve the occupation itself—higher quality recruits, better training, stiffer certification, and, it was hoped, greater public esteem.

Unfortunately, all such reforms are likely to be short-lived unless the conditions of work inside individual public schools are altered. Especially in the core of metropolitan areas, but also in the suburbs and rural areas, the years since 1960 have seen those conditions steadily deteriorate. It has long been known that, for whatever the reasons, the way schools operate deprofessionalizes schoolteaching, with the best teachers inclined to leave the field for other lines of work. The new literature of the 1980s joins the older studies in telling us that the frustrations of schoolteaching, especially in the secondary schools, drive many of the remaining teachers into passive timeserving and preoccupation with discipline and classroom order. The setting thereby undermines the efforts to make schoolteaching a profession, with all the advantages that are gained when work becomes a calling. Instead, the potential calling becomes a career, the career becomes a job, the job becomes a paycheck.

Something is fundamentally wrong. As pointed out by the Carnegie Forum in its 1986 report, "What must be done cannot be done within the constraints imposed by the system of public education that has been in place for many decades. A fundamental redesign of that system is needed." The Carnegie report further noted that schools should be restructured "to provide a professional environment for teaching" and offered the specific advice that school systems should "introduce a new category of Lead Teachers . . . to provide active leadership in the redesign of the schools." In fact, individual schools should be allowed "to design their own curriculum based on the teachers' view of what's best for their students."[8] But on how to bring this latter action to pass, the Carnegie Forum recommendations had little to say beyond exhortation.

To make serious headway, the school reform movement clearly needs a third wave of attention that focuses on the macro-organization of public schools and the composition of school districts. Are there high school structures—types of schools—that activate students rather than bore them? Can secondary schools move beyond bureaucracy to profession-oriented organizations that motivate teachers and elicit their commitment? Is the organization of school districts at the heart of the matter?

The studies that constitute the weightier part of the reform literature of the early 1980s touched upon various problems of school organization. The major books by John Goodlad, Ernest L. Boyer, and Theodore Sizer, published in 1983 and 1984, reported many operational features of public schools that dragged down teaching and learning.[9] Reflecting on the defects as he observed them, Sizer concluded that "better schools will come when better structures are built.

Those structures have no inherent merit, however: their sole function will be to provide apt and nurturing conditions that will attract students and teachers and make their work together worthwhile and efficient."[10] He praised public schools that tried not to be comprehensive but focused their character more selectively, generating what he later called "essential schools."

Out of the work of the Sizer research group there came in 1985 the powerful analysis of Arthur G. Powell, Eleanor Farrar, and David K. Cohen, in which the public comprehensive high school, struggling to provide something for everybody, was portrayed as a "shopping mall" in which many students wandered aimlessly.[11] Trying to be helpful by responding to various personal tastes and interests and myriad social problems, such as street gangs, drug and alcohol abuse, pregnant teenagers and unwed mothers, the individual school expands its mall, offering something here and something there and something else further along the way. The school loses unity and sense of purpose; teachers lose the moral authority of superior knowledge and wisdom. Critically, the lack of focus in the school leads to a lack of focus in the efforts of students. Coherent educational packages are not discernible; the motivating interests of students are not systematically tapped. Rather, attention is scattered and interests remain diffuse.

Notably, the unfocused setting encourages a downward spiral of compromise, a "treaty" between teachers and students: "If you do not bother me, I will not bother you." The classroom then undergoes a loss of intellectual content, a dumbing-down. These investigators recommend organizational changes that would create more "specialty shops" in which high school teachers and students would share a focus that would knit them together in a community of interest and enhance motivation all around.[12] The school specialty becomes the basis for meaningful student-teacher involvement in the educational process. Student interest in a particular specialty focus in *the* incentive to participate and to learn.

One year later, in 1986, a group of Michigan State professors, led by Michael W. Sedlak, offered a similar line of argument: in the vast majority of American public schools, teachers and students bargain away engagement in academic learning in exchange for social tranquillity.[13] Warning that the post–1983 reform initiatives fail to take into account the conditions in schools that promote this downward bargaining, they concluded that academic engagement and learning in the high schools will not substantially improve until those conditions are substantially changed. They portrayed the conditions as rooted in "three characteristics common to secondary schools in America: *universality* or the egalitarian commitment to everyone, *comprehensiveness* or the effort to educate students of different abilities and interest in the same facility, and a *bureaucratic structure* necessitated by universality and comprehensiveness."[14] In the individual comprehensive high school, the bureaucratic arrangements encourage a retreat to "institutional passivity and neutrality," a posture in which the school attempts to respond to diverse student interests and capabilities by increasing options, varying the paths to a diploma, and "not looking too closely at what was actually taught and learned in classrooms."[15]

In this insightful volume the faults of the public high school-as-shopping mall are again evident. The comprehensive public high school remains under systematic pressure from the school board, central district administrators, school administrators, and parents to be both responsive *and* less judgmental across diverse students. No wonder, then, that blandness is a widespread result, one noted by researchers and nonresearchers alike. Under modern conditions of student diversity, blandness is virtually a genetic defect of schools that attempt to do everything for everyone who comes their way.

The most fascinating part of the post–1985 literature on the reform of school organization has taken us directly to the high school-as-specialty shop, particularly those developing under the rubric of "magnet school." Magnet schools go out of their way to be attractive, to draw students by offering a distinctive set of courses that help to give the school a theme, a special self-concept, and a public image. A 1983 survey of public magnet schools showed that over 1,000 had developed, since their beginnings in the late 1960s and early 1970s, in more than 130 of the largest urban school districts.[16] These schools undoubtedly vary greatly in their intensity as magnets, from purely nominal to powerfully assertive. But as a type of school they are intentionally specialized, as opposed to schools designed to be comprehensive. Of course they have to teach the subjects deemed basic by the state. But their additional specialty gives them a focus, be it in science, the humanities, the arts, the health professions, commerce, the technical trades, or in variously labeled educational approaches, such as "individually guided education" or "open education."

The latest research (1986–1988) has provided some powerful insights into the nature of this type of school, highlighting features that lead an increasing number of reformers to look favorably upon their development. Leading the literature is the work of Mary Haywood Metz, which centered on in-depth observation of the interior lives of three public magnet high schools in a large city over a seven-year period.[17] Characteristically, as Metz showed so well, magnet schools offer choice to students and parents. As they do so, they set up competition among schools within a school district to attract students and demonstrate effective performance. Their specific, coherent purpose, compared with the all-embracing public comprehensive school, helps promote a unified school culture shared by teachers and students alike. Their special qualities give a boost to students', parents', and teachers' morale, enhancing pride all around. Notably, the schools she observed were able to instruct and integrate student bodies diverse in race and social class. Metz concluded that "something like magnet schools, with their official license and obligation to innovate, will be needed to create any serious innovation in high schools."[18]

At the same time, in the face of this need, there are strong opposing forces that continue to push for the standardized, traditional public comprehensive high school, on the bedrock of belief that the only way to guarantee an equal education is to attempt to guarantee the same education. In the traditional approach, there should be statewide and nationally distributed textbooks keyed to particular

grades and nationally normed tests that report student progress in grade equiv-
alents. High schools should be structured to be officially the same, from one to
another. This canon of the common school has a powerful hold on official doctrine
and public thought. But, as Metz has shown, it has been thoroughly undermined
by the reality that the public comprehensive high schools in any multischool
district are not the same and cannot be, despite any formal appearance of standardization.

Why? For the simple reason that comprehensive high schools are tied to
neighborhoods that vary enormously in their socioeconomic status and racial and
ethnic composition. The schools are thereby made very different on the fundamental parameter of student input, with all the attendant baggage of different
family backgrounds, cultural heritages, and neighborhood contexts. Metz has
stated well the American dilemma of comprehensive-school organization:

to live with this contradiction between officially equal education based on standardization
of curriculum and activity, on the one hand, and tremendous variety in the quality and
content of education arising from the linkage of public education to housing that is
segregated by social class as well as race, on the other.[19]

Magnet schools, then, "draw political fire because they bring this tacit contradiction to consciousness. In order to draw volunteers, they must be formally
nonstandard, different from other schools. They thus openly and officially violate
the rule that schools should be alike in order to ensure a fair race."[20] To add
insult to injury, they must be at least implicitly superior if they are to attract
students, and they are often explicitly so. This is too much for many public
school boards and central district administrators to bear. Better to wink at what
affluent neighborhoods and their schools do unofficially and nonexplicitly by
way of receiving extra resources and creating attractive conditions, than let
magnet schools do it formally and openly, and thereby force the community to
perceive the departure from the effort to effect equality through sameness.[21]

Powerful stuff, this, not least because it would plunge the reform movement
into controversial issues of power and control as well as bring to light fundamental
contradictions that school boards and educational officials would rather leave
implicit than have out on the table. And the work of Metz does not stand alone.
Again based on intensive work inside public schools, Linda M. McNeil has
brilliantly argued that minimum effort on the part of teachers and the offering
of "flattened content" in the classroom stem from complex organizational dynamics within schools and school districts.[22] The observations offered by others
in the past concerning ritualistic teaching and disengaging students in the traditional public high school are here linked to immediate underlying causes in
the organizational framework. Teachers find themselves under principals focused
on regularity, who see innovation, surprises, and diversity as inefficiencies. In
the schools McNeil studied, "the administration issued directions; teachers were
to comply."[23] Teachers saw that they were not valued for their expertise, that

subject competence gave them no added authority. In reaction, they engaged in "defensive teaching" and "defensive simplification," in which they met minimal formal demands of the state and district by watering down the work of the classroom, turning to lists of terms and to preparation for tests. As teachers defensively thin the subject matter, they engage in their own deskilling, their own deprofessionalization. The downward cycle becomes a vicious one indeed, especially when students then compare the "pap" they get in school with the information and discussion they get from the mass media, family, friends, and other outsiders. The very credibility of school knowledge is made problematic.

McNeil's perceptive analysis of such organizational dynamics in the traditional comprehensive public high school caused her to turn to the possibilities of magnet schools. In research on these schools, she found inventive teachers, committed to teaching. Teachers were allowed to be subject matter specialists. They worked together to develop a school curriculum, with personal specialties within it, that would reflect the distinctive purpose of the school. They then no longer taught defensively. They demanded more of students, not settling for minimum, passive compliance. They volunteered to be in magnet schools because then they could work as professionals, empowered rather than made impotent by the structure of the school. And to be with them, in a special setting, students with a given interest sought admission, even if it meant riding a bus for an hour or so each way between home and school.

Additional significant studies of school organization are now appearing or are in the offing that may help to shift the center of gravity in the school reform movement. In *The World We Created at Hamilton High*, Gerald Grant powerfully argues that public high schools labor under an increasingly massive superstructure, with principals having to serve as "middle managers who process directives issuing from a multilayered bureaucracy." For him, the two essential reforms are to let high schools shape their own destiny and to put teachers in charge of their own practice. This means that differences among high schools should be encouraged, a thrust reflected in "magnet-school programs or other plans that allow parents to select among a variety of schools at any given level."[24] The individual school needs the power "to make a world," to rebuild around a focus the moral and intellectual world that has been shattered in many contemporary public schools.

Along parallel lines, other investigators argue that public schools, having failed as protective monopolies, must be turned loose to compete with each other for faculty and students.[25] Every school in a participating district should become a magnet school. In a "universal magnet system" principals and teachers could choose, within broad state and district guidelines, each school's curriculum and specialties.

Finally, in a 1988 study, John Chubb and Terry Moe assert that specialized high schools have shown their superiority over public comprehensive high schools. But they also conclude pessimistically that the deeply entrenched political and administrative frameworks of American public education will probably block the needed evolution.[26] Albert Shanker, president of the American Federation of Teachers, has argued for several years in numerous articles, speeches, and newspaper columns that specialized schools offer much promise, not least in bettering the conditions of professional work and responsibility, and should be organized and turned loose under broad state and local school district guidance.[27]

One important implication of these studies is that the country may not need to turn to radical voucher schemes, currently being put forward, that would take school funds away from regular institutional allocations and simply give monies to parents and students to choose, as best they can, among private as well as public schools. Full-fledged voucher plans are a massive threat to the ideas and practice of public education. As such, they encourage maximum resistance. The approach suggested by the studies I have reviewed and by the perspective Shanker has adopted would still keep a global public school framework. Their thrust is not to abandon the public school but to restructure it.

TWO MIRRORS FOR REFLECTIONS

As we search for the underlying structural flaws of the American public secondary system, and for broad directions of change, school reformers can find additional insight in two forms of comparison. One is cross-national, in which they turn to the experiences of other countries; the other is cross-sectional, in which they turn to another level of our own educational system or another sector in our own society. In each case, we need not look for directly applicable blueprints. Instead, we can use the outside system more as a mirror that reflects what our own system is really like and thereby precipitates thoughts that otherwise might not occur to us. Sometimes in a mirror you see exactly what you are. In the cross-national mode, Japan has become the brightest mirror. In cross-sectional reasoning, American higher education highlights forms of organization and dynamics of change that are sharply different, with telling results, from those of secondary education. The implications for the school reform movement will be obvious.

The Japanese Mirror[28]

Americans often beg off from comparisons of the quality of American secondary schooling with European counterparts by pointing out that our system is for everyone and "theirs" is for only a minority of the age group, an "elite." But this tactic will not work for the Japanese case. Japanese secondary education is universal, and has a graduation rate exceeding that of the American secondary system. Japan also has moved deeply into mass higher education, with a diverse array of over 1,000 public and private universities, colleges, and community colleges. The American occupation following World War II caused Japan to formally adopt the comprehensive secondary school.

But the Japanese did not give up their older premise of differentiation at the secondary level. Schooling is uniform only through the first eight years. Like American counterparts, students in the early grades are assigned to schools strictly on the basis of areas of residence. But all this stops after grade 8; the secondary schools are not expected to be officially similar to one another in program and quality of institution. The comprehensive secondary schools are placed in districts that typically include five or more schools that are explicitly recognized as varying in quality. Indeed, high school entrance examinations "sort each age cohort into what amounts to an eight-to-ten-tier high school ranking system."[29] As students compete for entry to particular schools within a set of schools, they are torn loose from the limits of neighborhood and circulate within a larger catchment. How they are sorted is determined by educational criteria rather than neighborhood of residence. Since strict selection takes place again when students move from secondary to higher education, there is much downward influence across the educational levels. The university dominates the secondary school and the secondary school dominates schooling at the elementary level.

There are many things wrong with this system that give pause to Japanese educators and parents, but it clearly lets merit ride high in the saddle. Competition among the public schools, and between public and private schools, tends to raise academic standards and student achievement. The individual public high school scrambles to be perceived as better than others in order to attract better students. Since this ranking of public high schools has not been to everyone's taste, some Japanese reforms have attempted to make entrance to public high schools less competitive and to reduce the preoccupation with entrance exams. But this type of reform causes the top public high schools to decline—generating the boomerang effect for the public school system that parents then turn more to private schools.[30]

Observing this process, and reflecting on American as well as Japanese structures, Thomas Rohlen concluded that "the merit principle and hierarchical differentiation are inseparable in public education."[31] Efforts to make public schools identical work against high levels of academic excellence. Schools need to be different, with the differences leading to differences in prestige. Again, the medicine of reform seems bitter—until we note that the current American arrangement, in which schools are tied to segregated neighborhoods, actually sorts students more drastically than does the Japanese high school system. The Japanese sort openly, using educational criteria of achievement and ability, whereas "the sorting process in the United States is characterized by much less that is aboveboard, calculable, or based on objective measures."[32]

Reflections from the Japanese mirror promote tough thinking about what has gone wrong in the American provision of public secondary schooling. For one, we see further into the issue of sorting students by educational criteria against sorting them by neighborhood or residence. When so much depends upon where you live, as in America, equal access is out, made impossible by the neighborhood monopoly of each comprehensive public high school. To have students choose among distinctive schools, especially under broad district guidelines on student body composition, would certainly promote more genuine equality of opportunity, even as schools became dissimilar and ranked. Hence, charges of "elitism" made in the current U.S. debate against essential schools, theme schools, magnet schools, charter schools, and other kinds of educational specialty shops have it all wrong. It is in the current structure that elitism runs rampant. Behind the bureaucratic pretense that comprehensive schools are equal schools lies the unquestionable fact that millions of students from poor and minority families living in poor neighborhoods are held captive in schools that are nowhere near as good as those found in well-off neighborhoods. The irony is almost cruel: schools designed to be educationally different could promote equality of access better than do schools formally designed to be the same but that thereby tie students to the great inequalities of neighborhood locations.

The American Higher Education Mirror[33]

Even more telling is the startling difference in the way we in America organize higher education and secondary education. Higher education is diversified, organized in many different types of public and private universities, colleges, and community colleges. Secondary education is not, since it is fixed overwhelmingly in the single mold of the public comprehensive high school. Higher education is competitive and hierarchical; secondary education is not. As a result of its diversity and its competitive hierarchy, higher education puts a premium on institutional initiative and efforts to create a viable niche, place by place, in the ecology of the system. Secondary education has no such prods for local initiative and for the building of distinctive reputation and character.

Finally, American higher education is full of choice—for students, faculty, and administrators. Notably, prospective students can choose among a bewildering array of diverse institutions, public and private, large and small, religious and nondenominational, commuting and residential, within state and out of state, liberal arts and vocational, and so on, according to personal interest and material resources. Secondary education is woefully deficient in providing opportunities for choice among institutions and in diversifying institutions to offer meaningful educational alternatives. Instead, each high school is forced to pretend it can do everything within its own walls, right down to individualized instruction, thereby overdoing choice internally for its mandated student body and stretching itself willy-nilly into the shape of a shopping mall.

It is truly amazing that the two levels of American education could have developed so differently, with the one married to doctrines of diversity and the other to ideologies of sameness and administrative order. Diversity and competition have led the one to its place in the late twentieth century as the premier system of the world, with the international balance of trade in brains running heavily in its favor as students and faculty come here from throughout the world.

Sameness and administered order have led the other into its current morass and to a tellingly low international standing. Then, too, academic workers in higher education, rooted in disciplines and advanced professional fields of study, have a strong base for asserting professional rights and controls. In the better institutions, "shared governance" between faculty and administration is a fact of life, from the internal operation of departments to the campus level of administration, where the academic senate composed of professors typically has primary influence in personnel and curricular decisions. Teachers in secondary schools have a weaker subject base, one that is inherently less esoteric. They lose virtually all claim to subject expertise when materials are dumbed-down and taught in narrow segments specified by state prescriptions and district regulations. Professionalization reaches upward in the one case and downward in the other.

Intensive research in distinctive colleges that I carried out in the 1970s revealed the internal components of a focused and unified educational institution that is able to powerfully motivate both teachers and students. Of three leading colleges that were studied, each had its own way of implementing liberal education.[34] Around that distinctive way there developed a sturdy self-belief, a saga of success. The integrative belief, or institutional story, was anchored in the points of view of leaders, the separate but converging cultures of the faculty and the students, a social base of outside supporters, particularly the alumni, and in various special elements of the curriculum. Not every college or university is similarly positioned to stake out a special self-belief and public image. But the competition found in higher education pushes hard on institutions to make their own way; and virtually all, to one degree or another, lay claim to a unique role and character. The search for distinctive organizational character is part and parcel of the dynamics that cause American higher education to be adaptive and productive.

Among the institutions of higher education there is great variation in how much they function as educational "communities." In establishing favorable conditions for a sense of community, small size, institutional aging, and institutional isolation all help. But most critical is an educational focus embedded in the curricular and extracurricular practices of the campus as well as in the definitions of the institution that are found in the minds of students, faculty, and administrators. An educational community, an educational culture, requires an educational focus. It can be found in universities of 10,000 students. It can be found in many departments and professional schools within universities of 30,000 or 40,000 students. The effort to make a college or university (or a subunit thereof) distinctive from all others is simultaneously a way to promote a sense of commonness within. The establishment of a unique focus helps to create common interests, common problems, and even common enemies. Students are linked to one another and to faculty and administrators for their college years, and often for a lifetime as sympathetic and supportive alumni, as they are drawn into the overarching belief system and participate in the practices that presumably reflect it.

What would it take for public secondary education to reap some of the advantages that clearly obtain in the global organization of American higher education? Certainly an open willingness for public high schools to be different from one another. Certainly more autonomy for individual public high schools, operating as much as possible with lump-sum budgets. Certainly the right of the individual school to select its teachers and, within broad guidelines, its students. Certainly, then, on the part of all, a recognition that a competitive hierarchy of high schools can serve democratic participation. And certainly a realization that schools become integrative and stimulating communities of teaching and learning to the extent that they are rooted in a palpable sharing of interest. All things for all comers is the foundation for a shopping mall school. Specialized educational offerings for interested students and parents are the basis for a school functioning as a community.

As in real estate, the three rules of traditional school organization in America have been location, location, location. School districts relate students to schools in geographic zones. The three rules of the new required orientation should be program, program, program. Simply put, do we want school districts defined primarily by geographic locations or by educational programs? The trouble with the locational criterion is that it has no educational content, thereby weakening educational mandates and leaving the school climate exposed to the vagaries of neighborhood. Residential patterns, and the practices of realtors, then too often become more important over the long haul in determining the character of individual schools than the intentions of school administrators. For all these reasons, the traditional doctrine of the common high school needs to be replaced by the idea of the distinctive high school.

SIX PRINCIPLES FOR SECONDARY SCHOOL REFORM

What researchers have revealed at home and abroad about the effects of various types of schools has, by the end of the 1980s, progressed to the point where we can offer some broad principles of individual school and local school district organization that can extend and focus the school reform movement. Of course, specific prescriptions that can be made operative everywhere in a large country are not to be found, and no attempt should be made to manufacture them. Too often in the past educational administration has stumbled over specific assertions by practitioners and observers that there is a simple set of bromides offering the one best answer. But broad principles are another matter. There are general understandings that for a long time have undergirded and legitimated the comprehensive public secondary school. What might be the primary principles that underlie distinctive public secondary schools? Once extracted from ongoing research and practice, and assembled in a coherent fashion, such principles can serve as a doctrine that encourages an evolution from old to new forms. A theory of distinctive schools can add legitimacy to the efforts of many laymen, officials, and teachers, as well as those prominent in the reform movement, who have sensed that public high schools individually need a better focus than they have achieved under the older ideas and who are struggling to find new combinations. What, then, mignt the new principles be?

Principle 1. Diversity among public secondary schools should dominate uniformity across schools. It is more important that high schools be different than that they be similar. This fundamental principle applies particularly to sets of high schools in large school districts.

Principle 2. Differences among public high schools should be grounded not in the accidents of neighborhood location but in educational interests, approaches, and subjects. Individual high schools should strive to be distinctive in some important component of their educational makeup.

Principle 3. Decentralization of control is a necessary condition for diversity. School districts should be loosely coupled, delegating operational control to their constituent schools. Beyond funding schools, the districts should take as a central task the encouragement of school distinctiveness. Under broad guidelines, the individual public high school should have the dominant voice in arranging curriculum, selecting teachers, and admitting students.

Principle 4. School districts should be sets of competitive schools that earn their individual status by demonstrating educational merit. A central task of district authorities is to promote the competitive processes that will cause public high schools to ratchet upward rather than downward in the quality of their performance. High schools should be subject to the processes of quality control by means of differential prestige that serve powerfully in the vitality of American higher education.

Principle 5. A structure of dual authority or "shared governance" should characterize the new public high school. As individual high schools become more educationally distinctive, under conditions of enhanced autonomy, the professional authority of teachers takes its rightful and constructive place alongside the bureaucratic authority of the formal hierarchy.

Principle 6. Upper secondary schools should operate more like colleges and less like elementary schools. Toward this end, public secondary schools need administrative frameworks that free them from downward coupling to the canons of the elementary level. To help secondary schools develop distinctive character, K–12 districts may need to divide into elementary and secondary districts.

It clears the mind to realize that the school reform movement will basically move in one of two directions: toward more top-down dictate, under principles of uniformity and sameness; or toward more school autonomy, under doctrines of diversity, choice, and competition. The first, currently emphasized by the school reform movement, puts its money on systematic regulation by higher authorities; the second emphasizes professional control within schools and the play of competition among them. The theory of distinctive schools follows the second path, believing that the fundamental educational defect is the blandness that bores students and teachers alike when public high schools are forced to take on the official appearance of comprehensive sameness under close bureaucratic regulation by higher district, state, and national authorities. From the new point of view, efforts in school reform that add measurably to top-down mandates proceed in the wrong direction. They reduce the room in which schools have to maneuver, further squeezing the autonomy that schools must have if they are to construct vibrant institutional cultures and to bolster the conditions that will make possible a more serviceable profession of school teaching.

Of this we may be sure: while sameness spells massive bureaucracy, diversity spells the opportunity to build professional autonomy and control in the work place and institutional responsiveness in the broad marketplace of educational provision. It is time for enduring reform to find its bearings in the organization and culture of the individual public high school. For it is there that we find the immediate frames of achievement, for teachers and students alike. School structures have broad educational effects. This is surely the hardest lesson to learn in school reform.

For over half a century the public comprehensive secondary school has been tried and increasingly found wanting. However noble the dream behind it, its typical organization and structure have led the public secondary system into a bureaucratic morass. With all its attendant risks of turning the schools loose, the distinctive-school approach needs to be given the opportunity to show what school autonomy, initiative, and competition can do to motivate the hundreds of thousands of individuals who comprise the teaching corps and the millions of students for whom the whole enterprise exists. The "distinctive" high school offers the chance to move American secondary education out of its bureaucratic iron cage.

NOTES

1. National Commission on Excellence in Education (1983), *A nation at risk: The imperative for educational reform* (Washington, DC: U.S. Government Printing Office).

2. Rogers, D. (1969), *110 Livingston Street: Politics and bureaucracy in the New York City school system* (New York: Vintage Books), pp. 266, 492.

3. Lortie, D. C. (1975), *Schoolteacher: A sociological study* (Chicago: University of Chicago Press), p. 4.

4. Wise, A. E. (1979), *Legislated learning: The bureaucratization of the American classroom* (Berkeley: University of California Press).

5. Barr, R., & Dreeben, R. (1983), *How schools work* (Chicago: University of Chicago Press).

6. For example, Task Force on Education for Economic Growth (1983), *Action for excellence: A comprehensive plan to improve our nation's schools* (Denver: Education Commission of the States); College Entrance Examination Board (1983), *Academic preparation for college: What students need to know and be able to do* (New York: CEEB); Twentieth Century Fund Task Force on Federal Elementary and Secondary Education Policy (1983), *Making the grade* (New York: Twentieth Century Fund).

7. Carnegie Forum on Education and the Economy (1986), *A nation prepared: Teach-*

ers for the 21st century (New York: Carnegie Corporation); Holmes Group (1986), *Tomorrow's teachers* (East Lansing, MI: The Holmes Group).

8. Carnegie Forum, *A nation prepared*, pp. 26, 33, 59.

9. Goodlad, J. I. (1983), *A place called school* (New York: McGraw-Hill); Boyer, E. L. (1983), *High school: A report on secondary education in America* (New York: Harper & Row); Sizer, T. R. (1984), *Horace's compromise: The dilemma of the American high school* (Boston: Houghton Mifflin).

10. Sizer, *Horace's compromise*, p. 217.

11. Powell, A. G., Farrar, E., & Cohen, D. K. (1985), *The shopping mall high school: Winners and losers in the educational marketplace* (Boston: Houghton Mifflin).

12. Ibid., p. 316.

13. Sedlak, M. W., Wheeler, C. W., Pullin, D. C., & Cusick, P. A. (1986), *Selling students short: Classroom bargains and academic reform in the American high school* (New York: Teachers College Press).

14. Ibid., p. 170. Emphasis in the original.

15. Ibid., p. 158.

16. Lowry, J. H., & Associates. (1983), *Survey of magnet schools: Analyzing a model for quality integrated education* (Chicago: James H. Lowry and Associates).

17. Metz, M. H. (1986), *Different by design: The context and character of three magnet schools* (New York: Routledge & Kegan Paul).

18. Metz, M. H. (1988, January), In education, magnets attract controversy. *NEA Today*, p. 57.

19. Ibid., p. 59.

20. Ibid.

21. Ibid.

22. McNeil, L. M. (1986), *Contradictions of control: Social structure and school knowledge* (New York: Methuen/Routledge & Kegan Paul); (1988, January), Contradictions of control, part 1: Administrators and teachers, *Phi Delta Kappan*, pp. 333–39; (1988, February), Contradictions of control, part 2: Teachers, students, and curriculum, *Phi Delta Kappan*, pp. 432–38; and (1988, March), Contradictions of control, part 3: Contradictions of reform, *Phi Delta Kappan*, pp. 478–85.

23. McNeil, L. (1988, February), Contradictions of control, Part 2, p. 434.

24. Grant, G. (1988), *The world we created at Hamilton high* (Cambridge, MA: Harvard University Press), pp. 221, 223.

25. Kearns, D. T., & Doyle, D. P. (1988), *Winning the brain race: A bold plan to make our schools competitive* (San Francisco: Institute for Contemporary Studies).

26. Chubb, J. E., & Moe, T. M. (1988), *What price democracy: Politics, markets and American schools* (Washington, DC: Brookings Institution); Chubb, J. E. (1988, Winter), Why the current wave of school reform will fail, *The Public Interest*, *90*, 28–49.

27. E.g., Shanker, A. (1985), *The making of a profession* (Washington, DC: American Federation of Teachers), esp. pp. 14–16, on "expanding choices for parents, students and teachers."

28. See Cummings, W. K. (1985), Japan; and Clark, B. R., Conclusions, in B. R. Clark (Ed.), *The school and the university: An international perspective* (Berkeley, Los Angeles, London: University of California Press), pp. 131–59 and 290–325, respectively; Clark, B. R. (1985, February/March), The high school and the university: What went wrong in America, Part 1 and Part 2. *Phi Delta Kappan*, pp. 391–97, 472–75.

29. Rohlen, T. P. (1983), *Japan's high schools* (Berkeley, Los Angeles, London: University of California Press), p. 308. We can also recommend White, M. (1988), *The Japanese Educational Challenge* (New York: The Free Press).

30. Rohlen, *Japan's high schools*, p. 312.

31. Ibid., p. 313.

32. Ibid.

33. See Clark, B. R. (1987), *The academic life: Small worlds, different worlds* (Princeton: Carnegie Foundation for the Advancement of Teaching and Princeton University Press), Chap. 3, "The Open System."

34. The early research that led me to the idea of a "distinctive" organizational character in colleges and universities is in Clark, B. R. (1970), *The distinctive college: Antioch, Reed, and Swarthmore* (Chicago: Aldine); (1971, June), Belief and loyalty in college organization, *Journal of Higher Education*, *42*, 499–515; and (1972, June), The organizational saga in higher education, *Administrative Science Quarterly*, *17*(2), 178–84.

7 The Withered Roots of School Reform: An Organizational Perspective

Richard C. Williams

Before offering a perspective on the recent school reform movement, it is important to differentiate among the several school reform reports with regard to their scope and the kinds of changes they recommend.

Lawrence Cuban, a perceptive student of school reform movements, suggests that the reports' recommendations for change can be divided into "first order" and "second order" changes.[1] "First order" changes assume that our schools are failing to achieve excellence because they have strayed from accepted, well-established standards and practices that are associated with good schools. School improvement is essentially a quality control problem. "First order" changes call for more rigorous academic requirements, raising salaries, selecting better textbooks, extending the length of the school day and school year, assuring greater accountability through increased testing, and requiring more thorough teacher preparation in academic subjects.

"First order" reformers do not challenge the present school system in any fundamental way. They describe the qualities of an exemplary public school system, urge return to schooling practices that are tried and true but supposedly have been abandoned, and call upon the citizenry to ensure that educators attend to their business. A classic statement of this approach is the 1983 report *A Nation at Risk*, which calls upon school boards and legislatures to enact regulations and establish standards that assure the public schools will reach and maintain a high level of excellence. There is very little in the report about exploring new instructional approaches, developing innovative curricula, or reexamining the relationships between students and teachers, or teachers and administrators.

A Nation at Risk appeared at the right time. Many states had already begun school reform efforts, and this report provided federal encouragement for their efforts. The response to *A Nation at Risk* was quite remarkable. It focused a nation's attention on the need for quality education. Many states, using the report as a blueprint for school reform, passed regulatory legislation intended to improve the public schools. And, finally, the report spawned a series of innovations aimed at making sure the public schools were raising and enforcing standards.

In a similar vein, the U.S. Department of Education's *What Works: Research About Teaching and Learning* attempted to link traditional educational practices with research studies that supported the federal government's agenda for school reform. Very little in that volume counters traditional practice. Indeed, then Secretary of Education William Bennett stated in the foreword:

Most readers will, I think, judge that most of the evidence in this volume confirms common sense. So be it. Given the abuse common sense has taken in recent decades, particularly in the theory and practice of education, it is no small contribution if research can play a role in bringing more of it to American education.[2]

What Works does not deal with the potential impact computers might have on altering the basic structure of the classroom or how children learn, alternatives to the self-contained classroom, the uses of cooperative learning, or the negative effect of tracking. Nor does the document discuss differences in the research community over some of the topics, such as the role of phonics in reading instruction or the value of homework in schooling, and any connection the latter might have with "excellence." While there was much of value in *What Works*, the book was essentially an affirmation of traditional practice with exhortations to the public to see to it that the public schools are practicing the tried and true.

A different set of school reform reports recommended what Cuban has labeled "second-order" changes. These reports looked at our public schools, saw the same need for improvement, but produced a startlingly different set of recommendations. They saw an educational program that was failing because the curriculum was not attuned to modern societal and technological changes, the instructional program was limited and unresponsive to what research told us about how children learn, and the administrative and decision-making structure excluded teachers from any significant role in making decisions that impacted their professional work. They saw a public school system that had to be changed in fundamental ways if it was to meet the challenge of excellence of the 1990s. Accordingly, these reformers called for quite basic changes in the curriculum, in instructional methods, in the ways teacher and pupils relate to one another, and in the teachers' role in the schools' functioning and decision making. The following are some examples of "second order" reforms.

John I. Goodlad, the former dean of the Graduate School of Education at UCLA and an advocate of fundamental educational reform, dismayed by the sameness and emotional flatness that characterized the schools he studied and reported on in *A Place Called School*, calls for extensive rethinking of many schooling components, such as how schools are organized, how instruction is delivered, the ways in which students are grouped for instruction, and the mix of subjects in the curriculum. Albert Shanker, head of the American Federation of Teachers, also sympathetic to the school reformers' goal of excellence, advocates fundamental changes in the ways schools are organized and governed. He stresses a substantial increase in the teachers' role in determining the school's curriculum and instructional program. Based on his assessment of the supply of and demand for teachers in the decades ahead, he believes that public schools will have to change their governance and decision-making structure very fundamentally if educational excellence is to be attained. Deborah Meier is operating a secondary school in New York that radically changes the ways in which classes are scheduled, the organization of the school day and the curriculum, and the ways in which teachers interact with other teachers and students. Finally, Theodore Sizer has established a "network of essential schools" that are attempting wide-ranging, fundamental secondary school reform in the name of excellence in education.[3]

My perspective on school reform comes decidedly from the realm of "second order" changes. In my view, simply doing more of the same at a higher level of efficiency or for a longer period of time will not prepare our schools either for excellence or for the 1990s. I believe that we must reexamine what we teach, the way we teach it, and the roles various groups, *especially teachers*, play in deciding and implementing the school's responses to these challenges.

Calls for "second order" reforms are not entirely new. They did not originate in the reform reports of the 1980s. One can find calls for very fundamental school reform in the name of educational excellence during the post-Sputnik era and even earlier. During the 1960s many kinds of structural and institutional innovations were tried. For example, the nongraded school was advanced as a new structure that would allow schools to more effectively tailor their instructional programs to meet the pupils' natural growth and development while catering to individual differences.[4] And during the late 1950s and 1960s the universities and foundations were extremely active in sponsoring school curriculum reform—recall the "new math," the "new physics," the "new biology," and the "new chemistry" curricula.[5] In addition, the federal government became an active agent in encouraging innovations in public school practice. Through the National Science Foundation and Title III (later Title IVc) the U.S. Office of Education provided grants to the states that were to be used to encourage school districts and individual teachers to devise, test, and disseminate innovative curricula and teaching methods, especially in math, sciences, and foreign languages.

None of these reforms were fully and lastingly implemented. By and large public schools remained quite impervious to these fundamental attempts to reform and restructure education. Some innovations were attempted and in some instances they persisted for a while, but ultimately almost all schools "regressed to the mean"—they returned to more comfortable, traditional approaches. The lesson is that those who call for implementing lasting, fundamental school reform in the name of excellence face a formidable task indeed. As Cuban pointed out:

Since the turn of the century, successful school reform—that is, changes that have been incorporated into the routine operations of public schools—has generally been a series of first-order changes. On occasion, particular second-order reforms have been attempted in uncoordinated fashion. Such innovations as student-centered instruction, non-graded schools, team teaching, and open-space architecture have been tried but have had little enduring effect except in cases in which individual teachers and principals have selectively adapted them to local conditions.[6]

My purpose in this chapter is to present a perspective on (1) why it is so difficult to implement fundamental change in our public schools in general and (2) why the current school reform movement, more specifically, is going to have trouble implementing fundamental change in the public school. One can look at the public schools' intractability to change from different perspectives and likely reach different conclusions. An economist, for example, might see the problem as a school system with insufficient incentives to change; a political scientist might see how the competing and often incompatible demands from many constituency groups (legislatures, school boards, unions, special interest groups) severely limit the system's capacity to reform; a psychologist might see educators, as an occupational group, as being comprised largely of non-risk takers who are overly disposed to continue current practice.

I will be looking at the public school's inability to change from an organizational theorist's perspective, that is, I will be reflecting on how a typical public school's structure and functioning impede its ability to implement and sustain innovations. I will then draw out the implications for the current excellence movement. This is a large topic, so let me limit it to more manageable size. So far, much of the energy of the school reform movement has been focused at the secondary level; the reform of elementary schools has received far less attention. However, the greatest effort must be at the level of public elementary education. By the time high school is reached, the foundations for further education have been or have not been set. Our educational problems begin long before high school, and "the greatest effort, the greatest investment, must be at the level of elementary education."[7]

I do not intend to propose any blueprint for the reform of elementary education, as important as such a project is, but to outline some of the difficulties the reform movement will encounter when it turns its attention to the elementary school, as sooner or later it will have to do. My focus will be on the critical role of the conditions and practices in the individual elementary school site as constraining factors in educational reform. My thesis is that the typical public elementary school's organizational structure and mode of functioning severely limit its capacity to solve the substantive and procedural problems that would be presented by any reforms that fundamentally challenge current practice.

One reason for the nonimplementation of past reforms was not that the reforms were inherently badly flawed and failed appropriately. Some of the reforms were potentially very valuable. The problem, rather, was that individual school sites were unable to make the difficult adjustments in instructional methodologies, curriculum content, and working relationships that the reforms required. Teachers and administrators, like any occupational group, do not change long-cherished and imbedded practices easily, even when they want to. Innovations that call for fundamental changes, regardless of supporting research or compelling rationality, or even enthusiastic initial reception at the school site, often fail because the school's structure and daily manner of functioning do not allow the staff to accommodate to the innovation or fit the innovation to the school's specific milieu and circumstances. Thus legislatures and school boards often attempt to satisfy their constituents by passing laws or policies without considering the limits placed on implementing educational reforms by school structures and governance.

In presenting this perspective, I will first discuss the organizational conditions and practices that make long-lasting elementary school changes difficult; then I will discuss some structural and functional adjustments that are necessary if public elementary schools are to implement fundamental reform; and, finally, I will discuss the implications of this perspective for the current school reform movement.

Let me start by asking readers to think along with me as I address the following question:

Suppose you wanted to design an organization so that it would be maximally resistant to change and reform. What would be the characteristics of such an organization?

Here are five qualities I would build into an organization that would effectively immunize it against fundamental reform:

1. Isolate the most centrally important and knowledgeable employees from each other. This isolation during the regular workday would assure that employees could not exchange ideas, trade practical suggestions about how to do things better in their particular work station and in the larger organization, or discuss the relative merits of innovations or changes being implemented. Such isolation would virtually assure that no ideas for change or for more effectively managing the implementation of change would be forthcoming.

2. Keep the employees fully occupied with their main responsibilities. Make sure the work assignments provide little or no opportunities for the workers to consult with each other; allow no "slack time" for planning and considering problems the organization might be encountering. If the workers are provided with the time when they can get together to consider problems, make sure such meetings are scheduled late in the day, when the employees are tired and impatient.

3. Ensure there are clear negative consequences if the employees do not spend almost all of their time attending to their main responsibilities. That is, if employees direct attention away from their main, assigned tasks, make it clear that their inattention will be noticed and the consequences will be negative. The resultant anxieties will assure that the employees focus their energies on day-to-day, immediate, job-related

problems, thus leaving the organizational change concerns to others. The employees' attention devoted to change will be focused primarily on how better to perform immediate tasks—not on larger organizational change issues.

4. Provide employees with no training in or opportunity to develop skills in working collaboratively. Do not work with them in developing effective group process skills. Thus, if they do meet in committees or task forces, they will become frustrated by the inefficiencies of group work and meetings, and will eventually withdraw from such activities because they are viewed as a waste of time.

5. Do not inform the employees of the complexities of organizational change or teach them the various ways in which changes can be effectively implemented. Without an understanding of these complexities they will initially hold unrealistic expectations about what will happen when a reform is attempted. When the expected changes do not materialize quickly, they will seek to identify individuals, usually leaders, to blame for their dashed hopes; sometimes they will conclude that nothing will happen until a new, more perfect leader arrives.

That should just about do it. Any organization with isolated employees whose time is fully occupied with daily assignments, who suffer negative consequences if they do not attend to their main responsibilities, who have minimal skills and opportunity to learn to work together, and who do not understand the complexities of organizational functioning or organizational innovation ought to be so immune to change that the organization can indefinitely resist even the most promising innovations.

If your plan for a change-resistant organization is similar to mine, don't rush out to obtain a patent or copyright for the idea. Very likely you can find just such an organization in your nearby public elementary school. Let's review these qualities with a typical elementary school in mind.

1. Isolate the most centrally important and knowledgeable employees from each other. Teachers are clearly the most important members in an organization that has the central purpose of educating students. Elementary school teachers typically work behind closed doors in self-contained classrooms. Most of their time is spent with students. Their social and professional interactions with faculty colleagues are often limited to hurried lunch conversations or short meetings in the hallway or lounge. These brief encounters provide very limited opportunity or time to discuss important instructional or curricular matters or topics relating to the entire school's program.

2. Keep the employees fully occupied with their main responsibilities; provide little or no slack time. The teachers' job is to teach. Accordingly, their work day, week, and year are virtually identical to the students' school day, week, and year. Few hours or days in the teachers' contracted work time are available for them to explore new ideas or practices, to consult with colleagues in their own school or elsewhere, to attend workshops, or to observe and discuss each other's work in the classroom.

3. Ensure there are negative consequences if the employees do not attend to their daily teaching responsibilities or if they take risks by trying out new teaching approaches. Teachers feel considerable pressure to attend to their classrooms. First, if they are not prepared or the day is not appropriately planned, there can be disciplinary problems

or parent complaints, which, if they persist, can affect the teachers' evaluations and reputations, as well as their mental health. Increasingly, teachers are pressured to assure that their students perform well on district-adopted and nationally normed tests. With computers, administrators and school boards can easily aggregate pupil test performance to specific teachers. The visibility of these results assures that teachers will expend considerable energy and anxiety in assuring that their test scores are as high as possible. This forces the teachers' attention inward toward the classroom, not outward toward larger organizational problems or programs. It also dims their enthusiasm for new approaches that are not guaranteed to boost pupil test scores.

4. Provide the employees with no training in or opportunity to develop collaborative working skills. Teachers do not naturally work cooperatively. For many years we have known that effective committees and productive meetings do not simply happen; there are techniques and procedures that maximize the effectiveness of such cooperative enterprises. Executives and administrators often receive training in such techniques, but teachers are seldom given any training in how to lead and participate effectively in meetings and in how to work productively together. Teachers are expected to work effectively together simply because they are given the opportunity to do so. This is unrealistic.

   Similarly, because they work in virtual isolation from each other, and have little need to work cooperatively, teachers are often unaware of or are not particularly concerned about colleagues who might be "difficult" to work with. That is, teachers, like any employee group, differ in their temperaments and personalities. These difficulties have little impact on the school's functioning if the teachers mainly work independently and in isolation from one another. However, when teachers have to work cooperatively, these personal differences can have a profound effect on the ability of the organization to function effectively and implement change. There are ways of reducing and resolving these interpersonal differences and developing a sense of community in the organization, but these techniques must be learned and practiced; they do not occur naturally.

5. Do not inform the employees of the complexities of organizational change or of the ways in which organizational or programmatic changes can be most effectively implemented. Because teachers are relatively isolated from many nonclassroom activities, they typically do not have to attend to or get involved in many of the complex interpersonal exchanges and conflicts that mark the school's daily life. Their attention is focused primarily on the classroom. Further, most teachers seldom have the major responsibility for implementing educational innovation in a school. As a result, most teachers have a very narrow perspective on what it takes in terms of time and planning and patience to implement long-term, comprehensive change. Given their limited role in implementing change, one should not expect them to have a broader perspective. Moreover, their understandably limited outlook tends to make teachers impatient with the often slow process of change and the compromises that sometimes have to be made.

To summarize briefly, we have developed public elementary schools that do not provide the conditions necessary for change: free time, sustained professional interaction, knowledge of the change process, and cooperative work skills. The structure of our public elementary schools makes them highly resistant to any fundamental, sustained change in general, and more specifically to changes of a kind needed to meet the goals of "excellence." The consequences of this line of thinking for school reform, no matter how defined, are important. If any fundamental school reform is to succeed, it will be necessary to increase the teachers' involvement in decision making. We will need to increase teachers' opportunities to collaborate in school planning and ensure that the change strategies employed reflect the differing "personalities" of schools. In a similar vein, Chester Finn, one of the leading spokespersons for school reform, has cautioned that reformers who seek greater uniformity among public schools must be terribly careful lest they "level downward" through well-intentioned efforts that wind up sapping the vitality of the most effective schools rather than invigorating the others.

Let me utilize an aphorism from another setting to illustrate and reinforce my thesis. Experienced gardeners have a saying, "It is better to plant a $10 plant in a $100 hole than a $100 plant in a $10 hole." What they mean is that when putting a new plant in the ground, it is critically important to dig a hole that is sufficiently wide and deep for the plant's roots to grow and for the plant to obtain the nutrients that will enable it to grow and prosper.

The gardener must provide necessary nutrients and other growth-sustaining conditions, such as proper aeration and pH balance. Given these conditions, the plant's root system can grow and provide a solid foundation for the plant's future growth. Without these conditions, even the most expensive plant will either wither and die, or never fully realize its growth potential.

Inexperienced gardeners often underestimate the importance of providing these necessary conditions for the plant's root system. Instead, they concentrate their attention on buying healthy plants. Subsequently, they place their new, expensive plants in holes that are "good enough"—in which the plant roots will fit. But the planting holes are too small. No room is left for growth; little attention is given to nutrients or aeration. After they put their $100 plants in $10 holes, and the plants either wither and die or fail to realize their potential, the gardeners revisit the nursery, seeking new plants.

We would be making this mistake should we try to plant educational innovations and changes in our elementary schools as they are currently structured. We give most of our attention to the plant, or in this case to the new program or approach we want to implement in the school. We concentrate on the logic and rationale of the innovation. We may even initially try out the program in experimental pedagogical "nurseries" and collect data on its effectiveness. And in some instances our innovations prosper for a time in the "nursery." If properly implemented, these innovations could make an important difference in our schools. But few of them ever realize their potential in regular schools. Instead, they are often removed from the "nursery," planted with great fanfare in unprepared schools, and then wither away. When this happens, we return to the "nursery" looking for yet another approach or innovation that will beautify our pedagogical garden. Sometimes we look for a new gardener.

Instead of continuing this cycle, we should be looking for the reasons why seemingly endless efforts at implementing new educational programs and approaches do not survive. I maintain that the reason for our withering garden is that the basic conditions for our innovations and change to survive and prosper simply are not present in school sites. With no time or training or opportunity to work together or to understand the complexities of the change process and organizational functioning, the teachers, who must ultimately make most curricular and instructional innovations grow and prosper, cannot do so. We are indeed placing our $100 pedagogical plants into $10 holes. This being the case, we should continue to focus our attention on how we can develop more and better innovations, but we also must prepare our schools and teachers to be more receptive to change. We should explore how we can provide an environment in which educational innovations can set their roots, receive nutrients, and thereby grow and prosper, and enrich our schools and our children's education.

Let me move this discussion now from the abstract to the concrete. Improvement of students' writing skills is high on the agenda of the school reform movement. Let me briefly describe how the typical elementary school structure and governance limit the effective schoolwide implementation of a highly regarded elementary school curriculum and instructional approach that requires teachers to rather fundamentally change their assumptions about how children learn and the ways in which writing is most effectively taught. As an illustration, let us turn to the California Writing Project.[8] As part of California's curriculum reform efforts under State Superintendent of Schools Bill Honig, the state has adopted a novel approach to teaching writing. Originating in the Bay Area Writing Project, this approach changes the teacher's approach to writing instruction in important ways. Students learn to write by writing. They write almost daily in journals; grammar and syntax and spelling are taught in context rather than as separate subjects; students, through "read-around" groups, edit and critique each other's work; students learn the critical role that editing and rewriting play in the writing process. The fear and mindless drudgery are taken out of the writing process. The teacher's role is changed from one who reads and critiques every draft the students write to more of a coach and mentor who works with and through other students to develop each student's interest in writing and the ability to write.

This is a powerful instructional approach. However, this method changes the teacher's traditional role quite dramatically, and one does not learn to teach this way easily or naturally. Most teachers who want to adopt this approach go through an extensive training program, and those who complete such training often change their classroom methods and become more effective teachers of writing. But their changed teaching methodology is essentially limited to the individual classroom. The teachers usually have little or no schoolwide impact. Because of the conditions found in the typical elementary school, there is virtually no opportunity for these skilled writing teachers to share their expertise with colleagues in their school who have not been similarly trained, nor are there opportunities to solve the problems that schoolwide implementation would present.

The result is a school in which a few teachers are very good at teaching writing, but the remaining teachers continue to teach in the "traditional way." The school does not develop a sequenced writing curriculum which assures that teachers at the several grade levels provide a common writing program that reflects the California Writing Project's successful approach. Nor is it likely that the school's writing program is coordinated with the other subjects, such as social studies, science, and visual arts. And so, rather than having a comprehensive, schoolwide approach to writing, the school has the typical "loosely coupled" group of individual teachers in isolated classrooms. Thus, only those students who are assigned to these specially trained teachers profit from the program. The others do not. The school does not really have a schoolwide writing program. And a partially implemented program can confuse and harm students who from year to year experience teachers who approach writing in different and conflicting ways.

Of course, having some classrooms in which good writing is taught effectively is an important improvement over what was replaced, but the impact of a comprehensive, schoolwide writing program could be so much greater. It could be a "tightly coupled," developmentally sound program that is implemented throughout the school and provides all students with high-quality writing instruction.

Many readers would likely agree that such a schoolwide program should be implemented. Often what is missing is not the school's desire to implement such a program. What is missing is not the school's capacity to implement such a program. Fully implementing a schoolwide, comprehensive writing program would require extensive discussions, planning, peer coaching, and trial-and-error learning. This is what is missing. And given the characteristics of schools that I have described above, it is virtually impossible for schools to attend to such important matters. So the writing program remains an uneven patchwork, its full potential not realized. We have planted a $100 plant in a $10 hole.

The writing program described above is but one example of many curricular and instructional changes that have been urged by those seeking fundamental school reform in the name of excellence. Public schools, to take some other examples of reform, are struggling with how best to select and utilize computers and other instructional technology; they are trying to balance the curriculum so that it more adequately represents neglected subjects such as the arts. Yet the structure of our schools makes it virtually impossible for teachers to find the time to identify what needs to be done, to determine how they can respond, to acquire the training they require to respond successfully, and then to find breathing room to evaluate their progress and make the necessary adaptations.

What can be done? What steps can be taken to make our public elementary schools into environments where educational change can take root, receive nutrients, and flourish, and thereby provide the firm ground necessary to support fundamental, long-term reform? I suggest four changes that must be made or four steps that must be taken: break down teacher isolation; provide more "slack" time for teachers; direct teacher attention toward schoolwide concerns rather than individual classroom matters; and attend to procedures and conditions that will encourage and empower teachers to work cooperatively. Some public elementary schools here and there are experimenting with one or another of these innovations: Marsalis Elementary School in Dallas; Ganado Primary School in Ganado, Arizona; and Moyer Elementary School in Fort Thomas, Kentucky, among others.[9] In what follows we will concentrate largely on the experiences of Seeds University Elementary School (UES), the laboratory school of UCLA's Graduate School of Education, as it has attempted to provide an environment in which educational excellence could flourish.[10]

1. *Break down teacher isolation.*

Schools cannot function as unified organizations that confront issues and solve problems if the members of the team work in isolation from one another. Here the old adage "form follows function" applies most aptly. We must seriously confront the limits the self-contained classroom places on a school staff's interactions. So long as the organization's basic unit is built upon isolation and individualized effort in the single classroom, the school is confronted with a formidable barrier if it wants to encourage cooperative group work. The self-contained structure encourages and rewards isolation and independence. The school remains largely an accumulation of individual parts. It seldom becomes even the sum of its parts. The staff's energy and cooperative problem-solving capacity remain largely untapped. The educational version of the much heralded and highly successful quality circles used so commonly in Japanese industry, and increasingly in American businesses, is virtually impossible to realize in our schools, given their present structure.

One previously tried educational practice we must "dust off" is team teaching. This approach, in which two or more teachers work cooperatively as a team with a large group of students, was quite common in American public schools in the late 1960s and early 1970s. The reasons advanced for its use then were that it allowed for joint planning of lessons, allowed students access to the skills and approaches of more than one teacher, and permitted considerable instructional flexibility. The students could be taught in many different configurations (e.g., large group, small group). It encouraged—indeed, demanded—that teachers worked cooperatively. It reduced teacher isolation considerably.

Team teaching didn't last. It is difficult today to find schools that are organized on a team teaching format. Many of the open classrooms that were specifically designed to accommodate team teaching have been altered into self-contained classroom configurations. Many reasons have been given for the demise of team teaching, one of the most prominent being that the schools' culture, which had been built around the self-contained approach, rejected this approach. Teachers who had been trained to work in the self-contained setting and who had learned to prosper individually in their classrooms were not convinced that the problems presented and the changes demanded by team teaching were worth the effort. Also, the teachers were not granted the necessary planning time.

On the other hand, Seeds UES had been practicing team teaching since 1963. Seeds's teachers have experienced the difficulties that this arrangement presents. It requires time and effort for teachers to plan cooperatively; they must learn to accommodate to each other's habits and idiosyncrasies. But the school is convinced that the merits far outweigh the problems. Students have opportunities to work with several teachers, and teachers work with and learn from colleagues as a regular part of the school day. And this team teaching arrangement provides the essential building blocks for a schoolwide cooperative decision-making model. Teachers who team become accustomed to accommodating to the needs and plans of others. This isn't to say that team teaching is effortless or easily learned—it is not. But, as stated above, the benefits, at least at Seeds, outweigh the disadvantages.

2. *Provide more "slack" time for teachers.*

"Slack time," to many, raises the image of teachers sitting around wasting time—slacking off. This is not what is meant at Seeds. Instead, it means providing time for teachers to work alone, in small groups, and as a total staff in addressing institutional problems—problems that transcend the teachers' individual classrooms. Without providing such time as a regular part of their workday, it is quite impossible to ask teachers to become more engaged in solving problems that are primarily centered at the school rather than the classroom level.

Yet in most public schools, such slack time is rarely provided. Instead, teachers are held primarily responsible for meeting their daily classroom duties. They are given very little released time and, typically, they are asked to deal with institutional problems at contract-regulated, short teachers' meetings, usually late in the day when everyone is tired and preoccupied with facing the next day's classroom demands. Is it any wonder that teachers, however well intentioned or well trained, find it frustrating to attend to institutional problems? Is it any wonder that such unattended problems persist and fester?

The main problem is that the teachers' school year and the pupils' school year are virtually identical. When teachers are in school, they are continually confronted with the persistent demands that students present. Teachers must be provided quality time away from students. Let me suggest three ways to do this. Needless to say, all of them cost money.

One is to provide teachers with more pupil-free days. One of the greatest errors school reformers would make, if their call for increasing the length of the school year succeeds, would be not to call simultaneously for allocating a percentage of those additional days as pupil-free teacher planning days. We should, and can, begin urging such planning days now. This, however, would often require changes in educational codes in those states where funds are allocated on the basis of pupil average daily attendance. The appropriate number of such days should be determined by experience. At Seeds UES, there is a 180-day work year, but the students attend only 158 days. Those days when the pupils are absent are not considered a form of rest and recreation. At these times, for example, teachers and administrators meet as an entire staff and in smaller groups to address the critical issues facing the school and to explore and "fine-tune" changes that are being implemented in its program.

One problem with pupil-free days, of course, is that these days place a heavy child care burden on working parents. This problem could be handled in two ways. One, the more expensive, is to increase the teachers' school year beyond that of the pupil school year. For example, have the pupils attend school for, say, nine months and employ the teachers for ten months. This alternative provides more time for teachers without reducing classroom instructional time. Another way is to provide alternative programs for students on teacher planning days. This might include field trips or concerts, or special tutoring or enrichment programs, for full or half days, that are managed by special substitutes, aides, and parents. Indeed, school districts might employ a special team of teachers who go from school to school to provide special day-long programs for pupils, thus releasing the regular staff for planning and problem solving.

Providing slack time to school districts on a year-round schedule raises unique opportunities and problems. Districts with a year-round program have a unique opportunity to provide flexible scheduling for teachers during the teachers' "off" times. Again, this would require additional funds. The problem year-round schools face is that while it might be easier to provide a group of teachers with extensive time to plan and work together, it is more difficult, under some year-round plans, to get the entire school together because there is always a segment of the teacher population absent.

In summary, if teachers are going to be serious participants in the school's decision-making and planning activities, and thereby facilitate and contribute to the implementation of school reform, then they must be given the time to do so. Through additional pupil-free days, special programs, and year-round schools, such planning time can be provided. It will cost money, but it will be money well spent. If we continue to think only of more and tougher courses, higher standards, and standardized tests, and invest most of our resources at that level, we will continue to see important education reforms introduced, only to fade away. And we will continue to see teacher morale plummet.

3. *Increase teacher attention to schoolwide concerns.*

School reforms intended to be fundamental and lasting require that teachers no longer limit themselves to the confines of the classroom.

Teachers typically focus their attention primarily on their classroom activities. The school's budget, community relations, and interactions with other district schools and departments and community agencies, are generally considered the principal's responsibility. And the principal is expected to resolve interpersonal conflicts in the school. Such a viewpoint is, in my opinion, quite limited. It implies that what goes on in the classroom should, and can, remain detached from the other school functions, and that the classroom teacher can be successful—and the school can operate best—not as a coordinated entity but as a collection of autonomous units. It also implies that these other activities are peripheral to the school's main functioning.

Perhaps they were more peripheral in some past "golden age," although I doubt it. It is most certainly not the case today. The public school, like it or not, has assumed many additional tasks and responsibilities as the basic family unit has changed in our society. The family, community agencies, and other social agencies are a vital part of the school's total functioning and of the child's education and development. Schools do not function separately from these agencies; a child's education, especially in urban schools, often consists of the interaction of these various units. Similarly, teachers must be a part of the larger community. They must be aware of and interact with the administration and the community as a team in determining how the school can most productively educate its students. And as the problems and challenges facing schools will differ from community to community, so will the solutions.

One important implication of the above is that the public school in the community must function as an entire unit. If pupils do not achieve appropriately, it is the entire school's problem, not that of specific teachers. If a teacher is not effective, that is a school problem, not just the concern of the principal. If individual teachers or groups of teachers are not working cooperatively, it is the entire school's responsibility. This means that we must get away from our single-minded preoccupation with what happens in the isolated classroom. The unit of analysis, if you will, must shift from the individual classroom to the entire school. The school must face its challenges as a unit; the school must assume its responsibilities as a unit; the school must ultimately be judged as a unit.

4. *Encourage and enhance teachers' ability to work cooperatively.*

The California report *Who Will Teach Our Children?* urges that teachers be involved in a wide range of school decision making, including selecting new teachers, developing and coordinating the curriculum across grade levels and within departments, solving schoolwide problems, and developing programs[11] But groups do not naturally work productively together. Even when there are relatively consistent agreements over group goals and the need to move in a common direction, interpersonal differences and conflicts interrupt the organization's ability to achieve its goals. Committee meetings often have notorious reputations as being time-wasting exercises that produce wrongheaded decisions. Many are the groups, large and small, that are so torn by organizational politics that they have virtually given up on trying to work productively together. And top-down change is often resented. Schools are no strangers to these conditions.[12] Indeed, it is likely that, without attention to group dynamics, slack time will merely allow a school staff time to deepen its political divisions, become more entrenched in current practices, or fill the slack time with still more boring and ineffective meetings.

While these familiar characteristics are found in schools, as elsewhere, schools can learn to settle interpersonal and political differences and improve committee and group working effectiveness. There are techniques that enable groups to overcome interpersonal conflicts. There are time-tested, effective guidelines and methods that enable working groups and committees to operate efficiently and effectively. Executive training programs typically include such topics in their curriculum. Leaders are taught to understand the nature of complex organizations, ways in which people typically behave in complex organizations and small groups, and they learn techniques for resolving group conflict and ways in which to run efficient meetings and working groups.[13] Because the teachers' role has typically not included being directly or deeply involved in making schoolwide decisions, teachers are not routinely given training in these interpersonal and group-management skills, nor do they naturally develop them on the job.

If our public schools are to change and become truly excellent, they must include teachers in organizational decision making and planning, and they must do more than simply offer teachers the opportunity and time to do so. They must provide appropriate training so that teachers can better understand the nuances and complexities of organizational and group life.

One of the hard lessons learned at Seeds UES is that when the teachers' role in organizational decision making is increased, more serious attention must be paid to the personality and temperamental differences among teachers. When teachers limit their focus to classroom instructional matters, they can overlook or deal selectively with organizational interpersonal differences. To be sure, personal differences do have an effect on a "self-contained" school staff, but the differences generally have a limited impact on total school functioning. This is not so when a school moves to increase teacher influence over schoolwide decisions. A teacher with a strong pessimistic outlook or with an aggressive or argumentative style, or a teacher who will not listen, or a teacher who is passive-aggressive can have an inordinately powerful influence over group functioning and the decisions that follow. Individuals with such temperaments are found in all organizations, and generally they do not change their behaviors. Schools, like other organizations, must learn to live with such individuals and to appreciate the contributions they can make to the organization. Conversely, these individuals must learn how their behavior and attitudes influence the school's functioning. It is a two-way street—and a long and difficult street to travel. But travel it the school must.

Some argue that if organizations, including schools, are to be effective, they must ultimately transcend their traditional bureaucratic forms and evolve into new structures called "communities," in which organizations learn to celebrate and gain from the temperamental differences of their members. Once this is accomplished, the organization can really become a powerful decision-making and functioning entity. In fact, this is the direction in which we think the next phase of school reform should turn.

To summarize, my purpose here was to present an organizational perspective on why public schools have not responded to calls for reform and to suggest steps that should be taken if we want public schools to be more respective to needed fundamental reform. It is not enough merely to announce that teachers will be more involved in schoolwide decision making and that they will be given the time to do so. Teachers who are to be empowered must be trained in effective group methods, must be taught to understand the nature of complex organizations and how to work cooperatively with individuals having different personalities and temperaments. They must also be educated to understand how their own personality affects the organization's functioning. These techniques and understandings are not easily learned and applied; an organization's problems, not so easily solved. And in a very real sense, no organization really every masters its problems. New problems seem to appear constantly. But as the experience of Seeds makes clear, schools can function more effectively if teachers are involved in decision making, are trained in appropriate group management and interpersonal relations techniques, and appreciate the importance of their participation in all aspects of the school's functioning.

This chapter has been based on the premise that our public schools will have to change in rather fundamental ways if they are going to meet the challenges of the excellence movement and of a rapidly changing society. The key to educational improvement is not the testing of teachers or the abolition of the undergraduate education major or better academic preparation of teachers, as the Holmes Group or the Carnegie Forum on Education would have it. If we truly desire excellence in education, we need to consider fundamental, "second order" reforms in our schools' decision-making and governance systems.

Many spokespersons for school reform, realizing that past "top-down" educational reform approaches have had limited impact, and informed by research on the dynamic interplay between the planned change or innovation and the school organization and school site itself, have called for teacher empowerment, for greater teacher involvement in the reform process through involvement in school governance and decision making.[14] While such reformers have been insistent and eloquent in their pleas, most have been surprisingly silent about what is needed to bring such empowerment about. One sometimes gets the impression that they believe that simply offering teachers the chance to become involved in decision making will be enough. Given that opportunity, they assume that teachers will quite enthusiastically, skillfully, and easily become full decision-making partners with school administrators. Three years of experience in attempting to empower teachers at Seeds UES suggests that much more is required than good intentions.

One essential requirement is time. We simply cannot expect teachers to engage in the kind of extended, risk-taking, and creative discussions that are necessary for fundamental school reform to succeed if they are limited to casual hallway discussions. Ways must be found to provide teachers with extended periods of uninterrupted time, when they can set aside immediate daily classroom challenges and concentrate on the difficult tasks of implementing innovation. Another essential requirement is that teacher isolation must be ended or reduced. Teacher interactions on substantive and procedural matters must occur as a normal part of their daily work responsibilities. This can be accomplished in a number of ways, such as team teaching, cooperative teaching, or assigning teachers to committees that meet regularly and assume significant decision-making roles. In addition, teachers must be given the freedom and encouragement to take risks, explore the unknown, and try new approaches. They cannot and will not do so if they are constantly admonished to "keep the test scores up" and are encouraged to try only practices that are acceptable to the larger community. The ultimate outcome is that teachers will not become involved in decision-making activities and substantive explorations if they sense the outcomes are pretty well determined. Empowered teachers will not always conform to what others expect.

Finally, teachers must be given training and opportunities to develop essential organizational and group process skills. While it is important to provide teacher training in formal academic and instructional matters, it is equally important to provide in-service teachers and prospective teachers with training and practice in such areas as leadership, decision making, group processes, conflict resolution, and interpersonal communication. Bright, thoughtful, and creative people can, and often do, differ in rather fundamental ways about the best course to follow. These honest differences do not simply go away. Without the skills or know-how to resolve these issues, a group or organization will usually fall victim to intraorganizational conflict and feuding. Many are the business and other organizations, let alone schools, that are destroyed or rendered impotent by internecine conflict.

Through involving teachers in decision making and providing them with the necessary time, freedom, and training, public schools can become the kind of environment in which reform can take root and flourish. Without providing such an environment, public schools will continue to be the target of reform but will seldom implement reforms on any schoolwide or permanent basis. At best, the reforms will be implemented in individual classrooms for a limited length of time, and when the innovating teachers leave or lose interest in the reform, the innovative practice will disappear. The innovation will not be institutionalized. The lesson is clear. Our schools are complex organizations, and we must change how these complex organizations are organized and managed if we hope to implement long-lasting, fundamental reform. Continued limited focus on "first order" educational reform, whether in the name of excellence or of some other good, is not enough. We must also attend to the total setting or environment in which educational reform is to be planted if we expect it to take root and grow.

NOTES

1. Cuban, L. (1988, January), A fundamental puzzle of school reform, *Phi Delta Kappan*, pp. 341–44. We can also recommend, Chubb, J. E. (1988, Winter), Why the current wave of school reform will fail. *The Public Interest*, *190*, 28–29.

2. (1986), *What works: Research about teaching and learning*, (Washington, DC: U.S. Department of Education).

3. See, for example, Goodlad, J. I. (1984), *A place called school* (New York: McGraw-Hill); Boyer, E. (1983), *High school: A report on secondary education* (New York: Harper & Row); Sizer, T. (1984), *Horace's compromise* (Boston: Houghton Mifflin); Shanker, A. (1986, Fall), Our profession, our schools: The case for fundamental reform, *American Education*, pp. 38–44; Meier, D. (1987, June), Central Park East: An alternative story, *Phi Delta Kappan*, pp. 753–60.

4. Goodlad, J. I., & Anderson, R. H. (1959), *The nongraded elementary school* (New York: Harcourt, Brace & World), p. 15.

5. Goodlad, J. I. (1964), *School curriculum reform in the United States* (New York: Fund for the Advancement of Education).

6. Cuban, "A fundamental puzzle of school reform," p. 342.

7. Glazer, N. (1986), The problem with competence. In J. H. Bunzel (Ed.), *Challenge to American schools: The case for standards and values* (New York: Oxford University Press), pp. 225–30.

8. Honig, B. (1986), *Handbook for planning an effective writing program: Kindergarten through grade twelve* (Sacramento: California State Department of Education); (1987), *Practical ideas for teaching writing as a process* (Sacramento: California State Department of Education), p. 26.

9. Wayson, W. W. (1988), *Up from excellence: The impact of the excellence movement on the schools* (Bloomington, In: Phi Delta Kappa Educational Foundation), Chap. 8, pp. 152–64, and Chap. 9, pp. 192–98.

10. For a lengthy description of the collaborative efforts at Seeds UES, see Bank, A. (1987, Fall). Distributed leadership and the creation of a professional environment for teaching, *Focus*, *31*(2), pp. 31–32.

11. California Commission on the Teaching Profession (1985), *Who will teach our children?* (Sacramento: The Commission), pp. 31, 36; see also Boyer, E. (1988), *Report card on school reform: The teachers talk*, (Washington, DC: Carnegie Foundation).

12. Fullan, M. (1982), *The meaning of educational change* (New York: Teachers College Press).

13. See Meyer, J., Scott, W. R., & Deal, T. E. (1981), Instructional and technical sources of organizational structure: Explaining the structure of educational organizations, in H. D. Stein (Ed.), *Organization and human services: Cross disciplinary perspectives* (Philadelphia: Temple University Press), p. 27; Joyce, B., & Showers, B. (1983), *Power in staff development through research and training* (Washington, DC: Association for Supervision and Curriculum Development).

14. For example, in Goodlad, *A place called school*, the local school site is identified as the essential decision-making locale. E. Boyer, in *Report card on school reform: The teachers talk*, refers to the urgent need to make teachers partners in school renewal at all levels. The California Commission on the Teaching Profession, in *Who will teach our children?*, states that "teachers must participate in the task of managing and reforming

their schools'' (p. 33). Even W. Bennett, in *What Works*, urges school leaders to ''set aside time for faculty interaction and provide specific opportunities for teachers and administrators to work together on such tasks as setting school policies, improving instructional practice, selecting textbooks, and strengthening discipline'' (p. 51).

8   The Communal Ethos, Privatization, and the Dilemma of Being Public

Donald A. Erickson

One reason for the repetitious failure of school reform seems to be that the roots of our most serious educational problems are seldom properly understood. Reformers often oversimplify the dilemmas they attempt to solve.

In the current literature on public school reform, the oversimplification is manifested in two ways. First, though the school reform literature is complex and difficult to summarize, I share the impression of several other scholars that it focuses primarily on the need to restructure the curriculum, to lengthen the time spent on instruction, to shore up the disciplinary system, and to improve the quality of the people recruited into teaching, teacher training, and the level of financial support for schools. These things may be called technical requirements of schools. In contrast, only a few reformers emphasize the *communal* attributes of schools, which are at least as important as the technical; and those who do emphasize the communal seldom make realistic proposals for strengthening this aspect of the public school.

The technical emphasis often seems to involve the assumption that public schools are much like factories, with "inputs," powerful "throughputs," and easily measured "outputs." Schools are judged, from this viewpoint, largely by easily quantifiable outputs, such as achievement test results and dropout rates. In California, for instance, public schools can lose state money if their achievement test averages fall too low, or may gain state money if the averages improve dramatically. There is evidence that the resulting test score improvements are at least partially misleading, and many cases may mask serious learning losses that result from emphasis on testing.[1]

The logic of those who hope to reform our public schools mainly by technical means does not seem fundamentally different from the logic of the factory. Hire more intelligent workers. Train them more extensively. Motivate and empower them. Ward off disturbances. Focus worker energies on better assembly tech-niques and product designs. If all these things are in order, the largely inert material will be transformed into the intended product.

The viewpoint would be admirable if it were less fragmentary. Schools need all these technical things, but they also need a great deal more. Every school has a communal system, for example, that functions, either badly or well, much like a family or a little village. Most people in the school are members of various social groups. Often some people are outcasts. The groups reward some behaviors and punish others, and individuals conform to the group norms in varying de-grees. Student groups make explicit and implicit treaties among themselves and with authority figures such as teachers. Relationships among people range from friendly to hostile. Adults and students form emotional bonds or fail to do so. Sometimes schools have strong consensus and mutuality of commitment. Some-times they do not. In some schools the powerful groups cooperate impressively. In other schools they seem constantly in conflict.

Much evidence suggests that these communal attributes have strong effects on student learning. An adequate communal system will motivate both teachers and students in a manner no technical system can begin to emulate. The com-munal system can induce levels of productivity and cooperation that are impos-sible without it. It seems, in fact, that cohesive school communities produce surprising results even when the technical apparatus is inferior. The reason seems easy to discern: No matter how competent the teachers, how well structured the curriculum, and how lavish the physical accoutrements, learning will be deficient if teachers are dispirited and inconsistent and if students are part of an alienated, hostile culture that disparages the school and its purposes. But when people are bound together by affection and commitment to a common cause, they can overcome much adversity. One hopes, of course, for both technical and com-munal adequacy.

Two analyses conclude, in this regard, that in our public high schools teachers are forced, as a strategy of survival, to make treaties of mutual work avoidance with classrooms of students who are present under compulsion, have little interest in learning, and can easily make the teacher's day unendurable.[2] John Goodlad, for example, complains that high school teachers and students seem to travel on different tracks, with notably different interests.[3] Most teachers are preoccupied with instructional material, largely ignoring students' intense adolescent needs, while most students are preoccupied with their needs and largely uninterested in the instructional material. Other keen observers lament the tendency of Amer-ican public schools to shunt underprivileged students into special classes or curriculum tracks, to label them publicly as failures, and to exclude them from many social academic benefits.[4] Numerous studies document the frequent ten-dency of student peer groups to denigrate and even punish superior achievement, and the consequent "underachievement" of many students.[5] These and many other school woes are primarily consequences of lack of consensus, cooperation, and mutual commitment; but too many reformers are proposing technical solutions, and too many who hope for communal improvement are proposing unrealistic remedies.

In the communal view of schools, the teacher is a member of the family or little village—an adult role model embodying qualities such as sympathy, cooperation, and respect for others, desired in the student, and influencing the student not so much through the exercise of pedagogical skill (important though that is) as through interpersonal bonding. Student motivation is seen as resulting not primarily from curricular relevance and instructional competence (though both of these affect it) but from a desire to please beloved and loving adults, and from seeking approval and acceptance from groups that value and reward achievement. Students are viewed not as raw material or as clients or patients who may be dealt with segmentally but as crucial participants, members of the family or little village, individuals whose commitment and wholehearted involvement are essential to the school's success. Looking through the lens of the communal conception of schools, one becomes concerned about such issues as consensus, mutual commitment, the norms of powerful groups, implicit and explicit treaties among groups, the consistency of the values exemplified by staff members, the level of interpersonal caring, the development of affectionate bonds between teachers and students, the extent to which disadvantaged youngsters are granted respect and esteem and integrated into school social life, and the extent to which school and home are mutually reinforcing.

One study illustrates well the need to consider both ethnic and communal aspects when proposing school reforms. The author, Judith Kleinfeld, had noticed during more than a decade of experience with Eskimo adolescents that students from one particular high school—I will call it the Polaris School—did not fit the usual pattern among Eskimo adolescents of depression, alienation, and dropping out.[6] Polaris's graduates went to college more often than did Eskimo students from other high schools, and though entering college with the same low achievement scores, were far more successful there (55 percent succeeded, in comparison with 16 percent of Eskimo students from other high schools). After returning to their villages, Polaris's graduates were not the misfits that other high schools seemed to produce, but settled in comfortably and cooperatively. They seemed "well put together," with an "air of independence," an "aura of established values and secure identity, . . . fundamental self-confidence, the sense that they were at ease in their world and thoroughly in control of it."[7]

Kleinfeld was so impressed by these differences in graduates of different high schools that she attempted, through ethnographic research in Polaris and three other schools during a three-year period, to uncover the explanation. She found, first of all, that Polaris's accomplishments could not be attributed to what I have labeled the technical system. Polaris, lacking the carpeted libraries, controlled readers, vocational equipment, and art studios of the other high schools in the study, looked, she said, like "a poor relation outfitted from a church rummage sale."[8] It was housed in an antiquated, unattractive building. Much of its equipment was inadequate. Its student-teacher ratio was horrible. It lacked a structured program in English as a second language, which many educators would consider essential for Eskimo youth. Its teachers had no specialized cross-cultural training. It was administered autocratically. It was ignoring all the popular educational innovations. Its curriculum and instruction were resoundingly teacher-centered and traditional. Kleinfeld characterized many of its teachers as inept, inexperienced, untrained volunteers. Polaris operated on a ridiculous one-fifth of the per-pupil money the other high schools were spending. So much for the technical attributes emphasized in many current school reforms! The school most bereft of them—Polaris—was the most successful school by far in Kleinfeld's study.

At the heart of Polaris's success, Kleinfeld concluded, was the nature of the community in which students and staff members were ensconced. Teachers spent many hours with students outside the classroom. There was much touching. There were many lengthy, intense conversations between students and teachers about personal matters, as between close friends.

The coach of a visiting basketball team remarked that Polaris's female students seemed very close to their coach: "When they came up to her at time out, they would touch her and she would touch them back. There was a lovingness and a tenderness, a gentleness. I've been with my girls for two years every day and it doesn't happen to me."[9]

The social forces at Polaris were so powerful that Kleinfeld herself was affected, exhibiting more openness than at other high schools, more willingness to reveal personal experiences. The girls would ask her to eat with them, to walk with them to the village store, to try their shampoo. When she seemed homesick, they would ask why she was depressed.

The communal intensity was a major mechanism of influence in the school, Kleinfeld concluded. Since teachers and other staff members consistently embodied the values they sought to instill in the students, and interacted with the students extensively, the most important lessons were taught implicitly, through interpersonal exchanges in the classroom, the cafeteria, and many other settings. The intimacy that developed outside the classroom eventually seeped into the classroom, creating an atmosphere of unusual trust, warmth, and informality that counteracted traditional classroom structures. Competition gave way to mutual helpfulness.

Polaris embodied a definite ethic, a lucid conception of the person it sought to produce. Its image of admirable behavior was "perfectly clear" and generously rewarded. The school stressed concern for others, emotional stability, making a contribution—all values prominent in Eskimo culture and in the students' homes. It tried to promote qualities of leadership, but with the strong overtones of helpfulness without which Eskimos, with their aversion to authority, tend to reject leadership. It attempted to encourage attributes that would enable its students to stand on their own feet.

The school's message was communicated everywhere. The consistency of values here, in contrast with the situation in other high schools in the study, was "overwhelming." The maintenance man was as much an educator, Kleinfeld noted, as any teacher. Educational influences pressed upon students continuously, from all directions. The impact was not sudden and dramatic but "repetitive and cumulative, conscious and at the edges of awareness, extending over time and over many facets of experience."[10] It was much like the influence families exert on their members.

Kleinfeld encountered evidence at Polaris to corroborate her earlier observations about the superiority of the school's students. Her assistants noticed that students at Polaris showed up for research interviews enthusiastically and reliably, in marked contrast with students in other high schools, and were much more inclined to talk in complete sentences, to ask questions of their own, to open conversations voluntarily with strangers, to look directly at the interviewer, and to sit close by rather than across the room or behind a table.

It is important to note that the impact of Polaris did not show up in superior achievement test results, though I think it might have done so if the schools' technical system had been less deficient. Preoccupied with easily measured outputs, many contemporary reformers would classify Polaris as ineffective. But, according to Kleinfeld, the school produced profound, long-lasting results. Its influence was manifested mainly in the self-confidence, initiative, and social competence of its student, and thus showed up in superior success later—in college and in the Eskimo village.

I have discussed Kleinfeld's study because it seems unusually thorough and trustworthy, and because it illuminates the technical and communal aspects of a school so clearly. In other respects, the study is not ideal for present purposes, for it deals exclusively with schools for a special population of adolescents (Eskimos) in isolated areas. There are two other limitations that I have not yet noted. One is that all schools in the study were boarding schools (a frequent fixture in the education of U.S. native peoples whose populations are widely dispersed). I will discuss the additional limitation soon.

Were the major characteristics of Polaris's communal system largely a function of the special setting and student population? Apparently not. After scrutinizing a considerable body of literature, I have concluded that there are hundreds of schools, in every region of the United States and at both elementary and secondary levels, that embody essentially the same communal vitality and are unusually successful, numerous scholars have concluded, because of that vitality. Because of their communal systems, these schools appear to offer special advantages to underprivileged students, advantages reflected in higher achievement test scores (perhaps because these schools as a whole are stronger technically than Polaris was), lower dropout rates, more positive student self-concepts, greater success in college, and, according to one national study, greater occupational and social success later in life.

Recent years have seen much effort to understand the secrets of unusually effective schools. But are reformers lined up to analyze what makes schools like Polaris tick? Definitely not. Schools like Polaris have been distinguished mostly by neglect in the scholarly research about education in general and, with some exceptions (such as Gerald Grant), in the literature of the school reform movement as well.

The reasons for the neglect are clear but difficult to defend logically. First of all, educationists preoccupied with technical systems are unlikely to become excited about schools with particularly potent communal systems. Second,— and this seems the more important reason—the schools in question are mostly private, not public. Many researchers appear to assume that if there are any superior accomplishments of private schools, they result from taking unfair advantage (skimming off the easy-to-educate students, for example). Since the advantages enjoyed by private schools are deemed unfair, as definitely unavailable to public schools whose leaders play the educational game by superior rules, private schools are regarded as futile places to look for solutions to public school problems.

On the contrary, a careful examination of the strategies behind the communal strength of private schools reveals that all these strategies were used in this nation's public schools in the past but were abandoned because of well-intentioned but inadequately understood reforms; that some of the strategies are now widely used in other nations, in public schools that overshadow us in international comparisons; that some of the strategies have been readopted in special U.S. public schools (e.g., magnet schools) that seem to achieve unusual communal strength; and that all of the strategies are at least conceivable for reintroduction into the nation's schools as a whole. The Almighty did not prescribe immutably, on stone tablets, the current structure of U.S. public schools. But the structure has noble (sometimes along with ignoble) intentions behind it, and changes would involve important trade-offs, some of which I will discuss later.

The strategies that appear to produce unusual communal strength in many private schools are best understood in connection with the specific benefits they produce. Because of space constraints, I will limit discussion here to five of the many advantages identified in studies of the Catholic school, the most numerous type of private school in the United States and the one on which the best evidence is available. My analysis will be seriously incomplete, a mere fragmentary introduction to a much-neglected subject. The relevant findings are more fully documented, much additional evidence is added, and these and many other pertinent issues are far more extensively discussed in a book I have in preparation, *The Importance of Being Private, Even if You're Public*. The advantages discussed below, though sometimes produced and exhibited in different ways, seem to be found not only in Catholic schools but also in other major groups of private schools, though I cannot examine that aspect of the topic more than peripherally here.

The advantages in this particular set pertain to underprivileged children, often from minority homes, who are found in significant numbers in Catholic schools in inner-city locations. Approximately 50 percent of the many Black patrons of Catholic inner-city schools are not Catholics (many are Baptists, for instance, and are often bothered by the schools' religious emphasis). Many disadvantaged parents make considerable sacrifices to send their children to Catholic schools. Such patrons of the Catholic school system have characteristics that indicate upward mobility and unusually high educational aspirations for their children.[11] What is attracting them to Catholic schools when nearby public schools are available without the necessity of paying fees, arranging one's own transportation, and, for many parents, exposing their children to an alien religious influence, a transfer from one school to another, and the disruption of established friendships?

When one looks closely at the communal characteristics of Catholic schools as a whole, benefits that would be attractive to educationally ambitious parents of disadvantaged children are not hard to find. I must emphasize that the benefits seem characteristic of Catholic schools generally, especially in comparison with the public schools these underprivileged children would otherwise attend.[12] Not all the benefits are present in all Catholic schools, and not all are absent from all public schools.

The first four benefits discussed below, all closely related, will be listed first and then discussed together.

1. The disadvantaged child who attends a Catholic rather than a public school is less likely to be treated as second-class citizen, less likely to be excluded from full participation in school social life, denied an equal share of academic benefits, and negatively stereotyped.

2. The disadvantaged child who attends a Catholic rather than a public school is more likely not only to be a full participant in the social and academic life of the school, but also to experience a different emotional quality of communal life, to develop deeply affectionate bonds with teachers and fellow students; to experience an atmosphere of mutual helpfulness, respect, and caring; to encounter an emphasis on the importance in God's eyes of everyone's contribution, no matter how small; and to sense great stress on social justice and the evils of prejudice based on distinctions of race and family income.

3. The disadvantaged child who attends a Catholic rather than a public school is more likely to perceive that teachers are deeply interested in him or her, and will probably be given a great deal more individual attention.

4. The disadvantaged child who attends a Catholic rather than a public school is more likely to encounter attitudinal influences that are pervasive and highly consistent, since staff members will generally embody strikingly similar outlooks, since the character ideals of the school will generally be quite clear, and since the student's home will likely reinforce the efforts of the school.

Insufficient attention and supervision by caring adults, such as parents, uncles, aunts, grandparents, and interested members of the neighborhood, may impede the development of many children in underprivileged families. Such children may lack adequate exposure to adults who model the attitudes, understandings, and skills their parents hope to foster, and may be deficient in the inward security and motivation that spring from affectionate bonding to adults.

If these children are sent to schools where peers and teachers are unaccepting and distant, the above-mentioned problems may be exacerbated. But the evidence suggests that Catholic schools are more successful than public schools at integrating disadvantaged children into the social life of the school. One study found, in a systematic national sample of high school adolescents, that students with inferior academic achievement, inferior relationships with their parents, or both, were much more likely to describe themselves as near the center of social activity in Catholic high schools than in public high schools. As if to emphasize the importance of this finding, another national study found that people who had been given the benefit of supportive institutions early in life did better socially and economically later in life. A third study found that people who had been reared as members of a local religious minority had more psychosomatic symptoms of anxiety in later life than people who had been reared as members of a local religious majority. Social support during the early development years may be far more critical than is generally recognized.

There is good reason to believe that the difference in the socially integrative power of Catholic and public high schools occurs because public school teachers, in contrast with Catholic school teachers, are often afraid to voice values that seem religious or in other ways controversial, and thus stress academic achievement more exclusively, neglecting values that would bolster the acceptance and self-esteem of children who underachieve academically. Another reason may be a strong religious stress in Catholic schools on the "one lost sheep" ethic—the biblical concept that the disadvantaged deserve not merely equal treatment but more concern than the ninety and nine snuggled safely in the fold. The values found by Kleinfeld at Polaris would do much to explain the integration of underprivileged youngsters into school social life. Evidence concerning substantially the same values—the interpersonal closeness, the affectionate bonding of teachers and students, the caring, the mutual helpfulness, and the broad inclusion of the underprivileged—has emerged in other Catholic school studies, including several of national scope.

Two bodies of evidence, including evidence from the widely discussed High School and Beyond Survey, suggest that prejudice toward minorities is less pronounced in Catholic than in public schools. One major study specifically mentions the lack of negative stereotyping of low-achieving students in Catholic schools. Several studies indicate a strong aversion of Catholic school teachers to reducing the performance demands on underprivileged students, or even to learning which students are from underprivileged homes, in case the temptation to reduce academic standards might follow. Several studies cite instances in which Catholic school resources have been allocated in a manner that favors the underprivileged; for example, some Catholic schools provide smaller classes for remedial students than for honors students. One study indicates that the tendency to favor the impoverished and slow may be so obvious that it is a sore spot with many well-to-do Catholic school patrons.

Part of the explanation for the greater integrative power of the Catholic school's communal system resides, no doubt, in current Supreme Court interpretations of the First Amendment that prohibit official religious observances in public schools, and upon confusion among public school teachers as to what values may properly be emphasized. Another part of the explanation may reside in political realities, absent from private schools, that dictate allocative policies in public schools. But a major factor behind the lack of clearly enunciated, consensually sought nonacademic values in many public schools unquestionably lies in a lack of consensus in the school constituency. Teachers and administrators who sense great diversity of opinion in the constituency on critical issues of morality are denied a firm basis for emphasizing any such values at all on those issues, especially when the constituency is volatile. The investigations of Gerald Grant led him to comment that authority in U.S. public high schools once had a firm, easily identifiable center, like an avocado, but degenerated over the years to the condition of a cantaloupe, with a softer, more dispersed center, and later to the condition of a watermelon, with no discernible authority center at all.[13] Other studies similarly point to lack of patron consensus in public schools as the major explanation for the fact that public schools are notably more prone than private schools to internal disturbances.[14]

Differences in consensus between public and private schools, in turn, are easy to explain. Private school patrons not only are patrons by choice but face costs that induce them to take the choice seriously. A parent, knowing the local public school is closer at hand (in most cases) and available without additional cost, is not likely to go to the trouble and expense of sending a child to a private school unless the private school seems to be doing substantially what the parent wants. Minor disagreements (e.g., over religious dogma and ceremony) are tolerated only when consensus exists on issues far more important to the parent (e.g., issues pertinent to getting the child ahead academically). In public schools, on the other hand, the proverbial visitor from another planet could easily believe a prolonged, concerted effort had been made to minimize consensus, say, between parents and schools.

It is not enough, in an era of increasing neighborhood heterogeneity, that most parents are prevented or discouraged from seeking greater consensus by sending their children to public schools of their choice. The heterogeneity in the public school has been exacerbated in the last few decades by a nationwide consolidation and reorganization movement, based largely on a quest for greater strength in the technical system—a movement that, by making schools and school systems much larger (and ostensibly more capable of offering adequate programs), forced them to cast a much broader attendance net, drawing students from even more diverse environs and to bus many children from one neighborhood to another, largely in a quest for racial justice. One must admire both quests, but one also must ask whether the limited (in some respects, imperceptible) benefits begin to outweigh the huge cognitive and affective costs that appear to result from these assaults on community in schools.

The communal cohesion, extensive individual attention, and pervasive consistency of impact of the Catholic school depend as well on a two-sided selectivity of teachers. The often dismally low salaries of Catholic school teachers, while imposing such disadvantages as rapid faculty turnover, have one important benefit: They do much to ensure that teachers who lack a firm dedication to the special goals of the Catholic school will look for employment elsewhere. The pronounced religious emphasis of the Catholic school, similarly, along with its overt demand that teachers spend much time with students outside the classroom, should do much to discourage applications from teachers who find those approaches repugnant. Small wonder that many observers comment on the great similarity of background and outlook among Catholic school teachers and on extensive interaction between teachers and students outside the classroom.

The other side of teacher selectivity (in choice of a Catholic school in which to teach) is the deliberate selectivity exercised by Catholic school administrators. In this respect the Catholic school has two major advantages over the public school. First, since Catholic school staffs are rarely unionized, the school may make demands, at the time of employment and later, that have been outlawed through collective bargaining in public schools. Second, Catholic schools are not subject to the same statutory and case law strictures that govern public school hiring and firing. Increasingly, it seems, U.S. legislatures and courts are demanding that public agencies consider only the technical qualifications of applications for positions, ignoring all but the most odious considerations of character, ideology, and lifestyle. Lawmakers and judges have been abetted in that stance by educational experts who write and testify as if schools are exclusively technical enterprises. While the stance may be somewhat appropriate for public organizations in which the technical system is the overwhelming determinant of success, it seems destructive to organizations like schools, which depend extensively on their communal systems.

A number of studies of Catholic schools, along with one particularly outstanding study of another type of private school, cite as a major source of communal cohesion and consistency of impact the notable similarity of teacher backgrounds.[15] Regardless of the values and lifestyles a school may seek to promote in its students, its potency will be enormously reduced if the influences of different adults serve primarily to cancel each other out, and if its community is disconnected and conflict-ridden. The legislatures and courts are well intentioned in their efforts to ensure equality of access to public employment, but here again one must ask whether adequate recognition has been taken of the costs of this policy framework in organizations like schools. A different approach would be to reduce the financial and regulatory constraints that inhibit the creation and maintenance of schools that promote different views and, accordingly, dif-

ferent pools of applicants. Just as one's fiddle-playing competence may be irrelevant to an assessor's office but critical to a symphony orchestra, the values
and lifestyle of an employee may mean little in a factory but much in a school.

5. The disadvantaged child who attends a Catholic rather than a public school is likely
   to have the benefit of superior peers, that is, peers who respond better to the disciplinary
   system, place a higher value on learning, more often aspire to go to college, engage
   more consistently in instructional activities, and generally exhibit more productive
   attitudes and study habits.

The evidence suggests that disadvantaged students in Catholic schools are at
least twice blessed, insofar as their peers are concerned. First, their peers are
likely to be from somewhat higher socioeconomic strata and thus, on average,
to exemplify attitudes and behavior that are more educationally productive.
Second, even when Catholic schools are not selective socioeconomically (some
clearly are not, since the evidence shows their patrons to be fully as disadvantaged
as patrons of nearby public schools), their mechanisms of patron self-selection,
mentioned earlier, tend to guarantee that students from the lower social strata
who attend Catholic schools are strivers—more interested, like their parents, in
learning as an avenue of upward mobility. The disadvantaged student will have
the additional advantage, in many Catholic secondary (but not elementary)
schools, of peers who have been deliberately screened on the basis of various
estimates of ability or academic achievement.

There is much evidence to suggest that student expulsions are rare in Catholic
schools, but since it does not take many rebels to disrupt an entire classroom or
school, even the occasional expulsion can make a radical difference, and the
reality of the threat may help keep marginally rebellious youngsters in line.

Herein lies a major, broadly significant difference in strategy between public
schools as a whole and private schools as a whole. By dint of constitutional and
legislative mandates, court rulings, and a strong ideological strain in the public
school literature, individual public schools operate, by and large, on the premise
that with rare exceptions, they can handle the full range of student abilities and
interests found in the society outside. There is little deliberate specialization
among public schools, and perhaps less now than previously. There is little
deliberate effort to design some schools for the fast and highly motivated, some
for the slow and motivated, and some for the most difficult students of all—
those who seldom learn and do not care.

Some public school specialization occurs through housing patterns that seg-
regate students by socioeconomic status (SES), but since racial differences are
still strongly associated with SES in our society, efforts to combat racial segregation in schools—by means of busing, for example—have often served to
produce a more diverse mixture in individual schools along the lines of SES,
academic performance, and attitude, as have school reorganization and consolidation. The courts have intervened to demand more racial (and hence SES)
integration in formerly elitist institutions like the Boston Latin School. The

profound effects upon the communal life of schools seem seldom to be considered in these policy choices.

As if it is not sufficiently challenging for most public schools to be forced to deal with virtually everyone who comes down the pike, many school reformers are now demanding that public school teachers and administrators, already burning out in the face of impossible demands, start producing better results under even more difficult conditions—conditions imposed by the proposed abolition of internal school differentiation and specialization. The theory behind this demand is that since certain devices for handling heterogeneous students seem to have worked in some situations, according to research whose limitations are ever more widely noted, all schools must now mainstream, abolish tracking, and outlaw grouping. It seems that the ''specialty shops'' which one recent study identified as havens of productivity in otherwise lamentable public high schools may soon be doomed to the same fate as the school-by-school specialization that once produced renowned institutions of the Boston Latin School variety. Public magnet schools (discussed briefly later), justified on the grounds that they effect racial integration, seem to be one encouraging current exception, but they suffer the handicap of having to run the ridiculous ideological gauntlet of our times by trying to be special while pretending not to be better than the rest of the public schools.

The almost universal private school strategy, in contrast, may often be implicit and even unconscious, but nevertheless seems quite clear in the light of much evidence. It is a strategy based on the assumption that a school cannot be effective unless it targets a particular student population and designs its processes accordingly. Many high-tuition schools are unabashedly elitist. They are designed for the most capable students they can attract and, accordingly, not hesitant to screen their applicants both for attitude and for achievement. Similarly, many Catholic schools that admit without regard to academic ability or achievement make it quite clear that while endless effort will be expended to help the disadvantaged and the slow, students who do not work conscientiously at their studies will be shown the door. Furthermore, the affiliation mechanism of Catholic schools, as I have mentioned, is a powerful device for screening out parents and hence (in most cases) students who are not upwardly mobile strivers.

The importance of this exclusion of the worst troublemakers and of students with little interest in learning can hardly be overestimated. Excluding the emphatically uninterested parent and student means that teachers are no longer forced, as a way of surviving hours in crowded classrooms, to bargain for peace by making treaties of work avoidance. It means teachers have less reason to conclude that strenuous effort is futile because their students cannot or will not learn. It means that the pace of instruction, which does so much to determine the amount of student learning, may be more rapid. It means that the norms of student groups are more likely to support student efforts to learn. It means that much effort otherwise expended on discipline problems and often vain attempts to goad the recalcitrant is freed for more productive endeavors. It means that homes more consistently reinforce the efforts of the school. It means that the school's clients represent a far less turbulent political environment—one that does far less to consume administrator time and energy, undermine discipline, stir up conflict and dissension, harass teachers, and generally make schools into Grant's watermelons—entities with no firm center of authority, exceedingly difficult to govern.

These are some of the things, in fact, that many parents mention as reasons for patronizing Catholic (and other private) schools: better discipline, schools that run more smoothly, classrooms where students work, and teachers who demand that youngsters learn. Since parents seem almost universally concerned about the youngsters with whom their children associate, it is not surprising that those who have a deep interest in their children's education think deeply about the students with whom their children will associate in school. Since a peer group selected from homes where parents have an unusual interest in their children's education is one of the advantages that attracts parents to Catholic schools, the prevailing tendency, by Coleman and many others, to compare the achievement test results of Catholic and public schools while attempting to equalize home backgrounds is seriously misleading. It produces evidence completely useless to parents choosing between public and Catholic schools. It comes very close to asking, ''If the Catholic school lacked the advantages that attracted you to it, would it produce the result that you seek?'' It is interesting to note, in this regard, that most Catholic schools, financed at a meager level, lack many technical advantages that public schools enjoy. Seeking to make achievement test comparisons more fair, Coleman and others attempt to discount achievement gains attributable to the Catholic school's client-selection advantage, which is reflected in communal attributes, but make no effort to discount achievement gains attributable to the public school's financial advantage, which is reflected in technical attributes.

Controlling for student home background characteristics when comparing achievement in public and Catholic schools has another unfortunate consequence. It directs attention away from one important question this nation might illuminate through the comparisons. The question, far-reaching in its implications, is this: Do schools that specialize, systematically excluding parents and students they are not capable of serving, operate any better than schools that do not? An extensive examination of research on private schools, over a period of many years, convinces me that the answer is a resounding ''yes.''

I should emphasize, perhaps, that at the secondary level, both U.S. Catholic schools as a whole and public schools in nations that make us look ridiculous in international tests of student achievement (e.g., Japan) are overtly selective academically. The assumption here seems to be that as one moves to higher levels of competence and understanding in most subjects, it is not enough to screen for striving. The presence of beginners, whatever their motivations, will make it difficult or impossible to foster at all well the learning of the more advanced. This nation finds no fault with athletic coaches, piano teachers, ballet studios, and masters of the plastic and graphic arts who, while producing world-class performers, limit their instruction to the most talented youngsters available. But the same nation continues to expect its high schools (and often its colleges and graduate schools, one sometimes thinks) to hone the talents of the average student, to say nothing of the brightest and the best, while distracted by those who passed upward through the grades without learning much at all. And the nation now enforces increasingly the proviso—devised predominantly by people who have no responsibility for the day-to-day operation of schools, who almost always send their own children to elite schools, and who generally teach in highly selective institutions whose selectivity they work avidly to enhance—that the beginners who have been promoted willy-nilly must not be segregated within the individual building of the public school most children must attend.

The most important question for present purposes is how much of this private school advantage—the advantage of specialization and client selectivity—is exportable to the public school in the current U.S. context, as often it has been in other nations, and as it has been in the United States in the past. Client self-selection has often been an important element in public schools of choice, such as the current "magnet" schools and the popular public "alternative" schools of an earlier era.[16] To send their children to these schools, parents must make active choices and show considerable initiative. Parents with little interest in their children's schooling, and parents drastically out of tune with the particular thrust of a magnet or alternative school, are obviously screened out. It should come as no surprise, then, that public magnet and alternative schools have typically been depicted as enjoying unusually strong communal characteristics, such as consensus, social cohesion, highly motivated students, and involved, cooperative parents.[17] In one of my own studies, comparing "regular" public schools, "alternative" public schools, and private schools, private schools had dramatically different communal attributes than "regular" public schools, but the "alternative" public schools, as a whole, resembled the private more than the "regular" public schools.

Such similarity suggests that the adoption of private school strategies by public schools can do much to strengthen the communal system. In another of my studies, an opposite trend appears. In private schools that obtained generous tax support in British Columbia, the evidence suggests that several communal attributes were dramatically eroded during the first two years of tax support. Here, the adoption of public school strategies by private schools did much, apparently, to weaken the communal system. I do not have space in this chapter, unfortunately, to discuss the far-reaching importance of the source of fiscal support (taxes versus individual fees and donations) in public and private schools. I merely mention in passing that it seems that teacher attitudes shift considerably when school money, once derived from sacrificing parents, suddenly flows from government, a source that often seems limitless and warrants no tender concern.

The school reform movement, as Finn puts it, "is ambivalent to the point of schizophrenia in its attitude toward two radically different visions of what an ideal educational system would look like.''[18] That is, is an ideal system one in which schools are essentially the same or one in which schools are encouraged to be as unlike one another as possible? What if the nation moved entirely to a system of schools of choice? If the choice involved enough effort to induce parents to take it seriously, we would probably end up with much more consensus within individual schools, more mutual commitment, and a stronger basis for authority. Among public schools, then, as among private schools now (according to much evidence), there would probably be much more differentiation. Different schools would function in different ways, roughly in keeping with the interests of their selected constituencies. I wouldn't predict much widespread resistance to that.

The resistance arises rapidly, however, when one asks what may happen to students from the most underprivileged homes of all—the homes in which parents, partly because they are overwhelmed by problems of sheer survival, do not have the energy or disposition to show much concern about their children's schooling. If the more concerned parents are encouraged to filter off into special schools, those schools may indeed function well, but the schools concerned parents leave behind may be populated, more and more exclusively, by parents who are alienated and uncooperative, and by the difficult-to-educate students such parents typically produce—students almost nobody would want to accept. Some school reformers oppose a system of widespread choice because they fear that scenario. Similarly, some reformers oppose differentiation within schools because of the damage the differentiation seems to do already disadvantaged children.

But what can we do about the most seriously disadvantaged children of all? What suggestions do we have for the school reform movement? We cannot assign such children deliberately to the discard heap, giving up in our attempt to provide them with the most essential skills of good citizenship. One major clue to the answer, I think, is found in the conclusion of at least two prominent scholars who specialize in this area of inquiry—the conclusion that prevailing strategies for coping with the most difficult students of all, including the most widely touted strategies, are demonstrably inadequate and simply cannot work in the bulk of classrooms and schools. One of these scholars currently advocates one-to-one tutoring, the only approach that suggests that tutoring may produce results sufficiently dramatic to permit the reintroduction of these students into regular classrooms. I am not that optimistic, depending on the severity of the students' cognitive and attitudinal handicaps.

At any rate, I think it will become increasingly obvious that high-intensity, extremely costly educational techniques like individual tutoring will be needed to provide many of our slowest-learning youngsters with the most fundamental academic skills, and that some of them will not learn even then. The higher the costs, the more beneficial they will be in one important sense: They will force this nation's reformers to start addressing the cost side of the cost-benefit ratio involved in *all* reforms. The costs will force attention to the question of when it becomes unrealistic and self-defeating to insist that whatever seems good for the most underprivileged student must be done, even if that deprives everyone else. There must be a point when it is too much to expect virtually everyone to continue up the academic ladder. As a matter of fact, there is considerable arrogance in the tendency of most academics, including those in the school reform camp, to assume that more and more of what they think is valuable is exactly what everyone needs.

It is my conclusion, on the basis of the considerations examined briefly here, that most current educational reforms are doomed to fail, since they do not address at all, or do not address realistically, the communal problems that lie at the root of much school failure today. I can say little, in the space here available, about the reforms that *might* effect fundamental improvement, except to indicate what I think are four essential components of fundamental school reform.

One such component, as I have already suggested, is a radical shift in our posture toward the education of our most-difficult-to-educate students. At present, we largely fail them, but by keeping them in school we ruin the communal system for their peers, teachers, and administrators. I think we must identify clearly what we consider to be the most essential understandings and skills. We must then develop special high-intensity programs, certainly in special classrooms and perhaps, better still, in special schools—programs so intense, whatever the cost, that we can virtually guarantee the development of those utterly essential understandings and skills in any child who can be induced, through the many blandishments at our disposal in a powerfully financed institution, to engage in the necessary learning. Ironically, the considerable expense of high-intensity but generally effective programs for these students, if limited to the truly essential basics, could turn out to be much less than the muddle-headed cost, when properly understood, of keeping such youngsters in regular schools, year after futile year, where they consume vastly disproportionate quantities of staff time and limit the learning of everyone else. Many dropouts from academe that we now lament might then be cause for rejoicing.

Another component of reform that would work, I believe, would be a policy of ceasing to try to induce all youngsters, whatever their needs and interests, up the same academic ladder.One would scarcely guess, looking at our public schools, at the enormous diversity of rewarding skills available to the human being, at the great diversity of "intelligences" that human beings of different backgrounds exhibit, and at the dramatically different interests that youngsters naturally develop. I am aware, in fact, of the deliberate suppression of evidence along this line by academics grinding axes. If the state is to finance the extended learning of well-heeled youth in academic institutions (this policy, too, needs reexamination), then the same fiscal entitlement should be available in some form to every individual who has mastered the basics, regardless of how quickly the mastery was achieved. This entitlement, applicable to any selection from a wide variety of constructive learning activities, in any context, at any point in the life span, could prove a potent motivator for many youngsters who now lack one. Entry to learning experiences in academic and nonacademic spheres should be made easy for individuals at any time, so long as they exhibit the appropriate prerequisites and are willing to engage appropriately in the learning activities.

A third essential component of genuine reform, in my view—and here I agree with the mainstream of school reform thought—is to abandon the use of public schools as custodial institutions. Much of this abandonment would occur if youngsters uninterested in academic learning were permitted and encouraged, after they had mastered the all-important basics, to engage in constructive learning in many other contexts. It would take time and imagination, obviously, to encourage the widespread development of learning options in industry, recreation, the entertainment world, and elsewhere. One way or another, I believe we must recognize that instruction of any kind is impeded by the presence of individuals who must be kept on the scene regardless of their cognitive and attitudinal readiness to learn. Access to every learning context, with the possible exception of the high intensity, basic treatment for the most difficult students of all, should be voluntary and conditional.

Finally, I think we need a thorough airing—one that should be brought unapologetically to the attention especially of our courts and legislatures—of the benefits of strong communal systems in schools, and gradually (if need be) a consequent abandonment of the many school structures that now discourage not only parental choice but also program differentiation or specialization, consensus, commitment, consistency of interpersonal influence, the development of affection bonds between students and teachers, and many other vital communal qualities in our public schools.

NOTES

1. Fish, J. (1988), Responses to mandated standardized testing, Ph.D. dissertation, Graduate School of Education, University of California at Los Angeles.

2. Powell, A. G., Farrar, E., & Cohen, D. K. (1985), *The shopping mall high school* (Boston: Houghton Mifflin); Sedlack, M. W., et al. (1986), *Selling students short* (New York: Teachers College Press).

3. Goodlad, J. I. (1984), *A place called school* (New York: McGraw-Hill), Chap. 3.

4. Ibid., Chap. 5; Oakes, J. (1985), *Keeping track: How schools structure inequality* (New Haven: Yale University Press).

5. I have reviewed many of these studies in (1977), D. A. Erickson (Ed.), *Educational organization and administration* (Berkeley: McCutchan Publishing Corporation), Chap. 1.

6. Kleinfeld, J. S. (1979), *Eskimo school on the Andreafsky* (New York: Praeger Publishers).

7. Ibid., p. 4.

8. Ibid., p. 13.

9. Ibid., p. 31.

10. Ibid., p. 83.

11. Concerning the characteristics of minority patrons of Catholic schools, see Greeley, A. M. (1982), *Catholic high schools and minority students* (New Brunswick, NJ: Transaction Books); and Cibulka, J. G., O'Brien T. J., & Zee, D. (1982), *Inner-city private elementary schools: A study* (Milwaukee, WI: Marquette University Press).

12. My comments on advantages in Catholic schools are based on several references mentioned earlier as well as many other sources, including Levine, D. U., et al. (1972, Fall), The home environments of students in a high-achieving inner-city parochial school and a nearby public school, *Sociology of Education*, *45*, 435–45; Bassis, M., et al. (1976), *Achievement in the basic skills: 4th/8th grade, public and parochial schools* (Kingston, RI: Curriculum Research and Development Center, University of Rhode Island); Bryk, A. S., et al. (1984), *Effective Catholic schools: An exploration*, executive summary (Washington, DC: National Catholic Educational Association); Erickson, D. A. (1984), *Victoria's secret: The effects of British Columbia's aid to independent schools*, report to the B.C. Ministry of Education and the U.S. National Institute of Education (Los Angeles: Institute for the Study of Private Schools); National Catholic Educational Association (1986), *Catholic high schools: Their impact on low-income students* (Washington, DC: The Association).

13. Grant, G. (1981, Summer), The character of education and the education of character, *Daedalus, 110*, 135–49; Grant, G. (1984), Schools that make an imprint: Creating a strong positive ethos, in J. H. Bunzel (Ed.), *Challenge to American schools: The case for standards and values* (New York: Oxford University Press). Also relevant here, in the same volume, is Doyle, D. P. (1984), The storm before the lull: The future of private schooling in America. See also Grant's important new book (1988), *The world we created at Hamilton high* (Cambridge, MA: Harvard University Press).

14. E. g., Chubb, J. E., & Moe, T. M. (1986, Fall), No school is an island, *Brookings Review*, pp. 21–28; Scott, W. R., & Meyer, J. W. (1988), Environmental linkages and organizational complexity, in T. James & H. M. Levin (Eds.), *Comparing public and private schools*, Vol. 1, *Institutions and organizations* (New York: Falmer Press), pp. 128–60.

15. Peshkin, A. (1986), *God's choice: The total world of a fundamentalist Christian school* (Chicago: University of Chicago Press).

16. For example, Coleman, J. S., & Hoffer, T. (1987), *Public and private high schools* (New York: Basic Books).

17. Metz, M. H. (1986), *Different by design: The context and character of three magnet schools* (New York: Routledge & Kegan Paul).

18. Finn goes on to state, "I do not know whether a workable synthesis . . . is just over the horizon. I do know that I, like the excellence movement as a whole, am sorely vexed at having to choose between two models of reform that are both enormously appealing in different ways." Finn, C. E., Jr. (1985), The challenges of educational excellence, in C. E. Finn, Jr., D. Ravitch, & P. H. Roberts (Eds.), *Challenges to the humanities* (New York: Holmes-Meier), pp. 197–98.

9 Language-Minority Students and Educational Reform: An Incomplete Agenda

Concepción M. Valadez

A Nation at Risk and other national reports appearing since 1983 have indicted the nation's public schools. They have pointed out that, judging from the standpoint of achievement, the general student population was not being served adequately by the country's public school system. By the same standard, the educational achievement of minority students was even more dismal. Any discussion of the school reforms prompted by these reports must include an analysis of how those reforms have affected the minority public school population for at least three reasons. First, the reform movement itself has proclaimed a commitment to equity. Second, this country is based on principles of equality and justice. We have laws mandating equality of educational opportunities for all school-age residents. However, if, in violation of democratic values, we choose to ignore this second reason, we would still be compelled to attend to the quality of our minority population's schooling for, third, the survival of our country as a world power. The size of the minority population (23 percent and growing) makes ignoring it impossible. Improvement of educational achievement for minority students would result in benefits for the entire nation. If we do not succeed with minority students, we will certainly increase the danger, in the words of *A Nation at Risk*, to "American prosperity, security and civility." If it does not pay specific attention to the needs of the minority population, the educational reform movement has an incomplete agenda, to say the least.

Let us address the equity issue. In some circles talk of equity upsets people. They immediately raise the concern of excellence. They claim quality will be sacrificed if equality is enhanced. What does the school reform movement stand for? Excellence *and* equality? Two experts, in analyzing *A Nation At Risk*, reported that "By title and content, the report switched the attention of educational reformers and policy makers from equity to excellence."[1] However, as

Chester Finn, Jr., former assistant secretary of education and a leading spokesperson for school reform, has observed, equity and excellence are not antonyms in any dictionary. He adds, "The opposite of excellence is mediocrity; the opposite of equality is inequality or perhaps injustice. To pose them as contrasts with one another is to rob each principle of much of its power." Finn further notes that the contemporary debate about education reform commonly assumes that these two terms are "opposites, . . . as if daring the excellence movement to abandon the doctrine of equality of opportunity in pursuit of some elitist fantasy."[2] This is a dare that Finn rejects. We concur with Finn. The school reform movement cannot push for excellence while ignoring the needs of the less advantaged. The working blueprint of the school reform movement, therefore, should ensure that those minorities who have not been adequately schooled are brought into the excellence ranks by making quality education accessible to them. The school reform movement must give those minorities who have not been adequately schooled a chance to develop their abilities. The school reform movement must recognize that the nation cannot move forward by denying access to quality education to almost a quarter of its population.

This chapter addresses the severity of the problem of achieving excellence and equity for minority students, and concentrates on literacy acquisition as an area on which school reform must focus when the students are from a language-minority background. In particular we concentrate on the Hispanic or Latino student population. The use of first-language literacy for initial instruction, with subsequent transition to all-English instruction, is explored. We support bilingual education as a viable educational approach; our justification for this position will be presented. We understand that the audience for this book is not composed of researchers and specialists; thus we have attempted to keep technical language and the apparatus of research to a minimum. This chapter reviews theories of bilingual education and presents results of current research from an exemplary school district in southern California. The chapter ends with a synthesis of insights gained from research in bilingual education that, together with other theories on learning, should be applied by school reformers if they are indeed serious about excellence and equity. Our position is that unless the reform movement addresses the schooling of the language-minority student directly, the war against mediocrity in our schools will be lost and the school reform movement will severely compromise its proclaimed objective of excellence and equity.

Several innovations have already been prompted by the school reform movement. Graduation requirements have been raised. Core courses have been given more attention. Guidelines for curricula have been revised. School boards in Texas and California, among other states, have instituted tests of academic competency for student participation in extra-curricular activities such as athletics. Other school reforms have addressed teacher preparation and teaching. The University of California, Los Angeles, and the University of Texas at El Paso are among the teacher preparation institutions that have added basic skills tests to the admissions requirements of their programs. Money has been allocated for merit pay or mentor teacher programs. Several states have instituted teacher competency tests.

However, even with such reforms in place, the downtrend for large numbers of students, especially minority students, has not been reversed. In fact, a report by the Carnegie Foundation, released in March 1988, accused the reform movement of ignoring urban public schools. (And it is in the urban schools that 80 percent of the children from Hispanic families are found.) The report charged that "No other crisis—a flood, a health epidemic, a garbage [workers] strike or even snow removal—would be as calmly accepted without full-scale intervention."[3] Yet, the report declares, our most deeply troubled public schools are being allowed to remain characterized by unmotivated students and crumbling buildings where little more is being accomplished than keeping the youngsters off the streets.

Exactly how bad is the situation for Hispanics? In 1986 national figures indicated that Hispanics were completing twelve years of school at the unacceptable rate of 50 to 60 percent, while among Anglo students the public high school graduation rate was 83 percent.[4] The significance of the low achievement among Hispanics and its implications will be appreciated if we recognize that this population comprises an increasing proportion of the student population in the public schools of this country. Let's take California, the state that has one of the nation's foremost school reform advocates, Bill Honig, as its superintendent of schools.

If we study the growth of the minority component of California's student population from 1970 to 1990, we find that during this 20-year period the non-Anglo population will expand from 27 percent to 52 percent. In 1988 Hispanics alone comprised 30.7 percent of the state's total student population in the public schools. (Nearly 60 percent of all children in Los Angeles Public Unified School District schools are Latino; only 15.8 percent are Anglo.) The figure for the Anglo group is 49.2 percent, while those for the Blacks and Asians, the two other sizable minority groups in California, are 9.0 percent and 7.6 percent, respectively. The rest of the state's students comprised Filipino (2.2 percent), American Indian or Native Alaskan (0.8 percent), and Pacific Islanders (0.5 percent). Now let's look at the attrition rates for cohorts of Hispanic high school students. No one interested in education in general, or in the school reform movement specifically, can fail to see that our public schools are losing sizable numbers of Hispanic youth. Figures released in 1985 by the California State Department of Education showed that between the ninth and twelfth grades, the state loses 13 to 20 percent of its Hispanic students each year. In some high schools 50 percent of the Hispanic students who enroll as sophomores do not graduate. In others the figure is as high as 70 percent.[5] The reform movement cannot ignore these statistics or keep from being troubled by them. The questions to ask are "Why are these figures so high?" and "What can be done to reverse them?"

While several factors influence the decision of minority students to leave school, there is evidence that failure of poor academic achievement weighs especially heavily toward dropping out. In the revealing High School and Beyond Survey, with a sample of 30,000 students representative of all school-age persons in the country, poor grades was cited most often as a reason for leaving school, with 34 percent of the Hispanic males and 32 percent of the Hispanic females who had dropped out indicating that poor grades were a factor in their decision. (The study showed that poor grades were a major reason for Anglo students' school desertion as well.)[6] We have no quarrel with high standards; we welcome them. The point is to make these high standards accessible to all.

A frequently heard explanation for minority students' lack of success in public school is the home environment. There are indeed home and nonschool factors that affect school achievement. In this chapter we will not elaborate on this point except to say that readers should not think that Latino parents have low aspirations for their children. On the contrary, studies show that Latino parents want their children to be successful in school and reach higher levels of schooling than they did. Latino parents who do not speak English particularly set their hopes on their children's quick acquisition of English (and good grades) in public school. Therefore, no one is more disappointed than Latino parents who see their children getting into difficulties at school. If Latino parents themselves attended school in this country without finishing high school, they are frequently dismayed to see the pattern repeated with their offspring. The discrepancy between the aspirations and expectations of Latino parents and their children's school achievement must be addressed by the school reform movement. This may involve intervening in the nonschool environment. In this chapter, however, we focus solely on school factors.

We want to reemphasize that the school reform movement cannot claim to be committed to excellence and equity if a quality education is not being achieved by large numbers of minority students. Further, there are grave implications when large numbers of minorities fail to graduate from high school. If minorities are not completing high school, they cannot go on to college—just at the time that new jobs will be requiring college training. California State Superintendent of Schools Bill Honig points out the alarming situation in California, which may be a bellwether for other states:

The changes in our state's population—including the fact that one in four of our students comes from a home where a language other than English is spoken—coincide with a changing job market. As we approach the twenty-first century, most of the new jobs will require more than a high school education.[7]

Presumably the first phase of the reform movement was to establish high standards in our public schools. What is the second phase, then? "The second phase of our work is to ensure that these reforms are implemented in each and every classroom and that *all* students receive the benefits of our improvement efforts."[8] Honig is absolutely correct about the second phase, and we will emphasize his point. We have to assume that the reform movement has the will to impact positively upon our minority population in public school because it has repeatedly expressed that view. The second phase of school reform, however, will not become a reality unless the reform movement develops and provides the instructional programs necessary to make that positive difference.

On the other hand, the public must expect the reform movement to be concerned with finding instructional programs that will increase the chances of success of those minority students the public school system is now failing. One of the areas crying for special attention is literacy development of language minorities. Literacy is an area cited in *A Nation at Risk* as a major indicator of "risk":

Some 23 million American adults are functionally illiterate by the simplest tests of everyday reading, writing, and comprehension.

About 13 percent of all seventeen-year-olds in the United States can be considered functionally illiterate. Functional illiteracy among minority youth may run as high as 40 percent.[9]

Literacy is clearly the most critical requisite for academic success. Its acquisition must begin in the primary grades, for any subsequent school achievement depends heavily on reading and writing skills. Functional illiteracy is especially high among language-minority students. Why should literacy acquisition be particularly problematic for language-minority students? What is current research saying that can help the school reform movement understand the complexities involved in learning to read and write? Are there any breakthroughs that can guide instructional programs of the kind the school reform movement needs? This section focuses on reading acquisition among language-minority students. First we explore the nature of reading, which at first glance seems simple; then we go on to show how it is a rather complex activity. We use examples from current research, including some conducted by ourselves, with children who begin school knowing only Spanish and acquire mastery of spoken and written English. We then draw implications for the reform movement.

One definition of reading might be "the ability to obtain meaning from the written word." Let us consider what is involved in that apparently simple act. The basis for written language is the spoken language. We can find style differences between the way we normally speak and the way we express ourselves in writing, but the written form has been derived from how the language is spoken. The words we see or the sounds we hear can be language only if they symbolize thought, if they convey meaning. In turn, those thoughts are based on knowledge or experience or feelings. In order for a reader to be able to get meaning out of a written passage, he or she has to share not only a common language with the writer but also similar thoughts, or background and experience, or knowledge. In effect, reading can be characterized as an active and complex cognitive act involving conceptual and language processes. Thus it becomes clear why not everyone obtains the apparently easy skill.

Let's see where this leads. What are the implications for the school reform movement, especially as the reform movement turns its attention to problems of teaching and teacher preparation? In working with students who arrive at public school with very limited English, or with a dialect of English that is not the school standard, our teachers, who are typically monolingual English speakers, very often cannot tell what the experience base or the background knowledge of those students may be. They should not, and cannot, assume that the students' background has prepared them for the school curriculum. A teacher with a language or a dialect different from the students' will not have the tool of a common language to access the students' background. Nor can the teacher have any assurance that what he/she is teaching orally is being understood, much less learned. In the same way, except perhaps even more frustrating for them, language-minority students are likely to be unable to make any sense of the teachers' orally presented lessons or the written instructional material.

We would like to suggest an approach that the reform movement should consider in teaching language-minority or limited-English students, one that has been successful where appropriately implemented. Instruction begins by using the first or home language, with a shift to instruction totally in English as the students become proficient in English, their second language. Bilingual education, as this controversial instructional approach is called, has advocates and critics whose perspectives are largely politically based. Although our main interest is in explaining the pedagogical advantages of bilingual instruction, we will touch briefly on these issues because they so frequently surface in the press and on television, and even on the ballot, as recently seen in various state initiatives for English as the official language.

To understand the controversy over bilingual education, we need to examine our attitude toward the use of languages other than English. The use of a non-English language in public schools of this country is not new, nor is the level of criticism of this practice. Joshua Fishman, a noted scholar of language, tells us that our country began with several languages—English, Spanish, French, German, Russian, Swedish, and Dutch—the languages of the settlers who came to North America before the establishment of the United States as a nation. Although the last three languages mentioned rapidly lost colonial language status, except in a few isolated places, as the mother countries lost control of their fledgling colonies, the dominance of the English language, Fishman concludes, was not completely predictable. Shirley Brice Heath, another scholar of language, notes that in this country, from 1776 to the mid-nineteenth century, multilingualism was an accepted, even desirable, phenomenon, benefiting a nation of immigrants. At the time few fears were expressed about any potential threat of multilingualism to national unity. Eventually, helped by the benefit of numbers, of concentration and control of urban life and education, and of entry into service occupations, English took precedence over other colonial languages. English received important reinforcement in numbers by massive immigration from Ireland during the nineteenth century. What we find by looking at our language history is that because of a number of domestic factors as well as international events, the English language eventually became dominant in the United States.[10]

English has maintained its dominance in the United States without the country's having an official language policy. Research on language and cultural assimilation shows that the absorbing power of American society has been most effective where there has been an absence of, rather than the presence of, legal coercion and sanctions on the part of authorities against the use of ethnic languages. The anglicization of the non-English ethnic groups has occurred most rapidly when there has been free access to the "American" way without the need to reject the ethnic language and heritage. Public schools in Texas, for example, with the rule of "English only" prevalent through the 1960s, did not succeed in making Spanish-speaking Mexican-American students into proficient English speakers. Nathan Glazer, one of the nation's most respected students of the subject, has noted that characteristically America has been able to "[produce] *without* laws that which other countries, desiring a culturally unified population, were not able to produce *with* laws."[11]

The Constitution of the United States does not contain a language policy, but the country has English as its de facto official language. Why has the decade of the 1980s produced such a strong feeling against non-English languages in this country that the public is being asked to consider the passage of an amendment to the U.S. Constitution making English the official language of the country and restricting the use of other languages? Why is the public so adamantly against non-English languages now?

Current federal bilingual education legislation provides official blessing for the use of a language other than English in transitional instruction, a position that goes very much against the grain of segments of our population who speak only English, even if their ancestors came from a non-English-speaking country. These individuals oppose bilingual education, perceiving this educational policy as giving other languages equal importance to English. The proponents of the "English-only" state initiatives, for example, see the use of Spanish or other languages as a threat to the sovereignty of English. At the time of the writing of this chapter, sixteen states have approved legislation making English their official language. We should note that the position of "English only" has gained strength at the same time we are witnessing a large influx of non-English speakers into the country and some members of the ethnic minorities—who by the way, are dominant English speakers, if not monolingual English—begin to make some economic and political adaptation to the American society.

The major cities of the country are visibly culturally diverse; non-English writing is seen on store fronts. The commercial world is using non-English advertising. It is little wonder that the "English only" proponents may be expressing the feeling that the country is no longer theirs. The controversy, therefore, has to do with the open-door immigration policy we have in this country; the constitution that protects individual rights and the freedom of ethnic groups, including the right to freedom from discrimination on the basis of language; and the perceived threat to the dominant status of English.[12]

We should note at this point that the school reform movement itself is confused and ambivalent on the issue under discussion. For example, Chester Finn, Jr., and Diane Ravitch, eminent figures in the reform movement, concur with the statements in *A Nation at Risk* on the importance of starting foreign language learning in the elementary grades. However, the framers of that report suggest that foreign languages should be only for the collegebound students. Finn and Ravitch disagree. "Our view," they say, "is clearer and our prescription more demanding: every American should become proficient in at least one foreign language and while this must . . . begin before high school, it should continue in high school." Finn and Ravitch would like to see students leave elementary grades with basic control of the structure and mechanics of a foreign language, and then in high school develop the ability to read the literature in that language and the skills needed for the written and oral expression of more sophisticated ideas. These education reform leaders would like to have our students be able to grapple with the best that has been written in any language, and learn it to convey one's own best thoughts: "That is after all, what the humanities are about, and what education ought to be about."[13] On the other hand, the reform movement's leaders have not related this expressed desirable goal—for American students to master a foreign language—to the massive effort to eradicate the languages other than English arriving at our public school doors in ever increasing numbers every year! The contradiction between the two positions is ironic.

As a nation we are ambivalent toward the language diversity within our borders. Americans in general, like the school reformers, are not certain whether to view this phenomenon as a problem or as a resource. Perhaps a reason for our ambivalence is the lack of understanding of what is involved in learning a language. The language education literature has not been accessible to the public, and it is not widely known that the best way to learn a second language is to have a strong grasp of the first. Perhaps most adult Americans think they can't learn another language and would feel intimidated around those speaking a language they don't understand, even if these speakers are their own children. Finally, the wide resistance and suspicion toward use of languages other than English for instruction may also be due to the fact that the underpinnings of bilingual education have not been clearly explained to the public. This is our task now.

The rationale for first-language literacy instruction in bilingual education is based on a number of principles of learning that have been discussed in the relevant specialized literature. Among them is that a cognitively demanding skill like reading is easier to learn if it is taught in the language one speaks, the one used to communicate and share thought. Another principle we wish to call to readers' attention is that learning acquired through one language is not stored separately in the brain from that received through another language; rather, the human mind develops and underlying proficiency that can be accessed through any language the person speaks and understands.

A perception of the school reform-minded, monolingual public in this country seems to be that time is wasted on non-English instruction if the eventual goal is to be skilled in English-language curriculum. This view is based on the theory that a bilingual's proficiencies are developed independently and stored separately in the brain, the separate underlying proficiency (SUP) theory. Holders of this position maintain that if limited amounts of time and mental capacity are available, efforts should be concentrated on the development of proficiencies in English, the more educationally, socially, and economically useful of the two languages, whatever the other language. On the other hand, there is another theory, the common underlying proficiency (CUP) theory, which posits that a bilingual's proficiency in managing the linguistic demands of cognitively demanding, context-dependent tasks is interdependent across languages, and that development of proficiency through activities in one language is the equivalent of development of that proficiency in the other. This view holds that the ability to master tasks learned through the first (the home or parents') language will assist the bilingual in performing similar tasks in the other (the public school's) language.[14]

We would like now to describe an effective bilingual program supporting the theory of common underlying proficiency. Although the evidence comes from a small school district, we believe it has broader relevance.

A successful example of initial instruction provided in the first language, Spanish, with transition to all-English instruction can be found in the Montebello Unified School District in southern California.[15] A study conducted to identify the features that made this program successful included research on the relationship between language development and the acquisition of reading. The study took place in the kind of public school typically associated with low achievement: severe overcrowding (a school with 1,400 children), four tracks, year-round calendar, average class size thirty-two, 90 percent of the students Latino, 70 percent of the kindergarteners entering school with very limited English skills, the community a low-income one, and a 40 percent student turnover rate. Nonetheless, the school had a curriculum that had gained a national reputation for being successful with precisely the students we are concerned with here—the potentially nonachieving language-minority student, the Latino student from a low-income home, who begins school with little or no English proficiency. The National Council of Teachers of English recognized the school with an award for an innovative reading program in 1986, and the California Association for Bilingual Education selected it for an Exemplary School Award in 1987. The school was featured by the Achievement Council in its 1988 report, *Unfinished Business, Fulfilling Our Children's Promise*.

Here was a public school where the theoretical expectations of bilingual education were being fulfilled. The students were learning English while staying at grade level academically. The questions that led us into the classroom were to find out precisely what this school was doing right. We found the curriculum concentrating on development of high-level thinking and information-processing skills. These skills were being promoted in English or Spanish, or both. The school had the primary goal of ensuring that all students were English proficient and reading at grade level by the time they finished fourth grade. One of the key innovations we found at this school was a commitment on the part of teachers and administration to staff collaboration and staff development; the teachers continually sought to keep developing their skills. Most important, the administration and instructional personnel were convinced the children were ready to learn and wanted to learn. And both administrators and teachers understood that information, concepts, and even attitudes toward a subject learned in the first language, Spanish, would be useful when the children made the transition to English.

We followed a group of children from the start of kindergarten through the third grade. Their parents were interviewed and the classroom instruction was observed. Of particular interest to us was the development of reading and language skills. As part of the regular school procedure the children's language proficiency was assessed upon entering kindergarten by the IDEA Oral Language Proficiency Test; based on the results, each child was classified as English monolingual (English only), Spanish monolingual (Spanish only), or bilingual. If a child was bilingual, he or she was further classified as Spanish dominant or English dominant. The experiment began with ninety children, thirty each in the categories English only, Spanish only, and bilingual, with the latter subdivided into English dominant and Spanish dominant. Due to the high mobility of the student population, twenty-one of the ninety subjects were lost by the end of the first year. Nevertheless, the trends found in our analyses yield valuable information.

We were particularly interested in the development of reading; and because reading is an activity involving cognition as well as language proficiency and reading readiness, our study obtained baseline data on these areas for each of our students. The children were tested through the subtests of the Woodcock-Johnson Psycho-Educational Battery and the Woodcock-Johnson Language Proficiency Battery. We pretested the children one month into the start of the kindergarten year and posttested at the end of that first academic year. Unlike intelligence tests of bilingual children, where the primary concern is to establish language dominance before deciding upon an appropriate measure in one language, this study focused on determining the strengths and weaknesses in both languages, in order to be able to measure the changes in performance over time. Additionally, recognizing that progress in language development and reading not only involves instructional factors and maturity, but also is influenced by cognitive ability and home background, we obtained measures of home literacy, parent education, and nonverbal cognitive ability. Thus, the study could examine the relationship among home factors, cognitive ability, and primary language or language dominance at the onset of reading in a formal school setting.

We found that the children in the four groups (English only, Spanish only, English dominant, and Spanish dominant) began school with very similar general nonverbal cognitive ability, as measured by one of the most credible measures for this ability, Raven's Coloured Progressive Matrices. The highest mean score was obtained by the Spanish-dominant bilingual group (average score 16.7), while the lowest was that of the Spanish monolingual group (average score 14.2). The scores of the English-only children (average 15.5) and those of the English-dominant bilinguals (average 14.4) fell between the other two, but the differences between the groups were not significant.

However, there were interesting differences on the home background variables. A Home Literacy Scale was designed to tap adults' and children's reading habits, availability of reading materials at home, and accessibility of reading materials outside the home. Scores showed that the English-only homes had significantly higher rates of literacy than the Spanish-only homes. We also found that the homes of the English-dominant bilingual children scored very close to those of the English-only group. The Spanish-dominant bilingual homes also had higher scores than the Spanish monolinguals. The same order was found for the parents' education. This score was obtained by averaging the number of years of schooling completed by both parents. The highest average was held by the English-only parents (average score 14.4), followed by the English-dominant bilinguals, the Spanish-dominant bilinguals, and the parents who were Spanish monolingual (mean 7.0 years of schooling [standard deviation of 3.8]). All of this information is important to an understanding of the background of the children in these schools. Only if we know what the children come with can we determine the effect upon them of their school experiences.

We also obtained baseline data on the children's reading and language. We used the Spanish and English versions of the Woodcock-Johnson Psycho-Educational Battery and the Woodcock-Johnson Language Proficiency Battery. We selected these batteries because they have equivalent forms in both English and Spanish. On the pretest the monolingual children were tested in their language only, whether English or Spanish. The bilingual children were tested in both English and Spanish, regardless of their language dominance. At the posttest, the children who began kindergarten as Spanish monolinguals were tested in both Spanish and English.

At this school the traditional kindergarten curriculum was augmented by one hour. Instruction was provided in the children's dominant language, the English monolingual or English-dominant children receiving their instruction in English. Those children who were Spanish monolingual or Spanish dominant were instructed in Spanish. During the second semester the Spanish instructional group received thirty minutes of oral English as a second language three times a week.

Gains across one year of instruction were studied by comparing prescores and postscores for the children who were tested in Spanish and for the children tested in English. Everyone's scores improved. That indicated that some learning was going on, but when we took a closer look, we discovered that each group's improvement grew at a steeper rate when it was tested in its dominant language.

Since that dominance determined the language of instruction, that is not too surprising. However, there were also important gains even when they were tested in the weaker language, the language not used in direct instruction! We found the Spanish-dominant children with gains of 14.5 and 15.6 points in English oral language and English reading aptitude, respectively. These children were already developing the ability to access the common underlying proficiency. Naturally, the largest gains were found in the scores of the dominant-language children. For the English-dominant bilinguals these mean gain scores were 17 points in oral language, 18.4 in reading, and 18.1 in reading aptitude, scores that were very close to those of the English monolinguals: 19 points in oral language, 18.4 in reading, and 23.8 in reading aptitude. Among the children receiving instruction in Spanish, we saw similar gain scores, with the Spanish dominants making slightly greater gains than the Spanish monolinguals. The Spanish-dominant children had mean gain scores of 19.4 in oral language, 15.5 in reading, and 19.3 in reading aptitude.

The data demonstrate that time spent developing the critical cognitive and linguistic skills involved in reading in the home language will have a direct payoff when the student makes the transition into all-English instruction. It is the confidence in and security of having these skills that will make the student successful in the all-English environment.

The remainder of the program at this school is as follows: With a very energetic assessment program, children will continue to receive instruction in reading, math, and language arts in their dominant language. Every teacher is a trained English-as-a-second-language (ESL) instructor. Physical education, science, art, and social studies will be provided in settings where there is verbal interaction between the limited-English speakers and the monolingual English and dominant-English speakers. Thus an important part of the curriculum is provided in the students' dominant language with an ESL component until these children test at intermediate level (4 on a scale of 1 to 5) in oral English and grade level in first-language reading.

Other research has told us that the best predictor of how well these children will perform in English reading is their reading skill in Spanish. Ordinarily grade-level reading and the appropriate proficiency in oral English occur in the third grade. At that time the children are placed in a transition curriculum, a carefully designed reading program to assist them in transferring to English reading the skills developed in Spanish reading and adding those skills that are unique to English written language. In this school this program ordinarily takes twelve to fifteen weeks. At the conclusion of the program the child is expected to pass the assessment for that point and be reclassified. For the child who needs additional time, there are additional activities in the transition curriculum, but if assessment is done appropriately, few children need more than the three or four months to make the transition to English reading. Furthermore, the transition to an English basal book is usually within a half-year reading level of where the children were reading in Spanish.

Reclassification is an important event in the academic history of these children.

In the current official public school jargon, their records will show that they began as LEPs or NEPs (limited English proficient/non-English proficient) and now are FEPs (fluent English proficient). The records will also show the method used to meet the reclassification criteria. If one were to visit a fourth grade in this school in Montebello, the children who are smiling and feeling successful in an all-English curriculum are very likely those who began their career in this school as NEPs or LEPs.

We have provided a sketch of how children whose first language is Spanish learn English at a public school whose educational program is working. This school is taking current research on learning and successfully applying it to children who arrive at school without the prerequisite linguistic skills for receiving instruction in a traditional all-English classroom. We have shown that bilingual education can teach essential skills and subject matter while children acquire English at the same time. The school reform movement has not yet tapped the theories that undergird bilingual education, perhaps because of the political fears mentioned above. But the critical nature of the educational situation in the country and of its language-minority school population, no less than its proclaimed commitment to excellence and equity, should impel the school reform movement to look for assistance wherever it may be found.

Let us review the basic reason why the Montebello school is successful. The common underlying proficiency hypothesis has several related theories. Many researchers and scholars have written about the transfer of knowledge in learning and the transfer of skills. More specific to bilingual reading, Eleanor Thonis maintains that many skills transfer, but the most important thing that transfers is the joy of reading. To that we add that when students have developed a confidence in their ability to learn and feel that success in school is within reach, academic achievement through English is not seen as difficult or impossible, but as possible, probable, and enjoyable.

Bilingual education is not really a radical idea. It is simply using the students' native or first language as a tool for reaching for what he/she already knows and understands. The student is achieving cognitive growth in his/her stronger language. In the meantime the student is learning English in a nonthreatening environment. Eventually, all that had been learned in the first language is accessed through the second language, English. A transition period will occur around the third or fourth grade. The student's proficiency in the second language (English) will continue to grow, and by the sixth grade English will very likely become the dominant language of the student.

Bilingualism in this form serves as a bridge from the first or home language to academic success in English, the school language. At one time this author advocated bilingualism for all Americans, knowing there are cognitive advantages of full bilingualism. However, at the present time, given the critical condition of education of Hispanic and other limited-English students, we are confining ourselves to urging bilingualism as a way to keep these students interested in school. Currently such students are expected to learn skills, concepts, and knowledge in English without possessing the English proficiency to understand what is going on. This is unfair and inequitable. For Latino students the use of Spanish for initial instruction gives them a chance to be successful students while they learn English.

This country has undergone a soul searching since the publication by the National Commission on Excellence in 1983 of those unsatisfactory marks on our national school report card. Many efforts are under way to upgrade our public schools in the name of excellence and equity. Still, by all the standards of educational achievement, the educational condition of language-minority students has continued to decline. Academic standards are being raised with few or no practical measures instituted for language-minority students to reach those higher standards. In the meantime, employers are seeking employees with even higher levels of academic training.

The language-minority population is growing at a faster rate than the Anglo population. We hold that in order for the school reform movement to succeed with the language-minority population, it must utilize the practices that provide good results with language-minority students, whatever their source or label. Given its commitment to equity and excellence, the school reform movement has an obligation to search the literature for effective means of instruction for language-minority group members wherever they can be found. Then the reform movement must find the will and the resources to implement these measures.

NOTES

1. Clark, D. L., & Astuto, T. A. (1986, October), The significance and permanence of change in federal education policy, *The Educational Researcher*, *15*, 5.

2. Finn, C., Jr., (1985), The challenge of educational excellence. In C. Finn, Jr., D. Ravitch, & P. H. Roberts (Eds.), *Challenges to the humanities* (New York: Holmes and Meier), p. 198.

3. (1988, March 17), *New York Times*, p. 21.

4. Hodgkinson, H. L. (1986), *California: The state and its educational system* (Washington, DC: Institute for Educational Leadership).

5. The 1988 data for California appears in B. Honig (Ed.) (1988), *The California Schools*, *VI*(2), (Sacramento: California State Department of Education), p. 3. The attrition data appear in Cortes, C. (1985), The education of language minority students: A contextual interaction model. California State Department of Education, National Dissemination and Assessment Center, California State University, Los Angeles. (Sacramento: The Department).

6. National Commission of Secondary Schooling for Hispanics. (1984), *Make something happen* (Washington, DC: The Commission).

7. California State Department of Education. (1988), *The California Schools*, *VI*(2), p. 3.

8. Ibid. Emphasis added.

9. National Commission on Excellence in Education (1983), *A nation at risk: The*

imperative for educational reform (Washington, DC: U.S. Government Printing Office), p. 8.

10. Fishman, J. (1980), Language maintenance, in S. Thernstrom (Ed.), *Harvard encyclopedia of American ethnic groups* (New York: Cambridge University Press), p. 630; Heath, S. B. (1981), English in our language heritage, In C. A. Ferguson & S. B. Heath (Eds.), *Language in the U.S.A.* (New York: Cambridge University Press), pp. 6–20.

11. Glazer, N. (1978), The process and problems of language maintenance: An integrative review, in A. A. Lourie & N. F. Conklin (Eds.), *A pluralistic nation: The language issue in the United States* (Rowley, MA: Newbury House), p. 34. Emphasis in original.

12. For a review of the issues having to do with language and ethnic groups, a good source is McKay, S., & Sau-ling, C. W. (Eds.) (1988), *Language diversity, problems or resource?* (New York: Newbury House). See especially Ruiz, R., Orientations in language planning, pp. 3–25.

13. Finn, C., Jr., Ravitch, D., & Fancher, R. T. (1984), *Against mediocrity* (New York: Holmes and Meier), p. 260.

14. California State Department of Education (1983, 1984, 1986), *Basic principles for the education of language-minority students: An overview* (Sacramento: The Department). We also recommend Cummins, J. (1981), The role of primary language development in promoting educational success for language minority students, in California State Department of Education, National Dissemination and Assessment Center, University of California, Los Angeles. *Schooling and language minority students: A theoretical framework* (Sacramento: The Department).

15. There is a more complete description of the project in Padilla, A., Valadez, C. M., & Chang, M. D. (1988). *Young children's oral language proficiency and reading ability in Spanish and English*, Technical Report no. 11. University of California, Los Angeles, Center for Language Education and Research. (Los Angeles: University of California).

SUGGESTED READINGS

Achievement Council. (1988). *Unfinished business, fulfilling our children's promises.* A report from the Achievement Council by K. Haycock & M. S. Navarro. Los Angeles: The Council.

Arons, S. (1986, October 1). First Amendment rights are "crucial" in educating language minority pupils. *Education Week*, Commentary, p. 19.

California State Department of Education. Evaluation, Dissemination, and Assessment Center, California State University, Los Angeles. (1981). *Schooling and language minority children: A theoretical framework.* Sacramento: The Department.

———. (1983, 1984, 1986). *Basic principles for the education of language-minority students: An overview.* Sacramento: The Department.

———. Evaluation, Dissemination and Assessment Center, California State University, Los Angeles. (1986). *Beyond language: Social cultural factors in schooling language minority students.* Sacramento: The Department.

Cummins, J. (1981). The role of primary language development in promoting educational success for language minority students. In California State Department of Education, National Dissemination and Assessment Center, University of California,

Los Angeles, *Schooling and language minority students: A theoretical framework.* Sacramento: The Department.

Fillmore, L. W., & Valadez, C. M. (1986). Teaching bilingual learners. In M. Wittrock (Ed.), *Handbook of research on teaching* (3rd ed.). New York: Macmillan.

Fishman, J., et al. (1966). *Language loyalty in the United States.* The Hague: Mouton Press.

Grant, C. A., & Sleeter, C. E. (1988). Race, class, gender, exceptionality, and educational reform. In J. A. Banks & C. A. McGee Banks (Eds.), *Multicultural education, issues and perspectives.* Boston: Allyn and Bacon.

Heath, S. B. (1977). Language and politics in the United States. In M. S. Troike (Ed.), *Linguistics and anthropology: Georgetown University round table on languages and linguistics.* Washington, DC: Georgetown University Press.

Horowitz, R., & Samuels, S. J. (1987). *Comprehending oral and written language.* New York: Academic Press.

McKay, S. L., & Wong, S. C. (Eds.). (1988). *Language diversity, problem or resource?* Rowley, MA: Newbury House/Harper & Row.

Molesky, J. (1983). Understanding the American linguistic mosaic: A historical overview of language maintenance and language shift. In S. L. McKay & S. C. Wong, (Eds.), *Language diversity, problem or resource?* Rowley, MA: Newbury House/ Harper & Row.

National Commission on Secondary Schooling for Hispanics. (1984). *Make something happen.* Washington, DC: The Commission.

Padilla, A., Valadez, C. M., & Chang, M. D. (1988). *Young children's oral language proficiency and reading ability in Spanish and English* (Technical Report 11). Los Angeles: Center for Language Education and Research, University of California, Los Angeles.

Ruiz, R. (1988). Official languages and language planning. In K. Adams & D. Brink (Eds.), *Official English in the border states.* Tucson: University of Arizona Press.

Valadez, C. M. (1983). *Non-school factors in academic underachievement of Chicano/ Latino students.* Papers of the George Sanchez Seminar. Berkeley: Chancellor's Office, University of California.

———. (1986). *Effective teachers for language minority students, national needs.* Committee on Education and Labor, House of Representatives, 99th Congress, 2nd Session, Compendium of Papers on the Topic of Bilingual Education, Serial no. 99-R. Washington, DC: U.S. Government Printing Office.

10 Language Arts and Literacy: The Endangered Core of School Reform

Barbara Hecht

> The faculty of language stands at the center of our conception of mankind:
> Speech makes us human and literacy makes us civilized.[1]

In the past few years the nation has been inundated with gloomy assessments of the state of public education. At least nine major reports have documented the problems facing our public schools and have called for reforms that include higher expectations, more discipline, more homework, greater accountability and standards for teachers, the development of a core or basic curriculum, and a dedication to excellence.

The curriculum, what *A Nation at Risk* called the "very stuff of education," has been a central focus of the reform movement. Whether reformers call it the new basics (from *A Nation at Risk*) or traditional education (from *Last Chance for Our Children*, by Bill Honig), they agree that there is a basic foundation of knowledge and skills that every student and future citizen should master. Although there is some disagreement about the components of this basic curriculum, the reformers agree that language is at the core. As Ernest L. Boyer stated in the Carnegie Foundation's report on secondary education in America: "The first curriculum priority is language. . . . It is the most essential tool for learning."[2]

The National Commission on Excellence in Education compiled some statistics that illustrate the nature of the problem. In addition to widely reported declines in average SAT scores, 13 percent of all seventeen-year-olds and up to 40 percent of minority youth are functionally illiterate. Nearly 40 percent of seventeen-year-olds cannot draw inferences from written material, and only 20 percent can write a persuasive essay. Although oral language abilities are not formally assessed, teachers and business leaders complain that many students and graduates lack the ability to convey their ideas clearly and persuasively. Few high school graduates have given a public address, conducted an interview, or participated in a formal debate.

Increased proficiency in oral and written language is an unassailable goal. Language proficiency is essential—it is the underpinning of the entire educational process. Not only the reformers, but all educators, want students to be able to speak and write more clearly, to read with greater enjoyment and comprehension, and to listen with more attention and discrimination. No educator would dispute the importance of language skills. Unfortunately, the national reports calling for reform have been loud and clear about this goal, but virtually silent about the means for attaining it. The Carnegie report, for example, recommends that high schools require all freshmen to take a one-year basic English course with emphasis on writing, that all students take a one-semester speech course, and that speech and writing be emphasized in every class. Bill Honig, California superintendent of public instruction and a prominent figure in the school reform movement, has proclaimed that students should read great works of literature; that the English curriculum should include speech training, vocabulary development, and study of correct usage; and that teachers of all subject matter should emphasize oral and written language skills.

These recommendations from advocates of school reform like the Carnegie Foundation and Honig add up to little more than lists of subjects, topics, and skills. They are missing vital ingredients: concrete suggestions for improving classroom pedagogy. In many of the reports and documents calling for reform there is the implication that instructional methods need no improvement, that the organization of classrooms and the style of interaction within them are adequate to teach all students to read, write, and speak English fluently. In this chapter I argue that nothing could be further from the truth. More requirements and higher standards will not accomplish the goals of the school reform movement. Unless the reform movement focuses on methods for helping students to acquire greater language proficiency, it runs the risk of accomplishing no fundamental school reforms at all.

The lack of concrete strategies for improving pedagogy in language and language arts is particularly problematic for the education of low-income, minority, and other at-risk students. Indeed, the reform movement can be criticized for ignoring the problems of at-risk students in its calls for higher standards. Chester Finn, one of the leading spokesmen for the reform movement, has argued that excellence and equity are not mutually exclusive goals. However, neither he nor other leaders of the reform movement have offered any practical ideas for improving the educational achievement of minority students. He states:

I do not contend that no problems will arise if a sudden, sharp escalation of educational standards, *especially one unaccompanied by adequate efforts to assist people to meet those standards*, leads to failure rates that are both absolutely high and disproportionately experienced by members of low-income or minority groups.[3]

Finn does not explain just what those adequate efforts to assist low-income or minority group members would be. Current methods have failed large numbers of such students. Despite federally funded programs that provide additional tutoring and academic assistance to at-risk students, nearly 40 percent of low-income and minority students are functionally illiterate when they leave high school. Paying lip service to the need for "adequate efforts" to help such students begs the question: *How* do we help at-risk students to achieve excellence?

Language is fundamental. If the reform movement is to succeed in raising the level of academic achievement for all students, it must address itself to the special language problems of minority students. For many at-risk and minority students, the language or dialect learned at home and in the community differs from the language of the school. American educators have long recognized that English is the first priority for students who come to school speaking, for example, Spanish, Vietnamese, or Tagalog. What they have not always recognized or adequately addressed is that many low-income and minority students speak dialects of English that differ significantly from the Standard English dialect used at public school. Black English, Hawaiian Creole, and Appalachian English are just a few of the many varieties of English that are the "mother tongue" of vast numbers of American students.

The nonstandard dialects of English spoken by many low-income and minority students often differ significantly from Standard English. Linguists have discovered that low income and minority students who come to public school speaking nonstandard dialects do not speak an impoverished, incorrect version of English, but a dialect that differs in some important ways from the oral and written language of the school. A respect for the linguistic heritage of nonstandard dialect speakers does not imply that public schools should abandon the teaching of Standard English. Without proficiency in Standard English, many minority students will continue to face formidable obstacles to academic success. Just as a speaker of Spanish must master English in order to obtain access to the mainstream of educated, literate American society, so must a speaker of Black English master the Standard English of literature, textbooks, and classroom discourse. The many similarities between nonstandard dialects and Standard English should not mislead us into minimizing the difficulties that many young schoolchildren sometimes face when they try to read, write, and speak Standard English. There is much to be gained by considering some speakers of nonstandard dialects as (Standard) English-as-a-second-language learners who face many of the same problems and obstacles as any other non-native English speaker. The reform movement has not taken these difficulties seriously, and until it does, it will not adequately address the educational needs of vast numbers of our students.

Here, then, is the problem for the school reform movement: Current teaching methods and classroom practices have failed to provide large numbers of our students with the language arts and communication skills necessary for school success. How can these language skills be taught and nurtured in public school? Fortunately, scholars have learned a great deal in recent years about those factors which promote language and literacy development. This new knowledge is the result of more than two decades of intensive research in homes, communities, and classrooms in locations as diverse as London, Boston, Los Angeles, rural South Carolina, and Hawaii. Scholars trained in education, linguistics, psychology, sociology, and anthropology have contributed their expertise toward a greater understanding of the development of language and literacy. This research suggests that major changes will be required in the way that language is taught and used in the classroom if children's language skills are to improve significantly. True reform will require rethinking and restructuring language arts instruction, not just more of the same old thing.

There are three relatively new domains of knowledge that can provide important insights and directions for reform. The first concerns language development in the home. It may seem odd to begin a discussion of the reform of language arts instruction in public schools by examining, in some depth, the way that toddlers learn to speak in the home. But children's homes are the most effective language schools in existence. By examining the process of first-language development in the home we can learn a great deal about those factors which encourage and assist language development in any setting. These factors have received little or no attention in school reform proposals, yet research suggests that they may be critical for the accomplishment of a central goal of school reform: improved language proficiency.

A second important body of knowledge that has been largely ignored in the school reform literature concerns language use in the classroom. Considering the central role of the classroom in the educational process, it is shocking that proponents of school reform have focused so little attention on the classroom as a learning environment. How can the classroom be made a more effective locus for language learning? The most important ingredient for language development in the home—the opportunity for sustained, communicative discourse with more able speakers—is virtually absent in today's public school classrooms. The implications of this finding for the reform of classroom practice are clear and direct: students need more opportunities to speak and communicate if they are to develop the necessary skills.

A third critical topic is the development of literacy. Successful students come to public school with oral language skills and a set of early literacy experiences in the home that provide the foundation for mastery of the written language. Students whose home language differs from the language of the school and students whose early experiences do not include exposure to literacy may need the school to provide a very different form of instruction than is typical in primary classrooms. A number of new approaches to the teaching of reading and writing incorporate what we have learned about literacy development into successful language arts programs. These successful programs provide guidelines for a new language arts pedagogy. School reform efforts that do not encourage public schools to adopt the most important features of these proven approaches will be doomed to repeat the mistakes of earlier, unsuccessful attempts at school reform.

In the remainder of this chapter I will describe some of the knowledge that we have gained in these three related areas and show how this knowledge can be applied to the problem of language and literacy instruction. A greater understanding of language development in the home, language use in the classroom, and the development of literacy will help to explain how the language and literacy problems that have been identified by the school reform movement arose, the deficiencies in the current school reform agenda, and what must be done in order to promote effective and lasting reform of language and literacy instruction.

LANGUAGE DEVELOPMENT IN THE HOME

The process of learning to speak is one of the most mysterious accomplishments of early childhood. Within three years children advance from uttering a few simple words like "mama," "cookie," and "no" to producing complex sentences with conditional clauses and time connectives, like this one uttered by a child at his fourth birthday party: "If you give me the big present, I'll open it up right away so I can see what's inside, and *then* I'll open up *your* present." Children so young that they can't yet tie their shoes are able to master grammatically complex forms like those in the sentence above without any formal instruction. The apparent ease and speed with which young children acquire their native tongue is even more remarkable when we consider how difficult it is to learn a language in school. (It is well to remember how few students who *do* speak Standard English ever achieve even minimal levels of foreign language proficiency as a result of foreign language instruction in school!) It has been said—not entirely facetiously—that if children had to learn their first language in school, we would be a nation of linguistic incompetents.

What makes young children's language development in the home even more remarkable is that the ability to understand and produce complicated sentences is not simply the result of rote memorization. More than twenty-five years of intensive research has demonstrated that children actively engage in a process of understanding the complex grammatical rules that underlie their language. This knowledge is implicit—children cannot state the rules of grammar, but they use the language in a systematic, rule-governed way. Ironically, some of the most convincing evidence for children's implicit rule knowledge comes from the errors that they make. It is very common for young children to make mistakes like "two feets," "I goed there," or "I eated my ice cream." Errors like these are called overregularization. Children have actually figured out the regular rule for forming the plural or past tense and have applied it to irregular forms. They have, in a sense, improved upon the language. Systematic errors like the above in young children's language are a sign of progress, and they provide important clues about the process of language development.

These research findings have a number of implications for school reform. First, in the natural home environment children do not learn to speak through rote drill and memorization of isolated sentences. All of the major reports on school reform stress the importance of fluency and correct usage. Research on natural language development suggests that these ends can be achieved without resorting to the meaningless drills and rote memorization of isolated rules that were so odious to earlier generations of students and are still inflicted upon students. Second, grammatical usage is naturally learned in the context of interesting and meaningful conversation with proficient speakers. Meaningless drills of sentence forms or grammatical rules taken out of a conversational context are, at best, a waste of valuable time. There is no evidence that grammatical forms learned through rote drill ever carry over to actual oral or written speech. This is not meant to imply that practice is unimportant—to the contrary! Students must hear and practice well-formed sentences, but they must hear and practice them in the context of meaningful oral and written communication.

Another implication of this research for school reform is that children need not be "taught" grammar in order to learn the grammar of their language. Children can learn the abstract grammatical rules of their language without being able to state those rules explicitly. This is not meant to imply that grammar instruction should have no place in the curriculum. Virtually all of the reports on school reform highlight grammar as a critical component of the curriculum. Research on natural language development suggests, however, that students need not be taught grammatical rules in order to produce rule-governed oral and written language. In the natural process of language development, children develop this "metalinguistic" knowledge only *after* they have learned to understand and produce the relevant grammatical forms. Few educated people in this country however, have even a rudimentary understanding of the nature of human language, the principles by which languages change over time, or the often elegant rules underlying our own spoken and written language. Linguistic research has shown that English grammar rules, as they have been traditionally taught, are actually misleading and inadequate descriptions of the English language. They bear little resemblance to the fascinating and complex grammatical rules underlying the English language that linguists have discovered in this century. An introduction to linguistics, such as the instructional series called Awareness of Language, would be a valuable addition to the secondary English curriculum, and one that has been universally overlooked in the school reform movement.

Still another finding from child language development is that mistakes are often a sign of progress. Overregularization errors, for example, demonstrate the child's understanding of the basic grammatical rules. This implies that efforts at reforming the English and language arts curriculum will be most successful if errors are expected and tolerated in the course of language development. There is a danger that the quest for excellence emphasized in the school reform movement could lead to an intolerance for errors. Nothing could be more detrimental to language learning. Students who are afraid to make errors are afraid to speak. Errors are a normal and necessary component of language learning. Furthermore, since errors often reflect the generalizations that learners have made, they can provide useful diagnostic information for teachers.

There are a number of other discoveries about natural language development that are directly relevant to efforts at reforming the language arts curriculum. One rather unexpected finding concerns the role of praise or other forms of direct reinforcement in language learning. Many people assume that children learn to talk by being praised and otherwise reinforced for producing the correct words and grammatical forms. Surprisingly, explicit praise and correction are relatively unimportant factors in language development. In fact, adults rarely praise or correct young children's grammar and pronunciation. Instead, adults seem to look beyond the immature grammar and pronunciation to the meaning of children's utterances. Children often hear praise even when they produce incorrect forms. For example, when one child said, "Mama isn't a boy, he a girl," her mother quite naturally responded, "That's right." Children also receive negative feedback when their grammar is correct. When one little boy said, "And Walt Disney comes on Tuesday," his mother replied, "No, he doesn't." In those rare cases where parents do attempt to correct children's grammar, they discover that it is often a frustrating endeavor.[4]

Many proponents of school reform have stressed the importance of encouraging and rewarding student achievement. An understanding of natural language development in the home suggests that explicit praise or correction may be precisely the wrong method for encouraging achievement in language. Imagine what a deflating experience it would be if you were trying to tell your friend about a wonderful restaurant you discovered and your friend constantly interrupted you with statements like "Good talking!" or "You should say 'whom,' not 'who,' in that sentence." Students who are constantly praised or corrected can become self-conscious, reluctant participants in classroom interaction. It is not enough, then, for reformers to exhort teachers to reward good performance. Some attention must be given to the best means for encouraging students' often imperfect efforts.

If language is not naturally acquired by rote imitation, praise and correction, or learning grammar rules, how is it learned? In the past decade a number of scholars have discovered that parents and other caretakers use a very specialized speech style when they speak to children—a speech style that seems ideally suited to assist children in the language-learning process. Catherine Snow and Jacqueline Sachs, noted investigators of parent-child interaction, found that parents in our culture encourage development by treating even very young infants as if they are capable of intentionally participating in a conversation. They treat every cough, coo, and burp as a potential conversational turn, indirectly teaching infants a great deal about the structure of conversations.

As infants gradually progress from coos to babbles to syllables, parents encourage their verbalizations and (to the great amusement of onlookers) behave as if the infants are making meaningful contributions to the conversational exchange. When infants become toddlers, their conversational role increases. With a combination of gestures, babbled syllables, and words, toddlers are able to express a wide range of communicative functions. They use their limited linguistic repertoires to make requests and demands, to ask questions, and to initiate conversations. Parents encourage these efforts by responding and trying to make sense of their children's contributions to conversations.

In the successful home environment, proficient speakers encourage less proficient children to communicate. Adults give even the least proficient children extensive opportunities to participate in conversations. The implication of this finding for school reform is clear: Children must talk in order to learn to talk. This straightforward idea seems almost too obvious to state. However, in order to implement this idea, dramatic changes in our conception of the well-run classroom may be required. Students who are quietly listening to a teacher, occasionally raising their hands to answer questions with a brief word or sentence, do not have adequate opportunities to use and develop complex language. Opportunity to communicate with proficient speakers provides the foundation for language development, yet the school reform movement has virtually ignored the important role of conversation in the classroom.

In addition to encouraging children to talk, parents and caretakers provide other forms of assistance to young language learners. As soon as young children demonstrate some understanding of words, parents begin to use short, syntactically simple, well-formed sentences. They speak in higher pitch with exaggerated intonation, they use a simplified vocabulary, and they repeat and expand on their own and their children's utterances. These and other unconscious modifications of adult speech provide children with simple, clear, well-formed models of language—models that sometimes sound like miniature language lessons. Catherine Snow recorded one mother instructing her child to put away a toy: "Put the red truck in the box now. The red truck. No, the *red* truck. In the box. The red truck in the box."[5] This mother repeated words and phrases, accommodating her language to aid her child's comprehension. Although she certainly did not intend to teach language structure, her repetitions and paraphrases may have done just that by helping her child to pick out the individual words and phrases from the stream of speech.

The point is this: Adults modify their speech in order to communicate more easily with their children. How can this finding be translated into practice by school reformers? Fortunately, research suggests that public school teachers will not need specialized training in order to adapt their own language to their students' levels. All that is required is for teachers, like parents, to have ample opportunity to converse with students and a genuine interest in communicating with them. It is crucial to recognize that the helpful modifications parents make in their speech with children are natural and automatic only when they arise in meaningful conversation. Deliberate attempts by teachers to simplify their language that are not motivated by communicative need will justifiably be interpreted by their students as "talking down." Once again, the point to be made is that conversation is a vital tool in primary language instruction.

There is evidence that many other characteristics of parents' everyday conversations with children are helpful for language development and can be utilized by teachers in the classroom. Of particular importance is the tendency of parents to talk about topics that the child introduces or that are relevant to the child's focus of interest and attention. Conversations between parents and young children are in the "here and now," and are responsive to the children's communicative intentions. Parents clarify and expand children's utterances, provide models of appropriate adult sentences, and follow up on their children's initiation of topics. Investigators have discovered that children whose parents follow their lead in this way learn language more rapidly than those whose parents do not.[6] When adults assist children's comprehension and engage their attention by talking about topics of interest and direct relevance to the children, the children make more rapid progress in language development.

The implications of this finding for school reform are clear here, too, and its importance goes far beyond efforts to improve language proficiency. Students attend and learn best when they can relate the material being taught to their own interests, experiences, and prior knowledge. Many of the proposals for school reform emphasize the importance of helping students to establish these links. What they do not stress, however, is the need for flexibility in the curriculum to accommodate the diverse backgrounds and interests of students. Teachers must feel free to follow up on students' comments and expressed interests and occasionally to follow the students' lead in class discussions and in topics of study. The reform movement, with its emphasis on teacher accountability, is hardly conducive to this sort of flexibility. Teachers who feel pressured to "cover the material" will be reluctant to relinquish the floor to a student who is struggling to express a complex idea.

Parents and other caretakers do not make the sorts of conversational adjustments described in the literature on natural language development in order to teach their children to talk; their behavior is a natural consequence of trying to understand and be understood by children with limited language abilities. The goal of everyday interactions between adults and children is communication. The incidental consequence of this goal is a style that seems ideally tailored to fit the needs of a young language novice. Without any formal instruction, children learn the grammar of their language by hearing adult forms modeled, by having their own sentences expanded, and by using language in a variety of situations and circumstances. Most important, children learn to talk in large part because they have something to say. Roland Tharp and Ronald Gallimore, two researchers who have been concerned for many years with the language and literacy development of language-minority students, emphasize this point:

From the child's point of view, language occurs when and where there is something to communicate: "teaching" takes place in goal-directed activity. Language learning is not the goal: The child learns language as means to an end.[7]

To reiterate, communication is at the heart of language development in the home. Adults do not deliberately modify their language in order to teach, but in order to communicate better with their young children. When adults are genuinely interested in what their children have to say, the modifications in their own language that facilitate language development are unconscious and automatic.

Children's homes and neighborhoods are remarkably successful environments for learning a mother tongue—the language of the local community. But, as we noted earlier, the Standard American English necessary for school achievement is not the home or community language of large numbers of students in our public schools. These students must learn Standard English in public school. This is crucial for the attainment of both excellence and equity. Even those children who come from homes in which Standard American English is spoken have a great deal of language to learn during the school years. They must gain facility with relatively rare grammatical structures like passives and complex sentences with multiple embedded clauses; they must expand their vocabularies; and they must learn to use language as an effective tool for persuasion, explanations, directions, narratives, and a variety of new communicative ends. Finally, and most importantly, a major task for all students during the public school years is mastery of the written language.

If the school reform movement is to accomplish its goals, the public schools, especially the public elementary schools, must provide an environment conducive to language learning. All too often, however, schools fail at this task, since many students graduating from high school have not mastered Standard English—the language that will permit access to a rich cultural heritage, to higher education, and to a wide range of employment opportunities. Still other students cannot adequately use the written language. In order to understand the failure of many students to master both oral and written English, a number of investigators have turned their attention to the language environment of the classroom. A close examination of the way language is used in classrooms helps to explain this failure and demonstrates just how much work needs to be done in order to bring about effective reform.

LANGUAGE IN THE CLASSROOM

Language in the classroom, even in the elementary school classroom, differs markedly from language in the home. Thousands of hours of recorded classroom interaction demonstrate one major finding: Classroom language is nonconversational. Teachers do virtually all of the talking. John I. Goodlad, in *A Place Called School*, described the situation in the classrooms he visited: "We observed that, on the average, about 75% of class time was spent on instruction and that nearly 70% of this was "talk"—usually teacher to students."[8] Study after study has shown that the dominant form of classroom interaction is recitation. Recitation is a series of rapid-fire unrelated teacher questions that require brief factual answers in a display of student knowledge, frequently only a simple "yes" or "no." In a recitation only rarely are the teachers' follow-up questions responsive to the students' answers. The conversational role of students is limited to an occasional brief response, and some students say nothing in the course of the entire teaching period. The teachers set the agenda, ask the questions, and evaluate the answers.

Even in kindergarten, children have few opportunities to initiate discourse with adults. The goal of student interaction with a teacher is often not communication but the display of factual knowledge. Gallimore and Tharp conclude: "Five-year-old children . . . talk significantly less in the classroom than at home. The teachers tend to ignore children, talk over them, and generally dominate the proceedings."[9] The passive conversational role expected of students is so persuasive that teachers even judge school readiness by a child's ability to take on the role of the nontalker. An acquaintance of mine was recently advised by a kindergarten teacher not to enroll her five-year-old in kindergarten because "he asks too many questions."

This passive role of students, so consistently documented in American public school classrooms, may provide an explanation for the failure of large numbers of students to become proficient language users. Put quite simply—students have few opportunities to talk. They do not learn to develop ideas verbally, to relate events, or to use language to fulfill the range of communicative functions that constitute a complete command of the English language. Because they do not converse regularly with teachers or more able classmates, they do not hear their own utterances elaborated, nor do they receive feedback on their communicative abilities. On the other hand, teachers receive little feedback from students and thus have few cues to guide their own attempts to adjust their language to match students' abilities. And, since students are not encouraged to elaborate on simple answers to questions, they receive little assistance in establishing links between the teachers' topics and their own interests and experiences. We now know that these links can help to solidify students' comprehension and mastery of the material. By paying so little attention to the nature of classroom interaction, the school reform movement has overlooked a serious problem in the educational process that must be rectified before we can expect significant improvements in students' command of English.

When teachers use a recitation style of interaction, they often have an explicit answer in mind that they expect the student to produce. For students with limited English proficiency, this often results in a focus on the form rather than the content of the student's contribution. The following example of a conversation from a high school math class for English-as-a-second-language students, illustrates how ineffective the recitation can be:

The teacher wants the student to say "The sentences in Group A are number sentences, while the sentences in Group B are set sentences."

Ro: The group . . . the group A . . .
Teacher: The sentences . . .
Ro: The sentences . . . the sentences . . .
Teacher: in group . . .

Ro: of group . . .
Teacher: . . . in . . .
Ro: in group A is a number sentence
Teacher: . . . ses . . .
Ro: Sentences, while the . . . set B . . . is set . . . set
Teacher: (chuckles) Who can say it again? (Four more students are called on to produce the answer, only one of whom does it without error.)[10]

This is just the reverse of the situation in the natural language learning environment of the home. The teacher's focus on the form of the sentence obscures its meaning and discourages student involvement. But correction of form need not be so disruptive of meaning. Parents indirectly (and usually unconsciously) correct form by affirming the child's meaning and expanding or modeling the form. Fortunately teachers can, and sometimes do, behave the same way. Take this example. When one student in an elementary science class responded to a question by saying, "It might get ate," his teacher responded, "It might get eaten by something else, yeah." This teacher very naturally acknowledged the correct meaning contained in the answer while expanding and modeling the correct grammatical form. It is this kind of responsive attention to meaning that fosters both linguistic and conceptual development.

Unfortunately, this type of interaction is rare, especially in classrooms with disadvantaged or language-minority students. The very students who could benefit most from opportunities to engage in meaningful conversation with a teacher are the least likely to receive them. John Hyland, while conducting research for his doctoral dissertation at UCLA, observed hundreds of hours of classroom interaction in junior high school social studies classes in a large urban school district in which 90 percent of the students were Hispanic. Like Gallimore and Tharp, Hyland observed that sustained, communicative discourse between the teacher and students was virtually absent. "Teachers," he notes, "routinely ignored student utterances and seldom made use of student ideas as opportunities to engage in an exchange of knowledge."[11] In most classrooms for students with limited English proficiency, there is an emphasis on rote drill and memorization of isolated sentences, a focus on learning the grammatical rules, little tolerance for errors, and extensive use of explicit praise and correction. Thus, the very features that do *not* appear to be helpful for natural language development in the home are present in abundance in these classrooms. Communicatively driven conversation, the foundation of language interaction in the home, is virtually absent.

Teachers in the public schools who want to improve their students' language proficiency face a formidable set of problems. They are expected to teach students of widely varying experiences, temperaments, and abilities; to follow curriculum guidelines set forth at the state and local levels; to be accountable for student progress; and to monitor students' mastery of language as well as of specific subject matter. Proponents of school reform have not offered new techniques for solving these problems, but have simply called for *more*—more classes, more

homework, more instructional time, more rigor, more depth, and more accountability. What we now know about language development in the home and language use in the classroom suggests that effective reform will have to involve
rethinking and restructuring the nature of student-teacher interaction in the classroom.

What directions should such interaction take? One very effective approach is
small-group peer interaction or "cooperative learning" in which small groups
of students work together to solve problems and to master new material. Small-
group interaction has been used by many teachers in order to improve student
learning and motivation, and to help teachers manage large classes. This tech-
nique has the potential to enhance language development as well. Small-group
interaction can extend the number of opportunities that students have to engage
in intended and elaborated conversations. When students of varying abilities are
grouped together, less proficient students can benefit from the language modeled
by their more proficient peers.

Perhaps the most ambitious use of this type of small-group instruction is that
taken in the Kamehameha Early Education Project (KEEP). In KEEP, teachers
use a combination of whole-group and small-group activities, but at least half
of the children's day from kindergarten through third grade is spent in the small-
group learning centers. Some of these small groups are teacher-directed and
others are cooperative activity centers. Children in the cooperative activity centers
are encouraged to help each other and to discuss their work with each other.
Interestingly, children shift frequently from the role of the assister to the role
of the assisted. The cooperative behavior observed in the KEEP learning centers
is rooted in the children's native Hawaiian culture. Children with other cultural
backgrounds will often require teacher assistance and training in order to interact
cooperatively. But with a judicious selection of activities, materials, and problems, teachers can structure the centers to maximize cooperative verbal interaction. As we have seen, this sustained interaction is crucial for the students'
language development.

In the teacher-directed small groups at KEEP, teachers use conversation as
the primary medium of instruction. They help students to relate formal subject
matter to their own experiences through extensive discussion. These small-group
interactions are both subject matter teaching activities and language development
activities par excellence. Small-group instruction such as that developed at KEEP
holds great promise for improving students' English language skills, and deserves
a major place in school reform proposals.

THE DEVELOPMENT OF LITERACY

One of the primary functions of education is to teach literacy—reading and
writing. Although formal literacy instruction begins with a child's first encounter
with formal schooling, the roots of literacy can be traced to the preschool years.
The children who are best prepared for literacy instruction speak and understand

Standard English—the oral language dialect that most closely resembles written English. But there are other sorts of knowledge and experience that may be just as crucial. Those children who are best prepared to learn to read and write come to school already knowing some rather sophisticated things about oral language, books, and the printed word. They have learned about the structure of narrative by telling stories and recounting everyday events. They know that books contain stories, and that these stories can be read aloud and understood in much the same way that their own narratives and ordinary conversation are understood. They often know that utterances are made up of words and that the blank spaces that appear on the printed pages indicate word boundaries. Some children even know that words are spelled with letters that roughly correspond to the sounds in the spoken language. Most important, many children come to school with the expectation that they will learn to read and write—to decipher and produce the written code. They look forward to their initiation into the ranks of the literate. These children are prepared for school.

It is widely recognized that there is a great achievement gap between children who are prepared for literacy instruction and those who are not. Children with this sort of preparation can be expected to learn to read and write without serious difficulties, while those who do not have this preparation may experience frustration and early failure. What distinguishes the two groups? The prepared children come from homes in which exposure to the written language is an ordinary part of everyday life. They see adults reading for information and for pleasure, they are read to on a regular basis from the time they utter their first words, and they are encouraged to play with language—to produce nonsense words, rhymes, stories, and scribbled "words." The unprepared children have much more limited exposure to written language and are rarely read to. They are often not encouraged to make up stories or to recall the day's events in narrative form. Their early attempts at writing are ignored or discounted. Often the unprepared children speak one language or dialect at home and a different one at school. The effects of children's preschool literacy experiences on later school achievement are often profound. For example, it has been demonstrated over and over again that the number of books that children have and the number of hours that they are read to are among the best predictors of later reading achievement.

Disproportionate numbers of children who lack this sort of preparation come from low-income and minority homes. However, it is not income or ethnicity that determines preparedness, but the amount and kinds of early literacy experiences that families engage in. Tharp and Gallimore, the investigators whose work was described above, have focused on the educational problems of low-achieving minority children. They point out that the relative lack of literacy experiences in disadvantaged children's homes does not result from a lack of interest in or concern for school achievement at home. Instead, it seems to stem from a lack of experience with or understanding of the kinds of activities that promote children's literacy development. Tharp and Gallimore observe: "In our own work, it is evident that first-grade children who begin school in relative innocence of written language . . . first experience written text as unconnected to reality. These marks on paper or chalkboard are meaningful—if at all—only in their mysterious internal relationships.''[12]

Margaret Donaldson, an internationally renowned psychologist and student of language, has proposed three conceptual problems faced by such disadvantaged children when they first encounter written language. The children must have some idea of what reading is all about, they must be aware of words and that the marks they see on paper are versions of speech, and they must recognize the special purposes of text—that it can be an aid to memory, a means of recording speech, or a means of communicating over time and space. When the language of minority children's homes differs from the language of the school, these conceptual problems are compounded. Not only do minority children lack the rather sophisticated understanding of the functions and conventions of written language, but the written language appears to have no connection to the spoken language. How are these children to make the connection between written and oral language? For many of these children the reading activities in school make little or no sense!

The results of this lack of preparation for literacy can be devastating. Many minority and low-income students have great difficulty learning to read and write. Although the school reform movement has drawn attention to the sad result of this lack of preparation in the preschool years, it has not adequately addressed the causes of the problem or its solutions. In order for school reform to be effective for *all* students, the disparity between prepared and unprepared children must be eliminated. Until the school reform movement focuses on the early school years, there is little hope of changing the status quo. Efforts aimed at improving the written language proficiency of American students must begin by recognizing the difficulties faced by children with limited preschool literacy experience. Those relationships that literate educators take for granted, the sophisticated notions about text that many children have acquired before they start school, can no longer be assumed to be the background of *all* children who begin school. If some children come to public school without the necessary preparation for literacy, then the public schools will have to provide it, beginning no later than kindergarten.

But how can these problems be addressed in efforts to reform literacy instruction? Two recent approaches to literacy instruction hold great promise. The first was developed as part of the KEEP project mentioned earlier. Children in the KEEP project schools are native Hawaiians whose home language is Hawaiian Creole. Native Hawaiian children are among the lowest-achieving ethnic minorities in the United States. In the KEEP classrooms, reading, writing, and speaking are linked in early instruction. Children's oral language skills are developed in the instructional conversations that teachers lead during independent small-group interaction. The primary focus of reading instruction is comprehension, not decoding skills. Children are introduced to written text as an extension of their own jointly produced spoken texts. The first texts that they read are those created by small groups of children in the course of recording everyday experiences. Thus, the purposes of text are no longer mysterious. Children who have attended KEEP schools have markedly higher reading achievement levels than their counterparts in the community.

The other successful approach was pioneered by Donald Graves and his associates in New Hampshire. Their approach, recently adopted by the California Writing Project and writing programs in many other states, uses natural language development as the model for teaching reading and writing. Students learn to read and write by keeping journals that begin with their own drawings and gradually incorporate words, often in the students' own invented spelling. As students become interested in sharing their stories, their texts become a form of written communication. Invented spelling gradually disappears when students recognize the advantages of a conventional spelling system as an aid to communication. Students learn how to revise and edit their own written work. This form of literacy instruction encourages students to think of themselves as writers as well as readers, and one very important goal of this approach to writing instruction is to help students find their written "voice." Like that developed at KEEP, this method introduces reading, writing, and speaking as related activities with a communicative function. The students' first reading texts are those created by themselves and their peers.

These two approaches provide some guidelines for introducing students to literacy in a way that makes the functions of text, and its relation to spoken language, obvious from the outset. Although the school reform movement did not initially address these issues, a number of state and local school districts have begun to implement aspects of these approaches. California's new language arts curriculum guidelines, in fact, incorporate many of the key elements of Graves's writing program. The school reform movement can, and must, lead the way toward similar innovations in literacy instruction throughout the country.

CONCLUSION

Language is the core of the educational process. The school reform movement, while identifying some of the results of inadequate language arts instruction, has overlooked many of the underlying causes of the problem. The purpose of this chapter was to describe some of these underlying causes and to propose solutions based on what we have learned about natural language development in the home, the language environment of the classroom, and literacy development. This is knowledge that should be exploited by the reform movement in order to provide guidelines for effective reform of language and literacy instruction.

If the school reform movement is to be successful, it must, first and foremost, turn its attention to the early elementary school grades. It is during these years that the foundation of literacy is built. Beginning with kindergarten and continuing throughout the school years, the classroom must become a place where students are encouraged to communicate—in both oral and written form. All students, but especially those with limited English proficiency, must have opportunities for extended instructional conversations with teachers and peers. Language is learned in the course of conversation with more able speakers. Without opportunities for such conversation in the classroom, there is little hope that students will become proficient speakers of Standard English. When the goal of classroom talk is genuine communication and exchange of information between teachers and students, rather than recitation and drill, the classroom will become a successful language learning environment.

Those students who do not come to public school with the preliteracy background that is so beneficial for learning to read and write depend upon the public school to remedy this deficit. The programs that have been most successful have helped students to develop an awareness of the sounds of oral language, to learn the form of oral narratives, to become familiar with the purposes and joys of books and written language, and to appreciate the complex relationship between text and talk. Language arts and literacy instruction that incorporates a foundation in these prerequisite skills gives students the opportunity to succeed. The reform movement can and must turn to this new knowledge of language and literacy development. If it incorporates the important implications of these new discoveries, language arts and literacy need not be the endangered core of school reform.

NOTES

1. Olsen, D. (1977), From utterance to text: The bias of language in speech and writing, *Harvard Educational Review*, *47*(3), 257.

2. Boyer, E. L. (1983), *High school: A report on secondary education in America* (New York: Harper & Row), p. 103.

3. Finn, C. E., Jr. (1985), The challenges of educational excellence, In C. E. Finn, Jr., D. Ravitch, & P. H. Roberts (Eds.), *Challenges to the humanities* (New York: Holmes and Meier), p. 198. Emphasis added.

4. McNeill, D. (1966), Developmental psycholinguistics, in F. Smith & G. A. Miller (Eds.), *The genesis of language: A psycholinguistic approach* (New York: Cambridge University Press), p. 69.

5. Snow, C. E. (1972), Mothers' speech to children learning language, *Child Development*, *4*, 4.

6. Wells, G. (1981), Becoming a communicator. In G. Wells (Ed.), *Learning through interaction: The study of language development* (New York: Cambridge University Press).

7. Tharp, R. G., & Gallimore, R. (1988), *Rousing minds to life: Teaching, learning, and schooling in social context* (New York: Cambridge University Press), p. 95.

8. Goodlad, J. I. (1984), *A place called school: Prospects for the future* (New York: McGraw-Hill), p. 229.

9. Tharp & Gallimore, *Rousing minds to life*, p. 95.

10. Cazden, C. B. (1987), English for academic purposes: The student talk register, *English Education*, *19*(1), p. 33.

11. Hyland, J. T. (1984), Teaching about the constitution: Relationships between

teachers' subject matter knowledge, pedagogic beliefs, and instructional decision making (unpublished Ph.D. dissertation, University of California, Los Angeles), pp. 382–83.

    12. Tharp & Gallimore, *Rousing minds to life*, p. 98.

SUGGESTED READINGS

Donaldson, M. (1978). *Children's minds*. New York: W. W. Norton & Co.

Gleason, J. (1989). *The development of language* (2nd ed.). New York: Charles E. Merrill.

Graves, D., & Stuart, V. (1985). *Write from the start: Tapping your child's natural writing potential*. New York: NAL/Penguin. (Signet).

Hawkins, E. (Ed.). (1984). *Awareness of language* (series). Cambridge: Cambridge University Press.

MacLure, M., & French, P. (1981). A Comparison of talk at home and at school. In G. Wells (Ed.), *Learning through interaction: The study of language development*. New York: Cambridge University Press.

Olsen, D. (1977). From utterance to text: The bias of language in speech and writing. *Harvard Educational Review*, *47*(3), 257–81.

Snow, C. E. (1972). Mothers' speech to children learning language. *Child Development*, *4*, 1–22.

Tharp, R. G., & Gallimore, R. (1988). *Rousing Minds to life: Teaching, learning, and schooling in social context*. New York: Cambridge University Press.

11   The Politics of School Reform

James S. Catterall and Harry Handler

When Americans get serious about fundamental changes in their public schools, heated politics may be the only certain result. For one reason, the economic stakes are huge. School systems account for more than half of state and local government spending and employ more than one out of every twenty five adults in the national work force. For another reason, conflicting views of the good society are usually the true subjects of school reform debates. Just whose views (and whose children) will gain are inevitably the real topics of educational controversy.

The current "excellence movement" offers clear illustrations of both the importance we attach to our public schools and the stakes a host of players attach to the terms of educational change. In this chapter, we suggest that insights into the prospects for educational "excellence" can be gained through an analysis of the politics of school reform campaigns. The politics we describe are found in two arenas. The first concerns those people and groups who initiate calls for school reform and help to shape reform legislation. The second concerns the actions of those officials and professional educators who are required to implement school reform. We argue that politics molds both the substance of any school reform agenda (and ultimately the regulations that guide public schools toward change) and the reception given this agenda as school professionals proceed to carry it out. No reform is in place until both unfold. And both are fundamentally political processes.

This chapter is organized into three sections. In the first we present some critical lessons culled from the politics of previous attempts to "reform" the public schools. An overriding message stands out: if the past is any guide, we should be cautious about projecting grand reform expectations. We then turn to the politics of educational excellence. Drawing comparisons between this contemporary school reform campaign and earlier school reform efforts, we trace the emergence, adoption, and implementation of its unprecedented slate of standards-raising provisions, focusing on the key individuals and groups who contributed to the development or implementation of these reforms, and whose preferences or values have helped to shape the outcomes of the excellence movement thus far. In a final section, we discuss some emerging reactions to the excellence movement and speculate on what its longer-term effects may be.

Since we draw on experiences with recent reforms, we should begin by stating what is meant by the term "reform" and just which reform efforts have proved illuminating. There are two apparent definitions of reform, at least based on its application to our schools. One is that reform means changes of substantial magnitude, involving realignments of goals or governing values, or major restructuring of how schools are organized, staffed, or run. A second definition (more in line with Webster's) is that a reform is an exercise in improvement through the abandonment of imperfections or faults. This definition implies that reforms need not be large-scale, but may instead be concerned with some judicious pruning here and there.

Recent educational reform movements in the United States provide examples of both kinds of reform. Some school reform campaigns were broad in scope and promised effects throughout the system—the current excellence movement is surely one such campaign. Other heralded reforms, while of momentous importance to some constituents and perhaps to the annals of educational politics, were more narrowly focused. The National Defense Education Act (NDEA) of 1958, a program intended to cultivate the nation's top science and mathematics students, was one such reform. The federal Elementary and Secondary Education Act (ESEA) of 1965, especially its Title I program designed to deliver educational services to poor children, was another, as was the Education for All Handicapped Children Act (EAHCA) of 1975. While the emergence of these more selective programs taught us much of what we believe about educational reform, it is interesting that together they would not have accounted for more than 5 percent of educational expenditures and could not be classified as sweeping calls for innovation or improvement.

Our discussion relies on three principal sources. One is an accumulation of scholarly analysis concerning the conditions under which schools change (and do not change). We supplement this with perspectives on the implementation of public policies and the cyclical nature of public concern for pressing social issues, views generated largely in the works of political scientists. We also rely on firsthand experience with attempts at legislative change—in one case (Catterall) as staff and consultant to state legislatures and school districts, and in another (Handler) as the superintendent of the nation's second largest school district. We turn now to the lessons of school reform campaigns that preceded today's excellence movement.

Perhaps the most crucial observation concerning government attempts to redirect the public school is that the public's will to sustain pressure and support for change tends to be short-lived. A number of reasons for this are captured in what one political scientist calls "the issue attention cycle."[1] According to this theory, public attention to an agreed-upon need for reform proceeds in a series of steps: alarmed discovery of a problem, search for solutions, euphoric mobilization of resources, institutionalization of responses, harsh realization that answers will be expensive and progress slow, and ultimately retreat and a shift of attention to another problem fueled by another alarmed discovery.

A classic case of education reform caught up in the issue attention cycle was the provision for federal assistance to poor children passed as part of the 1965 ESEA. This legislation came on the heels of the civil rights movement and was a conspicuous element of the Johnson administration's War on Poverty. The enthusiasm that greeted its passage waned quickly as early results showed few educational gains associated with the program and as Congress wrestled to pay for the Vietnam War. Similarly, the optimism that launched the NDEA in the late 1950s was dampened by realizations that its "new math" taxed Johnny's ability to add and subtract.

The issue attention cycle points to a difficult hurdle set before these and all reform movements. This is the fluid motivation of political officials who must ratify and fund school reform programs. Simply put, legislators will attach themselves to issues as long as they are perceived to be hot in the public's mind; but supporters are also quick to abandon an issue in order to stake out a leading position on the next captivating problem. Some professionals somewhat cynically refer to this behavior as keeping our slogans in front of our performance. This suggests that whatever progress is to be made in an education reform campaign should be realized in the short run. The long run may bring shortages of interest and support.

Our examination of past school reform campaigns suggests additional generalizations about these campaigns, described briefly here. First, each of the initiatives cited above—NDEA, ESEA, EAHCA—occurred at a time of economic expansion. It is reasonable to expect that budgetary optimism is a necessary condition for large-scale attempts to alter schools. (It is perhaps ironic that when the economy is doing well, the public schools are perceived as doing poorly; see our discussion below of the ties between the economic system and concerns for school performance.) Furthermore, the fact that periods of business expansion are cyclical and self-limiting may contribute to the attention cycle we described above. Second, we also see that a catalytic event is frequently associated with the onset of reform activity. The NDEA followed the successful launch of Sputnik by the Russians, and was seen as a national response to the threat of Soviet technological superiority. The ESEA followed the passage of the Civil Rights Act. As we elaborate below, the present excellence movement was touched off by the publication of *A Nation at Risk*. And third, it appears that major school reform campaigns are spread out, coming along every ten years or so since the 1950s. This suggests a pattern in which precipitating conditions tend to accumulate until they reach a critical mass that touches off reform activity.

Federal attempts to sponsor improvements in the education of the urban poor in the late 1960s brought new ways of thinking about public policy processes in the United States. Critical gaps between passed legislation and institutional behavior puzzled analysts. We discovered that policies created by the top leadership of a system undergo various adaptations as they proceed toward implementation, for instance, in the nation's classrooms. This means that enacting a school reform law, for example, does not imply certainty regarding the practices or products that will emerge in the schools. Critical links in tracking reforms to classroom practices include the parochial concerns and perceptions of what is needed held by various intermediate players, such as state, district, and school level officials, as well as teachers, all of whom must interpret and act on laws and regulations.

Another source of uncertainty regarding implementation of reform is what has been called the "loosely coupled" nature of our school systems. Rather than displaying authoritative lines of command, local, district, and state education systems are characterized by semiautonomous professional levels that frequently operate with incomplete information and inadequate resources, and in an environment that requires building voluntary consensus in order to produce action.

Yet another piece in the implementation puzzle is the pocket veto available to teachers and school administrators, who may close their classroom doors and proceed to teach or run their programs unfazed by either larger political events or mandates from on high. All in all, implementation politics suggests that a package of reform legislation can be expected to bring uncertain and variable effects on the education of children and adolescents at the classroom level.

Observers such as Stanford's Michael Kirst have documented the arrival and quick departure of a host of reforms designed to make the public schools better. A legendary group of such reforms emerged in the 1960s when scientific management and rational policy analysis were hot public ideas. All were attempted and soon scrapped. The short lives of these and other public school improvements have prompted Kirst and others in recent years to sift the accumulated record for educational changes that managed to stick. What emerged were educational innovations exhibiting three common qualities: they were structural in nature (having to do with how things are organized rather than the content of instruction), they acquired a constituency within or attached to the schools (a group that has a stake in sustaining the change), and they were easily monitored.

One educational innovation that stuck was large-scale pupil testing programs, which added a layer of structure to the school system, produced a professional constituency (the testing directors and developers), and yielded results that were readily observed by educators and lay persons alike. The success of the EAHCA of 1975 was another; this created a small but vocal contingent of special education professionals in the schools. Some have suggested that the only major change to have affected our public schools in the last 60 years was the unbolting of school desks. The school furnishing lobby probably had something to do with the persistence of this reform! In contrast, reforms that promised to improve pupil learning simply by directing teachers or administrators to change their ways, such as the "new math" or team teaching, had dismal and short histories.

The experiences described above evoke doubts about the eventual success of educational reform movements, including the ultimate outcome of the present excellence movement. The issue attention cycle suggests that change must happen quickly, to capitalize on the fleeting attention and support of politicians. The realities of implementation suggest that even clearly designed and well-focused educational reforms may undergo adaptations as school leaders and teachers put them into practice. Will reforms retain their intended character through this process? The "top-down" direction of the present school reforms may serve to undermine their support at the bottom rungs of the system, where the programs will succeed or fail. Finally, reforms that have lasted do not appear to affect the fundamental goals and mission of the schools but to create new functions for the system. Pressure for educational excellence has shown great staying power thus far, but it will be a unique success story if its effects last. We turn now to the unfolding story of the excellence movement, and particularly its politics.

By the excellence movement we refer to the years since 1983 of sustained public pressure for increased academic standards in the schools. The chief item on the agenda of school reform in the early years of the excellence movement was more stringent requirements for the high school diploma. At least forty states added course requirements for graduation, such as extra years of mathematics and social studies. Many installed or beefed up tests that had to be passed in order to graduate. Most states also initiated campaigns to "smarten up" high school course content and textbooks, many of which, it was claimed, were "dumbed down" during the 1970s.

Once these standards-raising types of changes were legislated, the excellence drive in many states turned its attention to the teaching force. Efforts to improve teacher training, to screen out unfit teacher candidates, and to render the job more professional through career ladders or merit pay schemes became commonplace. A few states, such as Texas and Arkansas, moved to dismiss incompetent teachers already employed in the public schools through statewide competency tests.

In this section, we describe the political evolution of the excellence movement, depicting a decade's accumulation of pressures for change, the catalytic publication of a scathing national commission report, a maelstrom of legislative activity to respond to what had all the markings of a deep national concern, and the implementation politics of the fifty state school systems.

From the professional educator's viewpoint, the arrival of a reform movement takes on the characteristics of a volcano. There is a lengthy period of time during which pressures build up; then suddenly, without warning, there is an eruption and a flurry of activity. The publication of *A Nation at Risk* in 1983 could be described in such terms. Not only did the appearance of this report catch many school district and system leaders by surprise, but most superintendents, school board members, and teacher union leaders were completely unaware that the National Commission on Excellence in Education had been incubating such a document. However, all three groups did know that the public schools were in trouble. A ground swell of change had been mounting for a number of years.

Dating back to the early 1970s, a variety of indicators showed poor and falling marks for the nation's public schools. Widespread efforts to make the high school curriculum more relevant had met with limited success. Not only had dropout rates refused to decrease, but the resulting menu of course offerings in our public high schools became the object of ridicule—English III had given way to "film appreciation" and geometry to "the shapes around us." Financial support for the public schools had not kept pace with inflation, making the teaching profession progressively less attractive. Shortages of qualified teachers in mathematics and science were sharply increasing, raising questions about the capacity of our schools to train students for technological careers. Watered-down curricula coupled with limited financial resources had contributed to a dilution of requirements for high school graduation. Enrollment of students in private schools was increasing as parents demanded more academic rigor, more homework, and tougher disciplinary standards. New York, Chicago, Los Angeles, and numerous other urban school districts were experiencing steady increases in children from low-income families, minorities, and immigrant families who did not speak English. Scholastic Aptitude Test scores continued to decline. Colleges and universities, along with the business community, were becoming increasingly vocal about the lack of preparation of public high school graduates. The limited success of Blacks and Hispanics in college admissions and college graduation was gaining visibility. The gap between academic achievers and nonachievers was widening. In sum, a more auspicious environment for a galvanizing event that could precipitate education reform could hardly be imagined.

The publication in 1983 of *A Nation at Risk* is widely recognized as the beginning of the excellence era. The report, authored by the National Commission on Excellence in Education, established in 1981, stated in no uncertain terms that conditions in the nation's schools were deplorable. In our view, the power of *A Nation at Risk* as a primary mover of the educational excellence movement derived from its having captured and articulated a potent national sentiment. This sentiment had roots in the dissatisfactions with the public schools outlined above, but its real preoccupation appeared to be the sagging performance of the United States in the world economy. The trade deficit, the national debt, and the foreign, especially Japanese, competitive edge in industry and finance had reached intolerable proportions. The resulting national anxiety created a tremendous opportunity for the Commission on Excellence in Education upon which it shrewdly capitalized.[2]

The power of *A Nation at Risk* should not be underestimated. Nor should public sentiment. Abraham Lincoln once described the importance of public sentiment:

... public sentiment is everything. With public sentiment, nothing can fail, without it nothing can succeed; consequently, he who molds public sentiment goes deeper than he who enacts statutes and decisions possible or impossible to be executed.

It did not matter that many scholars in and outside the field of education questioned the factual matter and conclusions of *A Nation at Risk*. For instance, were its criticisms of the public schools excessive? Could economic stagnation really be pinned on individual productivity and not on such factors as capital investment or the terms of foreign exchange? The Brookings Institute's Paul Peterson concluded that nothing in *A Nation at Risk* permits the conclusion that our educational institutions have deteriorated badly.[3] But the sentiment and the report that enshrined it were facts of life by late 1983.

The response to *A Nation at Risk* was immediate and broad-based. One of its most distinctive characteristics was the curious lack of direct involvement of the federal government, together with an outburst of vigorous and parallel school reform activities in the fifty states. The state-level activities were in fact so similar to each other that one might have guessed that an external force, perhaps indirectly emanating from the U.S. Office of Education in Washington, was pulling strings tied to the state capitals.

The federal government was proud of its lightning-rod report but was in no mood to back it up with new federal programs. The nation was just recovering from an economic recession and still faced federal budget deficits approaching $200 billion. The Reagan administration had maintained a goal of shrinking government wherever possible, especially its social service agencies. Taking on an education mission, even one proclaimed as vital to the national interest, was not in the plans of the Reagan administration. The president's response to *A Nation at Risk*, signaling the direction his administration would pursue, was described in *Time* magazine:

Although the report was unveiled at a White House ceremony, the administration will evidently offer little more than verbal encouragement for reform. Even while praising the commission's work, President Reagan reiterated his belief that "parents, not the Government, have the primary responsibility for the education of their children."[4]

In the years that followed, President Reagan and especially his secretary of education, William Bennett, adopted positions as cheerleaders for education reform, articulating their views on educational improvement and urging the states to get on with their constitutional duties and make it happen. The federal role in education generally, and with respect to the excellence movement specifically, was a "bully pulpit," with Reagan and Bennett its ordained preachers. The Reagan style seemed keenly attuned to the importance of public sentiment on this score; the president (or, rather, Bennett) correctly banked on the likelihood that someone (the states) would act to accommodate the mood at the White House and the U.S. Office of Education.

Very early reactions by states showed confusion over who should bear responsibility for the national educational crisis, along with some sense that their own emerging efforts to change things had been eclipsed. Educators and legislators in some states that had already begun reform efforts were critical of the report, since it failed to acknowledge their earlier self-initiated efforts. For example, Governor George Deukmejian and State Superintendent of Schools Bill Honig led California's critical response. District school administrators and school board members were most skeptical because *A Nation at Risk* was silent about the resources required to implement its recommendations, and on how they would be generated. Urban leaders and others were concerned about the report's inadequate attention to issues of equity amid its siren song of improved student performance. Teacher union leaders were sympathetic with the report's overall goals but quickly identified substantial lists of items that would need to be negotiated, such as calls for a longer school year and longer school days, and merit pay for teachers.

In response to the federal government's hands-off attitude, literally dozens of state and local commissions were formed to pursue the need for school reform and to further the aims of the school reform movement. Four groups were particularly visible in this process: the governors, state legislators, business leaders, and private foundations. In addition, many scholars, such as John I. Goodlad and Ernest L. Boyer, had a running start, and their books were oft-cited contributors to the school reform debate. The net effect of this activity appeared to be a reinforcement of the essential message of *A Nation at Risk*; only now school reformers could depend for support on many different sources, not just the National Commission on Excellence in Education.

Since the most significant policy decisions were left to the states by default, the key players to surface were the natural heavyweights in state legislative politics: the governors (such as Tennessee's Lamar Alexander), state legislators (such as California's Teresa Hughes), and business leaders (such as Texas' H. Ross Perot). Politicians were quick to sense that education was now a glamorous issue and seized the early enthusiasm stage of the issue attention cycle. The business community came aboard in response to what it perceived as the decline of the United States in the international economy.

The politics of response to *A Nation at Risk* were dominated by bargaining over a set of critical issues by the chief parties to education reform, particularly between the public school systems and the state legislators and governors who channeled the public's enthusiasm for changes. One result was an exchange of promised reforms by professional educators for the additional financial support they felt they needed and deserved. The message from the state legislatures to the schools was clear: "If you want more money, then you must agree to reform." Texas businessman Perot put it this way: "Millions for reform, but not one dime for the status quo." And a state education commissioner was heard to say (though not for attribution), "What is educational excellence really about? It's about money."[5] And money the schools received: whereas total spending for elementary and secondary schools (in constant dollars) had remained level between 1978 and 1982, in the next four years real expenditures rose by 7 percent.

Another area of compromise between elected officials and the professionals in education was this: School districts would be held accountable for the implementation of reforms as well as for their outcomes. The full arrangement thus became "If more money, then reforms. If reforms, then demonstrate that they work." Even though school professionals accepted the demand for accountability, this part of the bargain presented some problems. First, many of the proposed reforms were suspected to have questionable value insofar as the needs of students were concerned. For example, would longer school days or school years contribute to learning when existing curricula were under attack as nonproductive? Second, the measures generally available to determine the effects of the reforms were thought to have questionable validity. Would tests designed to *compare* students show the effects of overall achievement increases? But teachers needed higher salaries and districts needed more money, and to resist reform and accountability was to ignore public sentiment. Stated another way, the stage had been set, and to oppose reform and accountability would have been politically stupid.

The need to document the effects of school reforms engendered perhaps the most heated and at the same time the least visible political struggles of the school reform movement. We think of the process this way: If educators are forced to accept accountability for a host of new programs, it is natural that they would attempt to shape the terms of the assessments used to reach judgements about them. In the public schools, attaching measured learning outcomes to individual components of a complex and cumulative schooling process is a tenuous business—just where would the effects of a required additional year of social studies or the identification and rewarding of mentor teachers be expected to show up? Probably not in general test scores, which fluctuate from year to year as pupil characteristics shift and because tests tend to be imprecise and unstable measures in the first place. What evolved, in part under the leadership of state school chiefs such as California's Bill Honig, was a move by the professional education community to install comprehensive sets of educational indicators for public scrutiny; these promised at least to show intermediate progress with the reform agenda and thus would build political support for reforms and for continued funding. The publication of indicators such as the number of students enrolled in advanced placement classes, number of students meeting state university entrance requirements, attendance data, and dropout rates became commonplace.

It is interesting to note that Secretary of Education Bennett in 1984 initiated this "multiple indicator era" with the issuance of the first of his department's annual "wall charts" of comparative state education statistics. On this document, some twenty statistics of educational performance (test scores), resources (e.g., per-pupil spending), and student background (e.g., percent minority) were arrayed. A glaring information shortage in this chart was immediately apparent to all—the only tests taken by students in all fifty states were college entrance examinations, the Scholastic Aptitude Test and American College Testing Service exam. Accordingly, scores on these tests were used in the wall charts. But state performance levels on each of these were proven in subsequent analyses to be largely a function of the percentage of high school students taking the tests. Where only a few students took the tests—for instance, to apply to competitive out-of-state colleges—state average scores were high. Where the tests were required for all in-state public college admissions, the numbers of students examined were high and the state average scores comparatively low. Most school professionals as well as testing experts in the universities concurred that as of the mid–1980s we had no way of comparing the education performance of state public school systems.

In response to this need, the country's major national achievement assessment program, the National Assessment of Educational Progress, announced plans to conduct its tests in ways that will allow for state-by-state comparison scores. This amounts to a political breakthrough of sorts. State education officials had long opposed state-by-state score reports on the national assessment because this would inevitably place half the states in a position of explaining why they were in the bottom half of the distribution. The collapse of this line of resistance can be interpreted as evidence of the power of the drive for accountability tied to the excellence movement.

Just how education performance data would be presented and interpreted was thus central to the politics of education reform. The debates extended beyond the larger questions of what types of tests and other measures to include, and whether comparative state-by-state measures would be useful. There were the finer questions of whether school districts or individual schools should be compared with each other. If we return to the impetus for accountability, there were good reasons to establish such comparisons. Low performing systems, whether states, school districts, or schools, would have motivation to do a better job if they were singled out in performance indicator schemes. They could face financial or other sanctions for poor performance, and their leaders could face possible removal from office.

But such comparisons, as we have implied, are difficult to make on a fair basis. The primary reason is that public schools serve pupil populations that bring with them different levels of skills, preparation, socioeconomic status, and home support for learning. Public schools also differ in the resources they have to work with. Attempts have been made to accommodate these differences by publishing, along with performance statistics, information about the backgrounds of a school system's students and the system's resources. But a no-win trade-off results. Simplistic comparisons, such as the publication of test scores with family education levels and per-pupil spending, do not fully account for background and resource differences and fail to support clear judgments about which schools are doing well and why. The alternative, including a dozen or more factors that could help explain performance apart from the school or the system having done a good job, creates an unwieldy and opaque performance report;

so cumbersome a document would prove difficult for even a seasoned education researcher to interpret, much less the news-reading citizen or legislator.

The net result was an ongoing series of struggles between schools, districts, states, and the federal government over how to report data, and particularly over how to group schools or school systems for comparison. Perhaps the only clear victor in the fight over pupil assessment indicators is the idea, described above, that selective indicators of implementation and pupil participation should be reported. These may have good prospects for suggesting gains under school excellence legislation, and therefore of being useful to professional educators as they seek continued support for public schools.

In the preceding section, we described some aspects of the initiation and implementation of the excellence movement with particular attention to its policies. Here we turn to observations about where excellence reforms have taken the public schools. We focus first on some of the "morning after" realities of implementation, foreshadowed in our discussion of previous reform movements. While much legislation has accompanied the drive for excellent schools, many observers of the American educational scene perceive gaps between the acknowledged purposes of excellence-in-education legislation and what the public schools seem to be delivering. We also discuss two fundamental reactions to the excellence movement. One is a resurgence of interest in students at risk of failure. Another is a surge of interest in a different kind of educational reform activity, which we will specify later.

School reforms made under the banner of excellence promised stiffer standards in the nation's public high schools, more rigorous course content, and more qualified teachers. We have noted that for a variety of reasons we often see slippage between school reform legislation and classroom practice. In fact, professional educators quietly expressed a number of concerns related to this problem as the excellence movement unfolded. Would setting graduation standards higher lead to higher performance or to a dilution of existing classes? If graduation hurdles should actually be set higher, would more students drop out? Would increased requirements for courses in mathematics and science lead to gains in these areas when qualified teachers were not available? Would merit pay and mentor teacher plans survive negotiations with teacher unions? Would longer school years and longer school days help if curricula were not substantively improved? Would requiring more courses or "seat time" in English, mathematics, history, or science guarantee that more content would be covered or that more would be learned? And would requiring the successful completion of proficiency tests prior to graduation ensure that necessary skills were learned by high school graduates, or would they show that the high schools had effectively aimed their curricula at the adopted test items?

Basic doubts about the effectiveness and "deliverability" of excellence-in-education state legislation were not the only shadows following the school reform movement. The local discretion built into many school reform laws created further uncertainties about what would actually appear in schools and classrooms.

Some calls for reform appeared as mandates; others were local school district options. School districts frequently were slow to implement or simply spurned reforms that were optional. As one example, some California districts felt that the school year and school day were long enough at their schools and elected not to accept the financial incentives to implement such changes. California's mentor teacher program, an effort to get extra pay to teachers who had been identified as excellent, provides another example. A major hitch in this innovation was that teacher unions and boards of education sometimes could not agree on a process for selecting mentor teachers. In some cases the school district administration did not wish to relinquish any of its authority in the area of personnel selection and assignment. In others, the teacher unions chose to hold the mentor teacher program hostage in exchange for some other item on the negotiating table. Problems like these contribute to the complexity and the unpredictable nature of the implementation of school reforms urged in the name of excellence.

Perhaps the most glaring example of the politicization of the educational excellence movement can be seen in the efforts of the state of Texas to administer a competency test to its public school teachers, one that would result in the firing of teachers who did not pass. The adoption and efforts at implementation of teacher competency testing in Texas led to intensive struggles over what exactly would be a valid test of teacher competency. The exam was simply a test of basic literacy and mathematical skills, the only common denominators to emerge in the state's quest for suitable content for such a test. Nonetheless, the teachers were steadfast in their objections to taking such an exam, a position that brought trouble to the profession. When their objections were juxtaposed in news accounts with some items from the test that looked like fifth grade material, public esteem for the state's public school teachers fell to new lows. Texas eventually administered the test and a small percentage of teachers, mostly minority group members, failed.[6] The exam that promised a more competent teaching force resulted, ironically, in a seemingly discriminatory purge of Hispanic and Black teachers.

While it may have sounded reasonable to assume that raising standards would improve performance for most high school students, it was also reasonable to assume that many students would need additional assistance if they were to meet the new requirements. Providing the additional support for one group of students would either cost more money or require redistributing existing resources. Tax increases are rarely popular, and redistributing existing resources, when the resource base is already thin, is also grounds for political disputes.

A growing professional and public perception holds that the excellence movement has neglected the low achiever. The years 1987 and 1988 have brought yet more reports from commissions and task forces, this time having to do with the at-risk student. The verdict of these reports is that the school reform movement appears not to provide added resources to help those students unprepared or underprepared to grapple with higher standards and tougher course requirements. The concern for at-risk students also stems from widely circulated reports on the numbers of educationally disadvantaged youngsters, particularly the poor and minorities who constitute a majority in some school districts and who will account for one-third of our pupils nationwide by the year 2000. While the effects of excellence legislation on at-risk and educationally disadvantaged students are only beginning to appear in the reports of researchers, professional educators, parent groups, and civic and philanthropic organizations are already telling us that we remain far from meeting the educational needs of such children and youth.

Furthermore, particularly for those who had been involved in the implementation of the ESEA of 1965, it appears that the excellence movement forgot the problems inherent in top-down mandates for school reform. Researchers had, in connection with ESEA, thoroughly documented the importance of local involvement and support to effect lasting change in the schools, but many of these lessons would apparently need to be revisited and relearned by the excellence movement.

Since most of the new school reforms had originated at the state level, they were perceived as authoritarian mandates that passed through or over the local governance structure, directly to the schools. This aspect of the top-down approach complicated the translation of the reforms to classroom activities. If state officials were writing the laws, and if teachers and youngsters were the ones whose behavior was slated for change, where did this leave school boards, school superintendents, and school principals? Who would serve as arbiter of community preferences or see that the schools were responsive to the parents? How would district officials convince their staffs and their publics that they were still in charge?

By 1985 a "local control" backlash to the top-down nature of the excellence movement was gathering force. It was expressed well in a report by the Committee for Economic Development and was echoed in similar statements in publications produced by governors and business leaders, as well as professional educators:

Our recommendations are grounded in the belief that reform is most needed where learning takes place—in the individual schools, in the classroom, and in the interaction between teacher and student. As businessmen worldwide have learned, problems can best be solved at the lowest level of operation. While structures are needed, bureaucracies tend to focus on rules and regulations rather than results, thus stifling initiative. Therefore, we believe that school governance should be retained at the local level, and not be supplanted by statewide boards of education or national dictates. However, states should set standards and provide the guidance and support to local schools that are necessary for meeting these standards.[7]

Efforts to decentralize the public schools took a variety of shapes. In Chicago, for example, an effort was initiated to establish a local board of education at each individual school site. In 1988 the California Business Roundtable recommended the establishment of a community board at every school with parents and community members serving on the board and teachers sharing in school governance.[8] The politics of shifting and/or sharing power was reminiscent of earlier eras in our educational history, including New York's Ocean Hill-Brownsville confrontations in the late 1960s, in which community control of schools was a rallying cry.

We have suggested that the rallying cry of local control was one reaction to the flurry of reforms hurled at the public schools. This proved to be only the first of now frequent calls for restructuring the school system, as opposed to more traditional standards-raising or curriculum enrichment reforms. This new phase of the school reform movement brought a pronounced market and business orientation to the debates about school reform. Continued concerns about the efficiency of the country's work force and frustrations about the pace of educational change under the first wave of reforms seemed to fuel this second wave of reform pressure.

There were certain parallels between the emerging corporate rhetoric of school reform and an ascending corporate philosophy in the United States. The latter was perhaps best articulated in the best seller *In Search of Excellence*, in which the authors claimed that excellent business firms were distinguished by ''the co-existence of firm central direction and maximum individual autonomy.'' If worker choice was good for McDonald's, it should be good for Washington High School. The Carnegie Forum on Education and the Economy summed up the new direction of education reform this way:

In the past three years, the American people have made a good beginning in the search for an educational renaissance. They have pointed to educational weaknesses to be corrected; they have outlined ways to recapture a commitment to quality. They have reaffirmed the belief that the aim for greater productivity is not in conflict with the development of independent and creative minds. There is a new consensus on the urgency of making our schools once again the engines of progress, productivity and prosperity.[9]

The emphasis in this passage on the words ''quality'' and ''productivity'' should not go unnoticed. While private sector support for public school reforms had been sustained since the beginnings of the excellence movement, the lexicon of the corporate world was clearly making an incursion into the debate about education. Quality and productivity were expected, and competition was to be a vehicle for success. A common ingredient in present demands for restructuring the school system is to give parents wide freedom of choice to decide which schools their children will attend. And the call for ''choice'' was heard not only from the business community. It was also a major plank of the National Governors Association's agenda for school reform.

The appeal of ''choice'' to the business community, and to many critics of the public schools, is clear. Providing school choice to parents would force public schools to compete for students on the basis of quality, and thus place educators in jeopardy of losing their market or clients; this threat, it was hoped, would force educators to greater efforts to improve the schools. Competition would also tend to drive down school costs or at least raise the productivity of existing resource allocations, again through the mechanism of competing for pupils. And if anyone was concerned that the resource infusions of the early phase of school reform would not last forever, the efficiencies promised through parental choice would at least cushion any setbacks.

Despite the growing appeal and support for choice, this is one issue that the education professionals have historically resisted and can predictably be expected to fight vigorously should legislation to enable choice be proposed. Previous attempts to promote tuition tax credits and education vouchers provide clear evidence of the professional educators' opposition to the provision of choice. Parental choice would undo the host of arrangements that now bind our public school systems; at stake are employment security agreements, job assignments, transfer policies, and the basic stability of the public school's organizational structure. Whether these cherished qualities of the school system are necessary ingredients of educational productivity has never really been tested. But beyond what might be interpreted as self-serving objections by the education profession, a legitimate concern about choice in education is whether it would prove possible to extend access to the same set of choices to all parents or families. In other words, many wonder whether choice schemes would tend to confer more advantages to parents and families already advantaged and confer more disadvantages to those already disadvantaged.

What of the future? It is difficult to predict the direction the reform movement will take next. The task is on a par with more general political prognostication, which experience warns us to avoid. We have already noted that recently the emphasis in school reform has shifted from a highly centralized and regulated approach to demands for decentralization, deregulation, and restructuring. In this shift, reform emphases have changed from raising standards for students, teachers, and administrators, and demanding school district accountability to facilitating teacher professionalism, accelerating efforts to meet the needs of students at risk, and providing parents with choice. While many of these recommendations appear to represent a desire to focus on ''bottom-up'' rather than ''top-down'' reforms, they are still being developed at the top and their ultimate impact on the public school remains an open question.

At the federal level, education was high on the agendas of 1988 presidential candidates George Bush and Michael Dukakis because of its salience to the general public and to the business community. But it remains unlikely that large-scale federal initiatives will be aimed at the public schools, not only because there is little recent precedent for massive federal involvement but also because federal budgets must accommodate the accumulated national debt, continued annual deficits, and competing demands for other services, such as defense. A federal tax increase for education seems farfetched at this time.

Continued education reforms are likely to emanate from the state level, because of the states' constitutional responsibilities for education, the high interest in the schools shown by state governors, and the comparative health of many state tax bases. But even in the states, interest in public school reform may wane. States must address many competing claims, including deteriorating infrastructures, overcrowded prisons, increasing numbers of the poor and homeless, and the health care needs of the young and the old. We should probably expect some tinkering with reform legislation to facilitate the newer directions we described: deregulation, decentralization, and perhaps limited parental choice. But it is difficult to envision any continued infusion of large sums of money to underwrite resource-demanding changes. We noted above that economic expansion has fueled post-World War II reform movements. The current American economic expansion is entering an unprecedented sixth year as of this writing, but most expect some sort of downturn in the next year or two. An added reason to hold limited expectations for the newer restructuring reforms occurs to us: The state superintendents of schools, state departments of education, and state boards of education may prove unwilling to relinquish the powers handed to them by the first wave of school reforms. Top-down directives may have their critics, but they are probably addictive to those at the top.

Leaders in the business community will undoubtedly continue their efforts to encourage public schools to become more efficient and productive. But if history is a guide, few public school systems will readily adopt the unorthodox organizational and management styles currently being suggested, and the educational enterprise is not likely to approach the business community's criteria for efficiency and productivity. Lack of progress on these fronts could lead to additional encouragement for the privatization of the public schools through competition-inducing choice mechanisms and perhaps through public support of private schools by means of education vouchers or tax credit systems.

Our guess is that the future course of education reform will be driven by the evolution of two sentiments that will come to dominate public discussion about our schools. First, to the extent that American business remains alarmed about the preparedness of high school and college graduates, pressures to enhance academic excellence and increase job readiness and technological preparedness will continue on the schools. If this alarm is sustained and if educational innovations in place produce flat results, more radical reforms may be tried. Second, to the extent that gaps between achievers and nonachievers remain wide or continue to grow, demands for equity will continue to be heard. And since by all projections the educationally disadvantaged will become a significant and increasing share of our labor force over the next decades, these two sentiments are bound to intersect. The net result may be sustained pressures for change— more protracted than in any past period of education reform.

In the process, the excellence movement in education as such may be transformed. We are likely to witness a heated national debate about the resources we are willing to provide on behalf of excellence, especially where they concern helping students at the bottom of the achievement distribution. And because traditional routes to school reform have met with multiple sources of resistance, we are also likely to witness continued debates over the lengths to which we are willing to experiment more radically with the structure, organization, and funding of our public schools.

NOTES

1. Downs, A. (1982, Summer), Up and down with ecology—The issue attention cycle, *The Public Interest, 32,* 38–50.

2. National Commission on Excellence in Education (1983), *A nation at risk: The imperative for educational reform* (Washington, D.C.: U.S. Government Printing Office).

3. Peterson, P. E. (1985, Fall), Did the education commissions say anything?, *Brookings Review,* 3–11.

4. McGrath, E. (1983, May 9), To stem a tide of mediocrity, *Time,* p. 63.

5. This statement was made at a UCLA research project advisory board meeting (attended by one of the authors) by the former commissioner of education of a large eastern state.

6. Shepard, L. A., & Kreitzer, A. E. (1987, August-September), The Texas teacher test, *Educational Researcher, 16*(6), 22–31.

7. Committee for Economic Development (1985, September 11), Quoted in "Investing in our children," *Education Week,* p. 17.

8. California Business Roundtable (1988), *Restructuring California education: A design for public education in the twenty-first century* (Los Angeles, CA: The Roundtable).

9. Carnegie Forum on Education and the Economy (1986), *A nation prepared: Teachers for the twenty-first century* (Washington, D.C.: Carnegie Forum), p. 2.

12   The School Reform Movement: A Comparative Perspective

Val D. Rust

Since at least 1983, the United States has been swept up in a major educational reform movement. Besides the more or less conventional reform issues such as demands for more or different courses, higher standards, and better discipline, a number of radical and controversial issues have appeared on the school reform agenda, including demands to institute a "basic" or "core" curriculum nationwide, implement national proficiency examinations for both teachers and students, and enhance parental choice in education.

The current school reform movement in America, according to one historian, is but the latest of a long series of "actions and reactions, of pendulum-like movements from academic traditionalism to permissive progressivism and back again."[1] Supporters of the current school reform movement indict the sins of America's "permissive progressivism" and claim their reform agenda will restore integrity, rigor, and "excellence" to American education. Opponents of the school reform movement have a different agenda. The debates over school reform remain grounded firmly within the American context. In this respect they are surprisingly provincial. This is unfortunate, because the debates over the current school reform movement deserve broader input; otherwise, the movement may come to represent nothing more than one more swing of the pendulum, while little of value occurs in terms of fundamental improvement of public schooling.

The educational experience of the Western European democracies is particularly relevant as a source of ideas for Americans. The central concerns of educational debates in Europe are remarkably similar to those in America. Just as in America, issues of parental choice, school-based local control, testing and assessment, public versus private schooling, and quality and equality in education are central to contemporary Western European school reform debates.

Familiarity with the context of these debates, the language of the debates, and the kinds of policy choices Europeans were confronted with, and made, could provide concerned Americans with a broader perspective while raising the level of discourse in the current debates about American education.

Americans who attempt to inform themselves about European educational reform activities may find their quest difficult, but sources of information are available. *The International Journal of Educational Research*, for example, published a special issue on "educational reform in international perspective."[2] In addition, journals such as *Comparative Education Review* and *Comparative Education* regularly publish essays on European educational reform activities with implications for developments in American education. These journals are, however, the outlets for specialists in the field of comparative education. Our intention in this chapter is to make the field of comparative education and developments in European education accessible to the concerned American public.

From comparative education's inception as a field of study, comparative educators, such as Professor Isaac Kandel at Teachers College, Columbia University, and Professor Nicholas Hans, at London University, gave great attention to the study of national systems of education in the context of their unique social, cultural, and political conditions and history. Many students of European comparative education continue to work in that tradition, and their work is invaluable for those American scholars, say, who are attempting to understand specific school-society relationships in specific European countries. However, the very emphasis of this tradition also defines its limitations: the focus on uniqueness of cultures and histories diminishes the possibility of useful comparative analysis.

More recently, another tradition has been established among comparative educators. "Comparativists" grounded in this tradition assume that there are educational regularities that transcend specific national contexts. They also maintain that an understanding of educational conditions in one country may be useful to those attempting to understand education in another country. Comparativists involved in this tradition have inevitably had their attention drawn to issues of educational innovation and reform. Comparativists having such an orientation insist that it is not sufficient to understand school-society relationships in one country; one must use this knowledge to provide insights or "lessons" about educational policy debates and educational innovation in other or "foreign" countries.[3] That will be our perspective in this chapter.

We shall engage in an analysis of certain contemporary educational reform movements in Western Europe, with the intention of drawing implications or insights from the European experience that might be helpful to Americans engaged in their own school struggles. Given the confines of a chapter of this size, however it is necessary to restrict ourselves to educational developments in two countries: Great Britain and Norway.[4] As in America, the political climate of these two countries has shifted to the right in the recent past; the new climate represents a decidedly conservative political orientation. More significantly, the

British and Norwegian educational reform debates are directly relevant to the issues being debated in America. In this chapter we shall deal with three specific issues: parental choice, local control, and curriculum reform.

Before we begin, it is important for American readers to understand something about the organization, structure, and governance of education in Britain and Norway. The British educational system has been administered through a shared governance principle between a central ministry, called the Department of Education and Sciences and headed by an education secretary, and the local education authorities (LEAs), which are, by and large, county school districts. Since 1944 British children have attended school from age five to age eleven in common primary schools, after which they have been separated, according to examination results, into secondary modern, technical, and grammar schools. Only the grammar schools have qualified a student for higher studies. Consequently the secondary school system has been criticized as corresponding to a rigid social class division. "Comprehensive secondary schools," which attempt to combine the three secondary school types under one roof, promised to provide greater social equality and became quite common—almost the rule—in Britain in the 1960s and 1970s, especially under successive Labour governments. As late as the 1970s, approximately 85 percent of secondary school students attended state-sponsored schools, most of which were comprehensive (and with which we are mostly concerned here), while 10 percent attended church-sponsored institutions and another 5 percent attended private independent schools.

The Norwegian school system, which originally was administratively decentralized, came to be highly centralized beginning in the 1930s under the Department of Church and Education. Since 1969 all children have attended a nine-year "basic school," which until recently featured a uniform or common curriculum, after which students attended secondary schools, all of which have vocationally oriented "branches of study." However, all branches of study qualify for higher education. As late as the 1970s more than 98 percent of the students attended state-sponsored schools.

In both Britain and Norway teachers have traditionally played a central role in policymaking. The teacher associations have come to maintain a formal relationship with the government in setting the educational agenda. In fact, in Norway, teacher groups could be described as an official branch of the government.

There has recently occurred in Great Britain and Norway (and it is not yet over) a heated controversy in which advocates of school reform emphasize greater parental choice in education—that is, greater freedom for parents to enroll a child in any one of a wide variety of schools, state or private, secular or religious—with support to come from public resources. Since parental choice has been particularly central in the current educational reform debates in England, the greater part of our discussion in this section will focus on that country.

In Britain, the public debate on parental choice evolved out of a broad campaign to discredit the state comprehensive secondary school. Beginning in the late 1960s, educational reformers in Britain began to rely on a language of "crisis" to attack the comprehensive secondary school. They argued not only that comprehensive schools were an educational disaster, but that school enrollment policies deprived parents of the right to choose the kind of school they wished for their children. At the same time, the conservative popular press, particularly *The Mail*, *The Sun*, and *The Express*, attempted to discredit the comprehensive school in the public mind by publicizing the connection between illiteracy among working-class youth, racially inspired violence, politically radicalized teachers, and the comprehensive secondary school.

The tactics used in the 1960s, not very successful then, were revived in the 1980s but with much more success. Conservative interest groups in England such as the Hillgate Group again relied on the language of crisis to highlight the plight of English secondary education. "Britain's educational system is breaking down," they asserted. Moral standards and civil behavior could no longer be taken for granted, students' talents were not being fully developed, and youth were not being prepared for work or advanced education.[5] Attacks on the comprehensive secondary school in terms of the need to reverse the educational decline represent but one side of the reformers' argument; parental choice represents the other side. In the second half of the 1970s, Conservatives in England gained control of the education agenda. Alongside the attacks on the comprehensive secondary school in terms of its educational inadequacy, they brought forward parental choice; parents should be free to choose which schools their children should attend, with the state providing the means to enable such choice. Thus the quality of education for all would be enhanced.

The arguments for parental choice were formulated by Conservatives based at private think tanks such as the Adam Smith Institute and the Institute of Economic Affairs, which popularized a special language based on a free-enterprise economic metaphor that has come to dominate the contemporary educational dialogue in England. According to the economic metaphor, a productive society is based on individual interest; people are able to "exchange goods and services" in the "open marketplace," to the mutual advantage of all. In this view, government must be constrained to narrowly defined functions such as supervision and licensing that protect individual (parent) interests and enable individuals (parents) to make free choices. In other words, private initiative and private enterprise are the sources of efficiency and productivity; government-run programs are inimical to efficiency and productivity.[6]

Conservative educational reformers in Britain charged that education had become a state monopoly controlled by the LEAs and organized to satisfy the needs of the "producers" of education, the education professionals and the LEA bureaucracies, and that it was imperative to transform the school system from a "producer" to a "consumer" or market orientation. The solution to the problem lay in "privatization"; the public sector had to be subjected to the market disciplines that have made the private sector so successful. Conservatives argued that if there were available a wide array of state and private schools from which parents are able to choose, education would be subjected to the "marketplace," so that schools, like any other business or industry that satisfied consumer demands would prosper, while schools that failed the test of the market would either take steps to satisfy consumer demands or would go under. According to advocates of market-or-consumer-oriented education, a system based on parental choice possessed a built-in mechanism to raise standards, because only quality schools would survive.

The arguments for parental choice were met with a barrage of counterarguments, particularly from the professional educators, who by and large were adamantly opposed to parental choice. Some of this response represented little more than pamphleteering,[7] but some of the opposition to parental choice reflected reasoned and thoughtful arguments. Stewart Ranson, of Birmingham University's department of education, for example, challenged the use of economic metaphors in education such as those described above, distinguishing between "consumers" and "citizens," and pointing out that consumerism is not citizenship. Ranson argued that parents-as-consumers express private self-interests and have little thought for public consequences, while parents-as-citizens must transcend self-interest and work with the well-being of others and the health of society in mind. According to Ranson, the marketplace may be an appropriate arena for consumers who wish to purchase products, which can be produced to meet consumer demand. However, education is not just a product, but a process that requires continual adjustment to meet individual needs. Education cannot be produced and marketed like a candy bar. True education requires "common" schooling concerned with the development of all children and youth, and an "enabling profession," made up of teachers trained to provide an education for citizenship in a democratic society.[8]

It is understandable that the professional educational establishment would react negatively to the school reformers. Not only were teachers becoming the scapegoats in the educational crisis, but few educationists were invited to join the ranks of reformers. The professional educators argued that the reformers had politicized education and debased educational dialogue. Of course, those in favor of the reforms were not just crude polemicists seeking to wrench control of education away from the education professionals. In constructing an economic metaphor for education, their works are filled with references to Adam Smith, John Locke, and John Stuart Mill.

There is an old saying: He who defines the agenda wins the argument. Conservative school reformers were definitely able to set the educational agenda to their own advantage. For example, they were able to pit the education professionals against the parents in a no-win situation for the professionals. One of the most effective lines of argument used by the school reformers was that parents, through the mechanism of parental choice, would be "more likely to achieve higher standards more quickly and more acceptably to the public than the collective wisdom of the present bureaucrats."[9] Labour Party-oriented politicians, who joined educationists in defense of the comprehensive secondary school, did not fare any better in the debate than the education professionals.

For example, in the "Great Debate" in the national election campaign of 1978, Labour tried to frame the debate over the comprehensive secondary school in terms of equality of educational opportunity. Conservatives were able to set the agenda by shifting the terms of the debate from equality of education to quality of education. They drew on international educational achievement studies to demonstrate how inferior British pupils of all ability ranges were when compared with pupils in competitor countries such as West Germany. Conservatives also drew on criticisms of employers, who complained that poor standards had led to young workers who possessed neither general nor vocational skills. Conservatives particularly emphasized the poor academic performance of the "bottom 40 percent," the children of recent immigrants from the former colonies, minorities, the poor, those on welfare. They complained that these young people were "shortchanged" and "neglected in most comprehensive schools" because the low expectations of teachers were all too often fulfilled.

Conservatives argued that two courses of action were necessary. First, all pupils, including the "bottom 40 percent" had to be given general academic training in a rigorous, mandatory curriculum, particularly in subjects such as mathematics. Second, stress on "development of personality" had to be balanced with "education for a job," especially in the schooling of children of minorities and the inner-city poor. Taking advantage of the high unemployment rate and the inability of young people to get jobs that required proficiency in academic subjects, Conservatives were able to argue the value of the academic side of education and skill training as an antidote to unemployment while disparaging the quality of education offered in the comprehensives. The Left remained wedded to "progressive education" and what was increasingly seen as a vacuous claim to be supporting the comprehensive secondary school in the name of a nonexistent equality of educational opportunity.

Two major educational innovations emerged from the controversy. First, a wide-ranging training program, known as the Technical and Vocational Initiative, sponsored by the Manpower Services Commission, a government body outside the educational establishment, was introduced in secondary schools to help school leavers become more employable. Second, the Thatcher government was able to get the Education Reform Act of 1988 through Parliament, an act grounded in parental choice that succeeded in a radical recasting of English education. The act is a sweeping and general one, so here we will concentrate only on the provisions for parental choice. When introducing the bill in Parliament, the education secretary stressed that it would give parents more educational choice, and encourage new types of schools, greater competition between schools, and the publication of more abundant information about schools—all of which would, it was hoped "galvanize parental involvement in schools" and result in raising the quality of education.[10]

The Education Reform Act does not provide for total parental choice, as might be available in a voucher system such as exists in the Netherlands.[11] However, under the act, local schools and local parents' associations begin to exercise much greater control over enrollment practices and recurrent expenditures than ever before. Parents are given the right to enroll their children in schools of their choice regardless of community boundaries, as long as those schools have room for additional students. Thus, argued its proponents, poor and minority parents would be able to place their children in better schools in better areas. The Reform Act also allows individual schools to opt completely out of the LEA in which they are located but still be financed by the national government. This was not just a symbolic gesture, for even as the bill was coming before Parliament, approximately 120 schools had already expressed interest in opting out of LEA control. Here is parental choice and local control with a vengeance.

In addition, private schools were given a number of benefits by the act. Because Great Britain does not have a tradition of separation of church and state, it is relatively easy for relationships between the state and the private sector to be cultivated in education, including private-sector religiously oriented schools. Thus, provisions of the Reform Act allow maintained (church) schools to make claim to state provisions and services in the same manner as those state schools that opted out of LEA control. In addition, parents who have children in private schools that are only partially supported by the state are given tax rebates for their schooling costs to encourage greater participation in the private sector.

While parental choice is also important in Norway, it has not been as central in reform debates there as in Great Britain. Furthermore, unlike Britain, where the deliberate policy was to enhance the private sector, parental choice in Norwegian educational debates has focused almost exclusively on the question of whether public resources should be given to private schools.

Private schooling played a major role in the earlier stages of modern Norwegian education, but as the Labor Party solidified its position in the middle of the twentieth century, the issue of national education for national unity took on overwhelming urgency. Unity to Norwegian educational policy makers became almost synonymous with centralization, standardization, and "sameness," and the parents' interests were viewed in negative terms. That is, the differing value orientations of different groups of parents were seen as an obstacle to national unity: something to be overcome rather than welcomed or encouraged.

The educational consensus arrived at in Norway after World War II was that private schooling was undemocratic, a carry-over from an earlier period in Norway's history when private schools were elitist enclaves that allowed wealthy parents to opt out of public schools. Successive Labor governments in Norway held that all schools must be under the control of "organs run by elected officials" and under "public control"; otherwise, the choices of self-interested parents in terms of schooling would continue to divide youth along social class lines and subvert Norwegian democracy. Such a negative attitude on the part of educational policymakers led to a dramatic decline of private education in Norway, so that by the end of the 1950s, for example, private primary schools had almost disappeared and less than 2 percent of the secondary school population was in private institutions. However, these few private schools were receiving substantial funds from the state because they were seen as satisfying important social needs in the public sector, particularly in the area of craft and industrial and commercial training.

A widespread debate on parental choice and private schooling was precipitated in Norway in 1961, when a small Seventh Day Adventist school applied for support, claiming that it was only fair that it be treated as other private schools that were receiving public assistance. This request subsequently led to the establishment of a parliamentary committee charged with the responsibility for recommending some general private school policy. The Norwegian Labor Party was traditionally opposed to private schooling, and since the committee was tilted toward Labor, the committee opposed the request, insisting that parents should send their children to designated "common" state schools that would expose them to different values and points of view, so that they would learn to be more tolerant of differences. The committee argued that private schools transmitted exclusionary points of view and should not be publicly supported. Before action could be taken on the report, the political climate had begun to shift, and still another parliamentary committee was appointed in 1965, one that was controlled by a politically conservative coalition that valued parental choice, minority rights, and the private school.

This committee recommended that parental choice be enhanced and that financial support be given to all private schools, mainly because private schools were in such a precarious financial situation that they would soon disappear and leave almost no alternative for those parents who did not wish to send their children to state schools. They also argued that private schools could act as a stimulus for new pedagogical ideas and satisfy unmet educational needs; private education could provide a leavening effect upon the whole public schooling enterprise. Opposition to this recommendation was led by Labor, which employed both ideological and more cynical or practical arguments. Labor maintained that private school support would be detrimental to Norwegian national and democratic ideals, and that it would become more and more of a drain on the country's financial resources because it would allow parents to opt for private schools, and increasing numbers of parents might do so. Interestingly, the professional teacher associations in Norway took no strong stance on the issue either way.

By 1970 the political climate in Norway had shifted even further to the right. By then the country had concluded a cycle of educational reform and experiment begun after World War II that culminated in a standard or uniform curricular program for all youth during the nine years of the "basic school," and legislation was under discussion that would provide universal higher secondary education opportunities in comprehensive upper secondary schools. Now, anticipating victory, Conservative politicians called for passage of a generous private school bill that would provide up to 85 percent of running costs to all private schools. Such a bill was passed in 1974. One of the consequences was an increase in the number of private schools from 117 to approximately 180. This represented a definite tendency in the late 1970s, but the actual numbers still remained inconsequential. In the 1980s, as Conservatives gained full control of Parliament, however, "privatization" began to take on great significance, as more and more parents demanded the right to enroll their children in private schools. What followed were some of the most heated educational debates in Norway's history.

The debates were fueled, as in England and in the United States, by a growing disenchantment with the quality of public schooling.[12] The media in Norway had begun to portray the mandated school curriculum as "watered down." A public perception began to emerge that students were being allowed to choose programs of studies that failed to provide the solid academic foundation that would help them make sound career choices. A rash of applications for private schools began to pile up in the Private School Section of the Ministry of Church and Education, which refused to act on most applications, thus preventing them from starting up. The ministry soon became the target of criticism for obstructing the rightful wishes of parents who wanted to opt out of public schools. Education Ministry officials responded to the claim that private education was necessary because of the poor educational quality in the public sector by advising parents of applicants for private schools to become involved in the public sector so that the state school in their local community would take on the value orientation they wished to propagate.

In summary, we see that arguments for parental choice in Norway have focused almost entirely on the issue of state funding of private schooling, and that the arguments for such funding have gone through two major phases. Initially, school reformers in Norway argued for private schools in order to give parents having a special or different value orientation than the majority the right to choose an alternative schooling program. Since the late 1970s, as a controversy has emerged about the quality of schooling in the public sector, school reformers have added the claim that since public schools have failed to provide the quality of schooling parents desire for their children, private schools ought to be made available to them. As Labor had predicted, as parents opted for private schools, it became a very expensive proposition. The government then appealed to parents to exercise local initiative to make state schools more responsive to their desires. Parental choice thus became closely linked with local control of public schooling, which in both Britain and Norway is another major issue in educational reform.

Local control of schools in Great Britain and Norway has two major dimensions: (1) decentralization of power from the central to the local level and (2) redistribution of power among school district officials, individual school officials, teachers, and parents. Reformers in Great Britain have focused on the redistribution of power, mainly because the British system already was decentralized,

while school reformers in Norway have focused most of their attention on decentralization.

In the 1980s British proponents of local control successfully linked the educational crisis with the professional educational establishment, which they identified as the LEAs and the National Union of Teachers (NUT). According to the
Conservatives, the LEAs and the NUT were destroying parental "trust" and
"confidence" in the quality of state schools, especially the comprehensive secondary school. What better way to restore trust and confidence in the comprehensives than to shift power away from the LEAs to the local, individual schools
and give the parents much of the responsibility to determine the nature and
curriculum of the schools their children attended? Thus, we see how local control
and parental choice are intertwined.

Surprisingly or not, throughout most of Western Europe parents have never
participated in schools as actively as they do in America. For example, until
very recently, British schools had been viewed as the domain of the education
professionals, and the role of parents was mainly to satisfy the demands of
teachers and to rear their children so that they would be orderly, well scrubbed,
and willing to conform to the school's requirements. Beginning in the late 1960s,
however, a change in attitude toward teacher autonomy began to take place. The
government began to implement schemes to increase parent involvement in
education, and soon parents were becoming formal members of school governing
boards and involved in the daily life of the schools. Such participation was
encouraged by officials at the highest levels of government. The major rationale
used to justify this shift toward parent participation was the recognition by the
government that state schools, especially the secondary comprehensive schools,
had lost much of their standing and authority, and parent involvement was
necessary to restore a sense of legitimacy to these schools.[13]

While parents came to play a larger role in school-based governance, the
teaching profession in England was first portrayed as the source of educational
problems and then as the potential savior of education. Initially teachers came
under heavy criticism for contributing to the crisis in education, but with the
passage of the Educational Reform Act of 1988 a new attitude toward teachers
began to emerge. Since the act provides only guidelines, for example, in the
areas of curriculum and assessment, which have to be developed or implemented
at the national or LEA level, the act helped shift the focus of attention away
from teacher incompetence or radicalism and toward the importance of the teacher
as a key agent in developing new curricula and drawing up appropriate assessment
measures. While teacher empowerment is actually being put forth by Conservative school reformers as absolutely crucial if the Reform Act is to be successful,
the reformers remain committed to the destruction of the NUT as a political
force. Teacher power will have to be shared with the parents, who, as we have
seen, have been given increasing informal and formal responsibility at the local,
individual school level.[14]

Just as in Great Britain, the rhetoric of recent educational reform in Norway has stressed "local freedom" and "local initiative." This has been one reaction to the Labor government's policy of national unity through education by which Norway instituted a comprehensive program intended to provide a standardized education throughout the country, even though much of the nation consists of isolated farms and fishing villages.

In fact, the movement toward national unity through education was always somewhat antithetical to the history of Norway, where almost every valley, because of its isolation and unique dialect, has maintained a tradition of autonomy and local control. While rural parents took pride in the quality of schooling the centralized government was providing for their children, they began to express concern about the impact of long travel, boarding situations, the large enrollment of the schools, and the regimented school programs on the mental and physical health of their children. They also began to express serious concern about the tendency of their children to become oriented to the more cosmopolitan centers where "basic schools" were located and to become dissatisfied with the villages and small towns from which they came.

In the 1960s these concerns began to be highlighted in the media, and a drive against centralized control and the large, consolidated or comprehensive "basic school" was launched. Parents complained that the consolidated school had come to represent a "foreign" element in their community. They demanded that the school must be reoriented through local decision making and become the focal point for the transmission of the local culture. Parents also maintained that because the large, consolidated schools were so detached and even physically distant, parents had little contact with the teachers, many of whom were imported from outside the locality and were unaware of parental interests, values, and attitudes. On the other hand, small, local schools, even those lacking modern facilities or a full program, it was claimed, could restore contact between teacher and parent and enhance local values.

Still another impulse for local control began to emerge out of the growing awareness that the traditional, highly standardized education was detrimental to minority group interests and the ideal of equality in education. Norway possesses two large minority groups: the Lapps in the far north constitute an indigenous population, while Pakistanis represent a recent immigrant group in the major urban centers. Throughout its modern history Norway has maintained a policy of assimilation with regard to its Lapp population, but in the 1960s some social scientists began to point out that a great injustice was being done to the Lapp population in the public schools, in that the Lapp children were achieving poorly in public schools, and Lapp parents were forced to endure the imposition of what they considered to be a foreign culture on their children. The arrival of a small but visible Pakistani "guest worker" population reinforced the notion that it was unfair to treat all students in the same manner. For example, Norwegians stress equality between the sexes, whereas equality between boys and girls contradicts some of the basic values of Pakistani culture. School reformers began to argue that programs of study must be developed that would help minority groups work productively in Norwegian society while retaining their unique character, and this could be accomplished only by allowing local communities to participate in defining the educational process.

The debate over local control eventually moved into the political arena and political parties began to formulate positions. The Center Party, representing rural farmers, focused on decentralization and the value of young people remaining at home and retaining close family ties. The Christian Party stressed decentralization and the value of schools in transmitting religious values and traditional culture. The Norwegian Communist Party also supported decentralization, claiming that the traditional stress on standardization and uniformity was but a ploy of the elites to maintain control of schooling. When a conservative coalition government finally came to power in 1981, it adopted a radical policy of decentralization, which almost immediately began affecting every facet of schooling in Norway. For example, the government decided to decentralize all central funding, so that central state subsidies for a whole range of local services were no longer given as earmarked funds for services such as education, health, and culture, but as a single block grant that was divided and allocated at the local and regional levels. Even the National Educational Research and Development Center, which had served as the experimental arm for educational reform in Norway, was abolished. Research was to be undertaken at the local level, addressing local needs and interests.

In 1987, with a downturn in the national economy, it became evident that major cuts would have to be made in the national budget, particularly for education. Conservative school reformers seized on the economic crisis as a means of justifying further decentralization by linking decentralization with efficiency. They promised that local control would increase efficiency, so that quality could be enhanced even while budgets were being reduced. If local schools could reduce vandalism, equipment, material, or personnel costs, they would be allowed to use the savings as they wished. On this issue, the education professionals raised a chorus of protest, claiming the cuts were forcing them to work as janitors and policemen.

In addition, since decentralization required them to devote considerable time to making decisions about the aims of individual schools, developing new curricula, and establishing new teaching strategies, teachers pointed out that the government was mandating so many additional responsibilities that they had no time for classroom teaching or for their students. The reformers countered that the education professionals were merely engaging in a "Pavlovian response" to the new direction education was taking. They argued that teachers resist educational change of any kind and must be compelled to become more innovative. In all of this, the public media appear to have played a rather balanced role in the controversy.

While school reformers in both Great Britain and Norway stress parental choice, local control, and decentralization, they differ completely with regard to measures dealing with curriculum and student assessment. Space limitations force us to deal more fully with curriculum matters than with assessment.

In terms of control of the curriculum, recent British educational policy has been dictated by a control-oriented segment of the Conservative Party. The British Conservative Party represents a fusion of two great political traditions. The more liberal wing of the party stresses a laissez-faire value orientation of free choice, free enterprise, minimal government, and individualism, while the more authoritarian and control-oriented wing stresses a strong centralized government. In order to arrive at an educational policy that would be supported by the majority of the party, some trade-offs were necessary. While the basic thrust of the present British education reform movement is for parental choice and individual school-based local control, the more statist or control-oriented wing of the Conservative Party has insisted that this "free choice" be accompanied by firm "accountability," which requires government control over the curriculum as well as an extensive national system of testing at ages seven, eleven, fourteen, and sixteen, so that parents can judge the ability of a school to "deliver the goods." One consequence of the emphasis on accountability is that for the first time in modern British educational history, the content of British schooling is now being structured according to a unified national curriculum.

In Britain, the local schools and their teachers have always been responsible for developing curricula. This tradition had become almost sacred in professional education circles, and in the past neither the education secretary nor his department had been seen as competent to challenge it. Even the central advisory councils and LEAs had been reluctant to encroach on teacher autonomy. However, the Conservatives relied on powerful scare tactics to shift the sentiment. They argued that "Curriculum is too important to be left to the teacher." They also claimed that radical, left-wing elements of the teaching profession, especially in the NUT, had been able to gain control of comprehensive secondary school curriculum-making. Teachers were portrayed as having disseminated a national program of studies in the secondary comprehensive schools that was called antiracist and antisexist but that in actuality inflamed racial and sexual antagonisms.

The curriculum content also was condemned by Conservatives as being hostile to law and order because it attacked institutions like the police. Conservatives depicted the curriculum as having been politicized to the point that it was indoctrination and Marxist indoctrination at that, rather than education.[15] Even subjects such as bilingual education and multicultural studies, which all camps supported as means of dealing with the enormous problems created for the schools by recent immigrants, have come under fire from Conservatives, who view the programs as too much slanted toward ethnic cultures and languages rather than rigorous study of English language, history, and literature.

Not all of the Conservative attack on the professionals in education was quite as polemical as just portrayed. Conservatives also argued that schools and teachers lacked the ability to deal with such controversial topics as racism, sexism, "peace studies," and nuclear disarmament, and in their quarrel with teachers and the NUT, the Conservatives were able to establish a connection between the radicalized curriculum of the comprehensive schools, the growing racial violence in the streets, and the widely perceived sense of deterioration of respect for law and order.[16] Conservatives declared that the teachers in the comprehensive secondary schools had to share part of the blame for what was happening and that the solution was clear—teachers must be relieved of the autonomy that they traditionally enjoyed. The government had to step in and assume responsibility for such important matters as the curriculum. That is, the curriculum would have to be "nationalized."

In fact, the 1988 Education Reform Bill mandated a standard national curriculum that would occupy 80 percent of the school week during the primary and secondary stages of schooling. The new curriculum will be phased in gradually, beginning with the introduction of foundation subjects (mathematics, basic science and technology, English) to primary schools in September 1989. Its emphasis, when complete, will be on traditional subjects (English, mathematics, the natural sciences, history, and geography).

The defenders of teacher autonomy in the area of curriculum construction were unable to mount a strong counterargument. During the consultative phase of the legislative process, the NUT strongly criticized the School Reform Bill for lacking flexibility (although, in a spirit of accommodation, the education secretary actually extended the amount of discretionary time in the school week when compulsory subjects did not have to be taught). Labour was not opposed to the nationalization of curriculum as such. It recognized that schools were failing to serve the growing minority population, that minority students were not learning to read, and an alarming number of minority youth were leaving school with no work skills. Their criticism, however, was leveled only against the manner in which the Conservatives had hurriedly translated their school reform agenda into legislative proposals. Other critics of the new national curriculum raised questions about the long-term implications of the curriculum reforms. With few constitutional checks to central authority by local authorities, teachers, or parents, some critics of the 1988 School Reform Bill argued that a precedent was being created under which future governments, whether Right or Left, could make ideologically based adjustments to the national curriculum. Such arguments, however, so far have been largely disregarded.

While attempts to implement a national curriculum are new to Great Britain, the curricular changes taking place in Norway must be seen against the background of a compulsory school program that had been strictly divided into traditional discipline areas, and which since 1939 had been mandated as a national curriculum as a means of forging national identity.

The standardized curriculum held up rather firmly through the decades, although beginning in the late 1960s there were signals of change, particularly the heightened sensitivity toward minority and ethnic group problems. For example, a 1969 law for the nine-year "basic" school had stipulated that "all children be given *approximately* the same instruction throughout all their years of compulsory education" (emphasis added). As the curricular plan for the basic school was being debated, the education professionals argued that the aims of the law could be met only if the children were placed in ability groups. However, the government argued that this was a form of discrimination and stipulated that the local community and the teachers in individual classrooms would be in the best position to work out some way to deal with individual differences. Consequently, the 1969 law stipulated that local school boards and teachers be given considerable authority to emphasize local imperatives and deal with individual pupil needs by integrating subjects of study, introducing more flexible and localized assessment procedures, and introducing thematic topics into the curriculum.

In the 1970s, especially after the passage of the 1974 Secondary Education Law, calls for decentralization began to appear more regularly on the school reformers' agenda. As Norway moved into the 1980s, a consensus had been established that the centralizing orientation of its recent past in education had to be curbed and new ways to establish viable, decentralized, locally driven programs had to be developed. As decentralization became an accepted educational goal, three major challenges to decentralization began to appear. First, decentralization placed too much responsibility on teachers and local school officials. With the demise of the National Educational R&D Center, much of the responsibility for experimentation and for reform of the curriculum fell on teachers or the local teacher colleges. Teachers complained that local communities were expecting them to become local historians and social scientists, for which they had little training. The teacher associations claimed that the teachers were already overburdened and could not be expected to undertake such overwhelming responsibility without enormous resources and compensation for the work they were expected to do. Among teachers, then, a general ground swell of unease has been developing with decentralization, and it is not yet clear where it will end.

Finally, many Norwegians worry that with school decentralization and local control, ideals of national education and national unity will be threatened. They are beginning to wonder whether or how, under conditions of decentralization, national unity can be perpetuated by the schools. Local communities, especially those containing large numbers of Lapps and recent immigrants, have already begun to focus on local ethnic issues that many consider to be antithetical to national unity interests. Even Steinar Riksaasen, the conservative superintendent of schools in Oslo, laments the loss of national curriculum content, compulsory subjects, stable student groupings, firm time schedules, and the loss of the inner unity of subject matter. In spite of these concerns, recent educational developments in Norway continue to accentuate the trend to local control of education.

In this chapter we have reviewed some educational reform trends in Great Britain and Norway and the main lines of debate that have emerged with regard to these reforms. We have found that both countries have undergone a "conservative" political reaction in recent years. Even a brief survey of the nature of school reform in the two countries has shown that we are dealing with a common conservative impulse expressed in distinct, national ways as well as different kinds of conservative reaction to earlier, social-democratic reforms.

Regarding the issues of local control and parental choice as well as curriculum and assessment, the central government policy in Norway has recently been to encourage decentralization and local control in all aspects of state education. This movement reflects what appears to be a growing organic conservatism in Norway, a conservatism that has grown from the localities, regions, and interest groups and that reflects some agreement between a variety of political parties on the need for decentralization. In its educational aspect, however, the movement toward decentralization is hardly conservative; in fact, it is in many respects quite radical. It has fundamentally altered Norway's formerly highly centralized school system. Norway's educational decentralization has not been perceived as radical, however, because it has occurred relatively slowly, over two or three decades, and it has been a relatively consensual process reflecting the renaissance of coalition politics at the central government level.

Our survey of recent educational reforms instituted by the Conservative Thatcher government in Great Britain illustrates a very different process of change. The goals of the government in England are in some respects similar to those in Norway, but the pace of change has been much faster and is continuing at a rapid speed, and the extent of change envisaged is much greater. When the Thatcher government came into power, there was some necessity to play off conflicting Conservative interests in order to gain broad party support. Parental choice and local control at the individual school level were the main concerns of the more liberal wing of the Conservative Party, while central control and nationalization of education were the main concerns of its more statist, control-oriented elements. The political solution arrived at was to argue for parental choice and school control but with "accountability," which would be ensured by shattering the tradition of teacher control of such educational issues as the curriculum, and the adoption of a national curriculum and of an extensive national student assessment scheme.

Our final task in this chapter will be to address briefly the relevance of our study of educational reform in Great Britain and Norway to educational reform in the United States. First, we wish to urge caution about any inclination to draw lessons or borrow educational policies or practices from other countries. One of the cardinal sins of comparative education is to draw lessons or borrow policy or practices indiscriminately without taking into account unique national contexts. We will try to exercise such caution here.

It should be reassuring for Americans to discover that their debates over parental choice, local control, decentralization, "core" curriculum, and national testing and assessment are not unique. The very issues being debated in America also take center stage in Great Britain and Norway. Educational reformers in

Britain and Norway are also emphasizing the need for educational quality and the school reforms required for reversing educational decline. They, too, have to answer the challenge of equality in education. They, too, are struggling to work out meaningful testing and accountability procedures for schools and teachers. They, too, are deliberating the question of to what degree a school's curriculum ought to be externally mandated and to what degree curriculum might be optional or locally designed. They, too, are struggling with issues of parental choice, freedom of conscience, national unity, and the function of public or state schooling in a culturally diverse society.

It is instructive, however, to find that identical issues can inspire quite different debates and different solutions in Great Britain, Norway, and the United States. This can be explained in part, of course, by different national contexts and different national styles of problem solving; but some general observations are possible. For example, we find that teacher organizations have been generally opposed to educational reform in Great Britain, Norway, and the United States, and we might ask ourselves why teachers resist school reform efforts. The simplistic answer might be that teachers tend to resist change because they are comfortable with established practices and routines. We are not prepared to make such a universal judgment about teachers. For example, in Great Britain and Norway parental choice and the extension of private schooling is not a great issue with teachers, while in America it is resisted by teachers. A more tempered judgment about teacher resistance to school reform might be that recent school reforms in all three countries were imposed from outside the profession, and any professional would tend to react against externally imposed change.

Americans can learn something from the manner in which educational issues are debated in Great Britain and Norway. The academic community and the public media become actively involved in addressing educational issues, and the debates on school reform in both countries are freewheeling and informed. In England, for example, *The Times*, *The Telegraph*, *The Guardian*, and *The Independent*, the great national daily newspapers, carry weekly sections devoted to education that are quite sophisticated. As a consequence there is a heightened public awareness about controversial educational issues and a high level of historical and theoretical understanding of these issues on the part of the public. Of course there is a unique context that makes it very difficult for Americans to focus their educational debates in the manner that is possible in relatively small countries such as Norway and England. American newspapers and journals provide extensive coverage of educational issues, but educational policy in America is not established at a national level; debates about school reform tend to be filled with exceptions and subtle differences from state to state, city to city, and even local community to local community, which diffuses public attention and tends to prevent the fixed focus on reform issues that is so prevalent in Britain and Norway.

In addition, the process by which educational policy or educational legislation is established in Britain and Norway might be instructive to Americans. Typi-

cally, in both Great Britain and Norway, when a significant educational policy
is proposed, commissions having broad representation are established and may
spend years accumulating information and debating the issue before the public.
The commissions will eventually draw up a tentative report that is widely distributed. Reactions to their proposals and even counterproposals are invited.
Summaries of these materials are ultimately included in any proposal for actual
legislation. The legislative process also is openly debated, and adjustments are
frequently made to whatever education policy is under discussion before legislative action is taken. The process just described is especially significant in
Norway, because there the educational decision-making process is consciously
designed to reflect a sense of consensus rather than to produce a winner and a
loser.

In the United States, educational controversies, like those having to do with
parental choice and private schooling, frequently end up narrowly focused on
legal and constitutional issues, and the courts are subsequently appealed to.
Public debates on many controversial educational issues are thus foreshortened
in America. Significantly, court rulings and legal entanglements are so rarely a
part of public educational policy formation in Great Britain and Norway that
they are scarcely ever considered in public debates on education. While there
are clear benefits in America's constitutional framework, the latter does present
a formidable obstacle in terms of our ability to fully and freely debate the potential
merits of controversial innovations like parental choice, and then settle the issue
by negotiation and compromise.

The experience with educational reform in England and Norway could provide
some empirical evidence on issues that Americans now argue mainly without
any evidence. For example, Americans heatedly debate the potential consequences of parental choice and public support of private schooling. Will parental
choice lead to a proliferation of private schools and undermine the public school
sector? Will it lead to divisiveness and undermine national unity? The English
experience with parental choice is so new that it is difficult to make any judgment
at this point in time. The Norwegian experience indicates that policies intended
to enhance parental choice do indeed lead to the enhancement of the private
school sector, although there is no evidence that the public school system or
national unity is thereby undermined. It must be admitted, however, that some
Norwegians are fearful of just such an eventuality.

Britain and Norway are already experimenting with certain educational policies
and procedures that Americans are still debating and that might serve as a sort
of "trial run" for us. A familiarity with the educational innovations recently
implemented in Britain and Norway might suggest potential problems that we
might avoid. For example, American school reformers and others who support
parental choice in education might learn something instructive from the problems
encountered by the British in allowing schools to opt out of LEAs while not
providing those schools which choose to do so with the kind of resources and
services they have come to expect from their LEAs. Finally, American school

reformers who believe in mandated uniformity in school curricula might benefit from the problems Norwegians experienced in the 1960s and 1970s in attempting to institute a national curriculum, as well as from the present British experience in trying to implement a national curriculum and national assessment procedures.

NOTES

1. Ravitch, D. (1988), The reform of secondary education in the United States: An historical perspective, *International Journal of Educational Research, 12*(2), 179.

2. Ibid.

3. Two older volumes are still useful as overviews: Bereday, G. Z. F. (1964), *Comparative method in education* (New York: Holt, Rinehart, & Winston); and Noah, H. J., & Eckstein, M. A (1969), *Toward a science of comparative education* (New York: Macmillan).

4. Because our discussion of the education situation in Norway is taken from primary source material in the Norwegian language, no sources will be cited here. I have a book in press, in English, on the history of Norwegian education: *The democratic tradition and the evolution of schooling in Norway* (Westport, Conn: Greenwood Press, 1989).

5. The Hillgate Group (1986), *Whose schools? A radical manifesto* (London: The Hillgate Group).

6. For example, Adam Smith Institute (1984), The Omega file on education (London: The Institute).

7. For example, Wolpe, A. M., & Donald, J. (Eds.) (1983), *Is there anyone here from education? Education after Thatcher* (London: Pluto Press).

8. Ranson, S. (1988), *From 1944 to 1988: Education, citizenship and democracy* (London: Local Government Studies), pp. 1–20.

9. Sexton, S. (1987), *Our schools—a radical policy* (London: Institute of Economic Affairs).

10. Department of Education and Science (1987, November 20), Education Reform Bill Press Release no. 343.

11. Beattie, N. (1985), *Professional parents: Parent participation in four Western European countries* (London: Falmer Press).

12. Scruton, R., Ellis-Jones, A., & O'Keefe, D. (1985), *Education and indoctrination* (Harrow, Middlesex: Education Research Center).

13. Palmer, F. (Ed.) (1986). *Anti-racism: An assault on education and value* (London: Sherwood Press).

14. Flew, A. (1987), *Power to the parents: Reversing educational decline* (London: Sherwood Press).

15. Scruton et al., *Education and indoctrination.*

16. Palmer, *Anti-racism.*

SUGGESTED READINGS

Adam Smith Institute. (1984). *The Omega file on education.* London: The Institute.

Beattie, N. (1985). *Professional parents: Parent participation in four Western European countries.* London: Falmer Press.

The Hillgate Group. (1986). *Whose schools? A radical manifesto*. London: The Hillgate Group.

Palmer, F. (Ed.). (1986). *Anti-racism: An assault on education and value*. London: Sherwood Press.

Ranson, S. (1988). *From 1944 to 1988: Education, citizenship and democracy*. London: Local Government Studies.

Scruton, R., Ellis-Jones, A., & O'Keefe, D. (1985). *Education and Indoctrination*. Harrow, Middlesex: Education Research Center.

Sexton, S. (1987). *Our schools—a radical policy*. London: Institute of Economic Affairs.

Wolpe, A. M., & Donald, J. (Eds.). (1983). *Is there anyone here from education? Education after Thatcher*. London: Pluto Press.

Selected Bibliography

Banks, J. A., & Banks, C. A. McGee, (Eds.). (1988). *Multicultural education: Issues and perspectives*. Boston: Allyn & Bacon.

Boyer, E. L. (1983). *High school: A report on secondary education in America*. New York: Harper & Row.

Bunzel, J. H. (Ed.). (1985). *Challenge to American schools: The case for standards and values*. New York: Oxford University Press.

Carnegie Forum on Education and the Economy. (1986). *A nation prepared: Teachers for the 21st century*. New York: Carnegie Corporation.

Coleman, J. A., and Hoffer, T. (1987). *Public and private high schools*. New York: Basic Books.

Cremin, L. A. (1988). *American education: The metropolitan experience, 1876–1980*. New York: Harper & Row.

Finn, C. E., Jr., Ravitch, D., and Fancher, R. T. (Eds.). (1984). *Against mediocrity: The humanities in America's high schools*. New York: Holmes-Meier.

Finn, C. E., Jr., Ravitch, D., & Roberts, P. H. (Eds.). (1985). *Challenges to the humanities*. New York: Holmes-Meier.

Fishman, J. A., & Keller, G. D. (Eds.). (1982). *Bilingual education for Hispanic students in the U.S*. New York: Teachers College Press.

Flew, A. (1988). *Power to the parents: Reversing educational decline*. London: Sherwood Press.

Fullan, M. (1982). *The meaning of educational change*. New York: Teachers College Press.

Glenn, C. L., Jr. (1988). *The myth of the common school*. Amherst, MA: The University of Massachusetts Press.

Goodlad, J. I. (1984). *A place called school*. New York: McGraw-Hill.

Gottlieb, J., and Gottlieb, B. W. (Eds.). (1987). *Advances in special education*. Greenwich, CT: JAI Press.

Graham, H. D. (1984). *The uncertain triumph: Federal education policy in the Kennedy and Johnson years*. Chapel Hill, NC: The University of North Carolina Press.

Grant, G. (1988). *The world we created at Hamilton High*. Cambridge, MA: Harvard University Press.

Maeroff, G. I. (1988). *The empowerment of teachers*. New York: Teachers College Press.

Medina, N., and Neill, D. M. (1988). *Fallout from the testing explosion*. Cambridge, MA: National Center for Fair and Open Testing.

Metz, M. H. (1986). *Different by design: The context and character of three magnet schools*. New York: Routledge & Kegan Paul.

National Commission on Secondary Schooling for Hispanics. (1984). *Make something happen*. Washington, DC: The Commission.

Oakes, J. (1985). *Keeping track: How schools structure inequality*. New Haven: Yale University Press.

Powell, A. G., Farrar, E. & Cohen, D. K. (Eds.). (1986). *The shopping mall high school*. Boston: Houghton Mifflin.

Ravitch, D. (1983). *The troubled crusade: American education, 1945–1980*. New York: Basic Books.

Rohlen, T. P. (1983). *Japan's high schools*. Berkeley: University of California Press.

Sedlack, M. W., & Schlossman, S. (1986). *Who will teach?* Santa Monica, CA: Rand Corporation.

Sewall, G. T. (1983). *Necessary lessons: Decline and renewal in American schools*. New York: The Free Press.

Sizer, T. R. (1984). *Horace's compromise: The dilemma of the American high school*. Boston: Houghton Mifflin.

Slavin, R., et al. (Eds.) (1985). *Learning to cooperate, cooperating to learn*. New York: Plenum Press.

Soltis, J. F. (Ed.) (1987). *Reforming teacher education: The impact of the Holmes Group report*. New York: Teachers College Press.

Tom, A. R. (1987). *How should teachers be educated?* Bloomington, IN: Phi Delta Kappa Educational Foundation.

U.S. Department of Education. (1986). *What works: Research about teaching and learning*. Washington, DC: U.S. Government Printing Office.

Wayson, W. W. (1988). *Up from excellence: The impact of the excellence movement on the schools*. Bloomington, IN: Phi Delta Kappa Educational Foundation.

Wells, G. (Ed.) (1981). *Learning through interaction: The study of language development*. London: Cambridge University Press.

White, M. (1988). *The Japanese educational challenge*. New York: The Free Press.

Wittrock, M. C. (1986). *Handbook of research on teaching* (3rd ed.). New York: Macmillan.

Index

About the Editors and Contributors

SOL COHEN, a professor in the Social Sciences and Comparative Education Division of the UCLA Graduate School of Education, is a past president of the History of Education Society (U.S.). His work in the history of education has appeared widely in books and journals published in the United States and abroad. He is the editor of *Education in the United States: A Documentary History*. He has published in *History of Education Quarterly* (U.S.), *History of Education* (U.K.), *Teachers College Record*, and *Harvard Educational Review*. He is completing a study of the "medicalization" of American education, a history of the influence of psychiatry, psychoanalysis, and the mental hygiene movement on American education.

LEWIS C. SOLMON, dean of the UCLA Graduate School of Education since 1985, has established a number of centers to enhance discussion between GSE faculty and southern California educators, and has encouraged GSE faculty to become more involved in local schools and statewide educational policymaking. As an economist, Dean Solmon is internationally known for his work in higher education. His current research focuses on cost-benefit analyses of foreign students in American higher education, as well as merit pay for teachers, among other issues in elementary and secondary education. Dr. Solmon has served as an adviser to the World Bank, UNESCO, the American Council of Education, and the National Endowment for the Humanities. Among his recent publications are (with M. La Porte) "The Educational Implications of the High Technology Revolution" (1987); (with W. Zumeta) "U.S. Science Manpower and R&D Capability: New Problems on the Horizon?" (1986); "Quality of Education and Economic Growth" (1985); and (with M. La Porte) "The Crisis of Student Quality in Higher Education" (1986).

JAMES E. BRUNO's specialty is quantitative methodology. He has served as technical expert and visiting professor, Economics Institute, Beijing, People's Republic of China; distinguished visiting professor, Melbow Chair, University of Southern California; and lecturer, Hebrew University, Israel. Professor Bruno's latest works include "The Instructional Audit in Urban School Settings" (1988), and "Design of Economics Education Curricula Using Information Referenced Testing" (1989).

JAMES S. CATTERALL is Associate Professor in the Administration, Curriculum, and Teaching Studies Division of the UCLA Graduate School of Education. In 1987 he was the first recipient of the Graduate School of Education's Susan and Mark Greenfield Award for Applied Research in Learning and Achievement. He is the author of more than forty articles, book chapters, and research monographs. Among his recent publications are (with Milbrey W. McLaughlin), "Notes on the New Politics of Education" (1984); "Politics and Aid to Private Schools" (1985); and "Dropping out of School as a Process: Implications for Research, Policy and Practice" (1987).

BURTON R. CLARK is Allan M. Cartter professor of higher education and sociology and chair of the Comparative Higher Education Research Group at the UCLA Graduate School of Education. He taught previously at Stanford and Harvard Universities, the University of California, Berkeley, and Yale University in departments of sociology and schools of education. From 1974 to 1980 he was chairman of the Yale Higher Education Research Group. His publications include *The Distinctive College* (1970); *Academic Power in Italy* (1977); *The Higher Education System* (1983); and *The Academic Life: Small Worlds, Different Worlds* (1987). He also has edited three volumes: *Perspectives on Higher Education* (1984); *The School and the University* (1985); *The Academic Profession* (1987).

JOHN E. COULSON received his Ph.D. in experimental psychology from Columbia University. He has been associated with the Rand Corporation and the Systems Development Corporation, managing and conducting applied research and development in instructional technology, with particular emphasis on public education and complex training systems in military and industrial settings. He has headed research teams conducting national evaluations of such large-scale, federally funded programs as Head Start, the Special Services for Disadvantaged Students Program, the Job Corps, and the Emergency School Aid Act Program.

DONALD A. ERICKSON has sought to illuminate issues of school organization and administration through comparison: between regular and "alternative" public schools, between public and private schools, and between private schools under conditions of private and public financial support. His "Choice and Private Schools: Dynamics of Supply and Demand" contains some of his earlier views on choice and private schools. Of Professor Erickson's many works the most recent, all to appear in 1989, are a chapter in a book on private school research and a chapter in a book on educational policy issues. He is currently completing two books, one, *The Importance of Being Private, Even If You're Public*, and the other (coauthored with Mary Peter Travis), interpreting research on Catholic schools.

HARRY HANDLER is adjunct professor at the UCLA Graduate School of Education, where he teaches courses in urban education, school organization, and evaluation. Before joining the Graduate School of Education faculty in 1987, Dr. Handler was superintendent of the Los Angeles Unified School District, the nation's second largest school district. Dr. Handler's affiliation with Los Angeles schools spanned thirty-five years and included roles as teacher, counselor, director of research, and various senior administrative posts before he became superintendent in 1981. Dr. Handler has received numerous awards for his service to education and youth.

BARBARA HECHT is Assistant Professor in the Educational Psychology Division of the UCLA Graduate School of Education. She received her Ph.D. in linguistics with a specialization in child language development from Stanford University in 1983. Her research and teaching interests include language and cognitive development in normal and language-impaired children, assessment and remediation of language disorders, and the relationship between children's oral and written language development. She is coauthor (with Susan Conant and Milton Budoff) of *Teaching Language-Disabled Children*. She has contributed to *Annual Review of Psychology* and *Issues in Special Education* as well as *Journal of Applied Psycholinguistics* and *Journal of Child Language and Cognition*. Her current research interests focus on the home language environment of developmentally delayed children.

FRANK M. HEWETT is a member of the Educational Psychology Division of the UCLA Graduate School of Education. He also holds a joint appointment as professor in the UCLA Department of Psychiatry. His research and teaching interests relate to the development of educational programs for severely emotionally disturbed children and youth, and more generally to the development of an ecological orientation for the field of special education. He is coauthor (with Steven R. Forness) of *Education of Exceptional Learners*, now in its third edition, and (with Frank D. Taylor), coauthor of *The Emotionally Disturbed Child in the Classroom*, now in its second edition.

VAL D. RUST has published in *Comparative Education Review*, *Comparative Education*, *Phi Delta Kappan*, and *Teaching and Teacher Education*. He is the author of *Alternatives in Education: Theoretical and Historical Perspectives*, and *The Democratic Tradition and the Evolution of Schooling in Norway*, which received the International Book Award honoring Norway's celebration of 250 years of public education. Professor Rust is president-elect of the Comparative and International Education Society.

HARRY F. SILBERMAN has conducted research on instructional technology and the educational effects of work experience. He edited the *Yearbook on Education and Work* for the National Society for the Study of Education in 1982. He served for five years as a member of the California Employment Services Board for the state's Employment Development Department; was chairman of the National Commission on Secondary Vocational Education, which published *The Unfinished Agenda: The Role of Vocational Education in the High School* in 1984; and received an outstanding service award from the American Vocational Association in 1987. Most recently Professor Silberman has worked with the Institute of Industrial Relations at UCLA to upgrade the training of blue-collar workers from the Van Nuys (California) General Motors plant in order to prepare them for transition to a more participative management system.

CONCEPCIÓN M. VALADEZ is Associate Professor, Graduate School of Education, UCLA, and associate director of the UCLA Center for Language Education and Research. Her research has focused on issues affecting language-minority students and academic underachievement. Among her recent publications are (with J. McNeil), *Reading Skills of Minority Bilingual Personnel and the Reading Demands of Work* (1983) and (with L. Fillmore) "Teaching Bilingual Learners" (1986).

VIRGINIA de R. WAGNER is a doctoral candidate at the Graduate School of Education, UCLA, in special education/administration. She is an experienced teacher and resource specialist in the area of the learning handicapped. She has taught at the Clearview School for the Severely Emotionally Disturbed and was a demonstration teacher at the Grace Fernald School at UCLA.

CARL WEINBERG, author of several books on humanistic education, has been involved during the past few years in research on at-risk teachers, the clarification of concepts leading to the identification of at-risk students, and the learning processes involved in artistic development. His most recent publication on the subject of artistic pedagogy is "On Becoming an Artist: Implications for the Development of Classroom Teachers" (1988). Professor Weinberg's paper on the meaning of the concept of "serious emotional disturbance," as used to legally identify at-risk students, will be presented at the annual meeting of the Council for Exceptional Children, San Francisco, Spring 1989.

RICHARD C. WILLIAMS is a Professor in the Graduate School of Education's Division of Administration, Curriculum and Teaching Studies. He has served since 1984 as director of Seeds University Elementary School, the laboratory school of UCLA's Graduate School of Education. His current research and theoretical interests center on the relation between school structure and governance and educational innovation. His recent publications include (with Adrianne Bank) *Inventing the Future: The Development of Instructional Information Systems* (1987); and (with K. Moffet and B. Newlin) "The District Role in School Renewal" (1987).